DIVERSIFICATION AND INTEGRATION
IN AMERICAN INDUSTRY

NATIONAL BUREAU OF ECONOMIC RESEARCH
NUMBER 77, GENERAL SERIES

Diversification and Integration in American Industry

By MICHAEL GORT, 1923 -

A STUDY BY THE
NATIONAL BUREAU OF ECONOMIC RESEARCH

PUBLISHED BY
PRINCETON UNIVERSITY PRESS, PRINCETON
1962

Printed in the United States of America

RELATION OF THE DIRECTORS TO THE WORK AND PUBLICATIONS
OF THE NATIONAL BUREAU OF ECONOMIC RESEARCH

1. The object of the National Bureau of Economic Research is to ascertain and to present to the public important economic facts and their interpretation in a scientific and impartial manner. The Board of Directors is charged with the responsibility of ensuring that the work of the National Bureau is carried on in strict conformity with this object.

2. To this end the Board of Directors shall appoint one or more Directors of Research.

3. The Director or Directors of Research shall submit to the members of the Board, or to its Executive Committee, for their formal adoption, all specific proposals concerning researches to be instituted.

4. No report shall be published until the Director or Directors of Research shall have submitted to the Board a summary drawing attention to the character of the data and their utilization in the report, the nature and treatment of the problems involved, the main conclusions, and such other information as in their opinion would serve to determine the suitability of the report for publication in accordance with the principles of the National Bureau.

5. A copy of any manuscript proposed for publication shall also be submitted to each member of the Board. For each manuscript to be so submitted a special committee shall be appointed by the President, or at his designation by the Executive Director, consisting of three Directors selected as nearly as may be one from each general division of the Board. The names of the special manuscript committee shall be stated to each Director when the summary and report described in paragraph (4) are sent to him. It shall be the duty of each member of the committee to read the manuscript. If each member of the special committee signifies his approval within thirty days, the manuscript may be published. If each member of the special committee has not signified his approval within thirty days of the transmittal of the report and manuscript, the Director of Research shall then notify each member of the Board, requesting approval or disapproval of publication, and thirty additional days shall be granted for this purpose. The manuscript shall then not be published unless at least a majority of the entire Board and a two-thirds majority of those members of the Board who shall have voted on the proposal within the time fixed for the receipt of votes on the publication proposed shall have approved.

6. No manuscript may be published, though approved by each member of the special committee, until forty-five days have elapsed from the transmittal of the summary and report. The interval is allowed for the receipt of any memorandum of dissent or reservation, together with a brief statement of his reasons, that any member may wish to express; and such memorandum of dissent or reservation shall be published with the manuscript if he so desires. Publication does not, however, imply that each member of the Board has read the manuscript, or that either members of the Board in general, or of the special committee, have passed upon its validity in every detail.

7. A copy of this resolution shall, unless otherwise determined by the Board, be printed in each copy of every National Bureau book.

(Resolution adopted October 25, 1926, as revised February 6, 1933, and February 24, 1941)

Contents

Tables

APPENDIX TABLES

Charts

Acknowledgments

I owe much to George J. Stigler for valuable advice at several stages in the preparation of this study. I am also indebted to Ralph Nelson, Thor Hultgren, Willard L. Thorp, S. H. Ruttenberg, Theodore O. Yntema, Frank J. Kottke, and Donald Dewey, all of whom read the manuscript with great care. Their numerous suggestions for its improvement have been invaluable.

Rosanne Cole assisted me in developing the basic data for the study and performed most of the statistical work. Without her skillful assistance and good judgment, the preparation of this study would have proved far more arduous. Robert Kinsey, Shirley Montag, Jurgen Greif, and Prakash Mathur also gave valuable assistance in preparing the data.

I am grateful to Howard C. Grieves, Maxwell R. Conklin, and Julius Shiskin of the Bureau of the Census for making unpublished tabulations available to me. All of the tables in this study which were developed from unpublished census data were prepared in accordance with the Census Bureau's requirement of secrecy. By law, the Census Bureau is prohibited from publishing any statistics that disclose information reported by individual companies.

The manuscript was edited by James F. McRee, Jr., and Joan Tron. Charts were drawn by H. Irving Forman.

MICHAEL GORT

Foreword

THERE never was a business with only one productive process and one final product; there never will be. A firm that merely bought and sold the same commodity would find that it was engaged in a host of different productive processes—collecting information, lending or borrowing, keeping records, safeguarding goods or the titles to goods, making tax returns, and what not. A firm that appears to make only "one" product almost always makes this product in a variety of qualities, with differing sizes of order, speeds of delivery, period of payment, etc. Diversification and integration in the strictest sense are universal.

Diversification usually connotes more than the performance of a variety of productive activities within the firm—in some sense the activities are not closely related in a technological or economic sense. When Willard Thorp made the first statistical study of the structure of manufacturing companies, he distinguished five kinds of relationships between the plants belonging to one firm:

1. Uniform functions—the plants make the same product.
2. Divergent functions—by-products, joint products, similar production processes.
3. Convergent functions—complementary products, auxiliary products, similar markets.
4. Continuing functions—vertical integration.
5. Unrelated functions.[1]

Of these, only the fifth class might be termed "pure" diversification. Thorp found such unrelated activities to be rare, and essentially accidental.

On this pure view of diversification, where the concept does not include even the dissimilar products with a common market, diversification is necessarily an act of pure investment, devoid of any operating connections (other than those entailed by common ownership) between the plants. This, however, is probably still an unimportant category—usually it is possible to find *some* connections: use of the same salesmen, appeal to the same customer, utilization of the results of a research laboratory, and so on.

And if we view diversification broadly as the encompassing within a single company of two or more activities each of which constitutes the sole activity of more specialized companies, diversification is a very widespread phenomenon. How widespread it is, of course, depends upon how finely we divide the activities (or "industries"). In our first census of

[1] *The Integration of Industrial Operations*, U.S. Bureau of the Census, 1924, p. 161.

companies (as distinguished from plants) in 1954, it was found that of the 263,100 companies assigned to manufacturing, 259,700 operated in only one industry—where the industry was a fairly broad "3-digit" industry, to be sure. But the 3,400 companies operating in more than one industry had more than one-third of the employees in manufacturing; and of their 9.1 million employees—an average of almost 3,000 per company— 3.6 million were in nonmanufacturing industries. On the other hand, a seventh of the employees in manufacturing worked for companies assigned to other areas. And the role of diversified enterprises would of course be larger with a finer (4-digit) underlying industry classification, which one would prefer to use.

Michael Gort now provides us with the first comprehensive study of the interindustry structure of the large, diversified enterprise. In order to trace the history of diversification as well as to analyze the causes which have been proposed for its development, his basic statistical record covers 111 of the largest companies in the country, for which the product structures in 1929, 1939, 1947, 1950, and 1954 have been compiled. These enterprises do not exhaust the list of even diversified large companies, since it was advisable to cluster the sample; but judged either by their own importance or as samples of all diversified enterprises, Gort's record makes an essential and illuminating contribution to our knowledge of the area.[2]

These 111 companies were operating in an average of 9.7 (4-digit) manufacturing industries in 1954, and 36 per cent of their activity (measured by payrolls) was in the nonprimary industries. They were making an average of 15.6 products, in addition to operating in another 4.8 nonmanufacturing industries. There is some evidence of a recent acceleration in diversification: these companies together added 40 to 50 products a year from 1929 to 1950, but twice as many from 1950–54.

How can we explain this increasing and (among the 111 companies) even accelerating diversification, when one of the most famous theorems in economics says that the division of labor increases with the size of the market? There are, of course, contrary hypotheses—such as that businessmen wish to achieve a greater stability of operations than specialization allows (Gort finds that the product additions are generally in relatively

---

[2] In a recent unpublished Columbia University dissertation by Jerome Strong, a somewhat less intensive study has been made of diversification of companies of smaller size— most of Gort's companies are among the 200 largest in the country, whereas Strong's are on average nearer the 800th largest in rank. Although diversification was much less extensive among these medium-sized companies (they produced an average of 3.8 4-digit products in 1954), they displayed the same acceleration in recent years as the large companies.

unstable industries, however), or that businessmen seek entry to young, rapidly growing industries. (He finds such a tendency, but with no resulting relationship between diversification and profit rates.)

One more attractive explanation lies in the ability of large companies to raise capital at relatively attractive terms. The industries which the diversifying firms enter commonly have large average sizes of firms. In addition there is a strong tax incentive to diversification: if a corporation invests in a new industry instead of paying out its earnings and allowing stockholders to make the investment, the stockholders are postponing personal income taxes (and perhaps converting income into capital gains).

Gort's is only the most recent of a long series of National Bureau studies dealing with the firm structure of industries and the product structure of firms, a series which in recent years has included Rosenbluth on concentration and Nelson on mergers. But the forces of diversification seem to be much stronger in economic research even than in large corporations: it is instructive that the problem of industrial organization insists on spilling over into areas such as business finance, taxation, and technological advance, so that a full list of the National Bureau's relevant work would be a tolerable sample of its entire research program.

I suspect this is a sign that we are progressing in our understanding of the structure of our surpassingly complex economy. The initial studies of a subject concentrate upon its most immediate and dominant characteristics, and only after these begin to be understood and measured do the subtler and wider-flung relationships beckon for attention. When Gort fixes the main contours of diversification and raises a host of questions on its relationships to other aspects of economic life, he is illustrating the most fundamental characteristic of the scholar, for whom research means much more the discovery of relevant questions than the giving of conclusive answers.

GEORGE J. STIGLER

DIVERSIFICATION AND INTEGRATION
IN AMERICAN INDUSTRY

CHAPTER 1
Introduction

ENTERPRISES that produce diverse goods and services are not a recent phenomenon. In the early sixteenth century, the firm of Jakob Fugger II was engaged on a large scale in mining, real estate, banking, and the spice trades; and the famous trading companies, such as the British East India Company in the eighteenth century, embraced a vast range of activities. More recently, large American manufacturing firms had fairly varied product structures at the outset of the period covered by this study, 1929. In the 1950's there was some acceleration for these firms in the trend toward product diversification, but the basic phenomenon is of long standing.

Let us say that the primary industry of a company is one which accounts for more of a firm's output, or payrolls, than any other activity in which the firm is engaged. The greater the volume of output or payrolls within the primary industry relative to that outside it, the less diversified is the firm.[1] Thus for large firms the movement toward more diversified product structures can be placed in perspective by the fact that for 111 of the largest manufacturing companies the average ratio of payrolls within the primary industry to total manufacturing payrolls declined from 69 per cent in 1947 to 64 per cent in 1954. It is clear that this change did not radically transform the structure of the 111 firms. On the other hand, if the same rate of change continues, the cumulative effect over a longer period of time should prove substantial.

What are the consequences of diversification? These can be examined both for the individual firm and the economy as a whole. For the individual firm, one of the most important results is that its long-run growth becomes less dependent on the trend in demand for products within its primary industry. Thus the link between the fate of firms and the rise and decline of particular industries is—at least partially—severed. In addition, diversification increases the range of a firm's investment opportunities, since it permits a company to take advantage of the more profitable opportunities in sectors of the economy in which it has previously had no activities. However, as evidenced by the record of product abandonments (described later), firms sometimes diversify into markets in which they are unable to survive.

From the standpoint of the effects of diversification on the economy, the reduced dependence of firms on growth in demand in their primary industries has the effect of reducing changes in the composition of leading

[1] Alternative definitions of diversification are discussed in Chapter 2.

3

firms. An important source of these changes is the rise and decline of particular industries. The broadening of the investment horizon of individual firms is also likely to increase the sensitivity of capital flows to differences in profit rates between industries. To the extent that a wider range of investment projects is examined, capital funds generated in one sector of the economy are rendered more likely to move into other sectors where investment opportunities are more attractive. An increase in the heterogeneity of the output of firms also tends to reduce those differences in the profit experience of firms that arise from the varying profitability of their primary industries.

Diversification diminishes the effect of adverse circumstances in one of a firm's activities on the firm's total performance. Thus it reduces the risks associated with unpredictable changes in the profitability of particular industries. The effectiveness of diversification as a countercyclical device, however, largely depends upon the cyclical stability of industries into which firms diversify. Since peaks and troughs in demand for several products normally will not coincide perfectly, a random selection of products for diversification will, on the average, tend to reduce the amplitude of fluctuations in sales. However, entry of a firm based in a stable industry into a cyclically volatile one may destabilize the firm's total sales. Our data show that firms did not systematically select the more stable industries as outlets for diversification.

This study shows that companies have diversified largely into industries characterized by rapid technological change. Entry into many of these industries requires substantial amounts of capital—a fact which frequently constitutes a barrier to newly formed firms. Thus it seems plausible that diversification by large firms has facilitated the flow of capital into these industries and in this way contributed to the latter's growth. Many instances of diversification have been initiated through merger. The acquisition of existing property in an industry does not in itself change the volume of resources therein; it merely alters the combination of properties under common ownership. However, mergers and purchases of property frequently initiate further subsequent expansion in the newly entered industries.

Many instances of diversification involved entry into industries in which a few firms accounted for a large proportion of total output and sales. Frequently, the new entrant grew to relatively large size, and in a significant proportion of these industries, the entering firm became a leading producer. Thus, to the extent that entry and growth were accomplished by means other than merger, diversification has proved to be an important source of new competition.

In the 1929–54 period, the overwhelming majority of increases in number of products produced by a sample of 111 companies can be characterized as diversification. However, there were also frequent occurrences of integration—that is, the production of goods or services that are merely stages in the output of common final products. The effects of integration, important though they may be, are harder to assess than those of diversification. This is because the effects hinge upon a wide range of special circumstances. For example, the acquisition of sources of raw materials or of distribution facilities may render possible more orderly planning of production and a consequent reduction in costs. On the other hand, these advantages may be offset by possible diseconomies resulting from entry into activities in which the firm has had no previous experience.

The most widely discussed effects of integration are those upon competition. While a discussion of this subject is largely outside the scope of the present study, it may be noted briefly that these effects vary greatly with circumstances. Generally, if integration leads to substantial control of scarce resources by a few producers, entry into industries employing these resources is rendered more difficult. Competition, actual or potential, may thus be reduced. Without control over scarce resources the effects of integration on competition are difficult to predict and, doubtless, are frequently negligible. There is also some discussion in theoretical literature of the effect of integration on final prices when competition is absent at each of several successive stages of production. However, even under this highly restrictive assumption, there has been no general agreement about probable effects.

The demand for goods and services at each of several stages of production must ultimately depend upon the demand for the final product, and hence will fluctuate in response to fluctuations for the latter. Thus integration cannot reduce the instability in a firm's earnings by generating offsetting increases in sales for random or cyclical contractions in primary industry demand. Exceptions, however, may arise if alternative markets exist for component or auxiliary goods and services. Moreover, special circumstances can alter the consequences of integration for the problem of instability. For example, if all marketing outlets were owned by competing producers, a manufacturer who did not own marketing outlets would be in a weak competitive position during periods of falling demand and widespread excess capacity in the industry. As another aspect of the relation of integration to instability in demand, the acquisition of supplies of raw materials may protect a manufacturer against rapid rises in raw-materials prices during periods of peak demand. On the other hand, it deprives him of the opportunity to shift backward, in the form of lower prices for raw materials, the effects of temporary declines in demand for final products.

Integration is sometimes undertaken simply as an investment outlet for accumulated business savings. In this respect, the data show that the more integrated firms tend to diversify less than those with a smaller volume of integration activities. Thus, integration appears to compete with diversification for capital or managerial resources.

Except for the work of Thorp and Crowder,[2] studies of diversification and integration have concentrated largely on individual industries. Both the data used and the focus of Thorp's and Crowder's work differ materially from ours. Their data relate entirely to single points in time; in contrast, a substantial part of our information concerns changes over time. A major effort in the work of both Thorp and Crowder is devoted to developing a detailed breakdown of the nature of relations between products found under common ownership. In our own analysis, most of these are subsumed in the categories of technical propinquity and integration.[3] The primary focus of our work, apart from measuring trends in diversification, was that of defining two sets of relationships. First, what are the economic characteristics of diversifying firms? Second, what are the economic characteristics of industries that are frequently entered by diversifying firms?

A rapidly growing industry tends to attract resources from existing firms based primarily in other sectors of the economy as well as from new firms or from those within the industry. This result is supported by the relatively high growth of most industries used as diversification outlets by our sample of firms. Also, in most instances, firms diversified into industries with a higher growth rate than that of their primary activities. Thus capital funds generally moved from the less to the more rapidly growing sectors of the economy. The most decisive influence in the choice of an industry as a diversification outlet, however, was not its growth rate but its rate of technological change. Diversifying activities were heavily concentrated in industries associated with rapidly changing technologies. These industries usually require highly specialized managerial and technical skills. In consequence, firms that employed in their main activities a relatively large number of technical personnel were in a stronger position

[2] Willard L. Thorp, *The Integration of Industrial Operations,* U.S. Bureau of the Census, 1924; Walter F. Crowder, *The Integration of Manufacturing Operations,* U.S. Temporary National Economic Committee, Monograph Number 27, 1941.

[3] However, our categories and those of Thorp and Crowder do not altogether overlap. For example, we have attempted to deal with a class of technical propinquity not examined in the two earlier studies—namely, that of common technical and managerial skills required for two or more products.

to enter industries that had proved most attractive as diversification outlets, and thus diversified more frequently than other firms.

For reasons indicated in Chapter 8, it is easier for a firm to grow faster than industry demand in an industry in which all sellers are small than in one in which the leading firms account for a large proportion of total sales. In consequence, firms whose managers seek rapid growth will be more prone to diversify if their primary activities are in industries with a relatively high degree of large-seller dominance. The data show that the degree of large-seller dominance[4] in a firm's primary industry was positively associated with the extent to which the firm diversified.

In the twenty-five years from 1929 to 1954, the trend for large manufacturing firms was unmistakably in the direction of more diversification. This trend proceeded at a somewhat higher annual rate in the 1930's than in the 1940's, but appeared to accelerate again in the 1950's. However, it cannot be firmly established from our data that firms in manufacturing as a whole became more diversified on the average, as it is possible that greater diversification for existing companies was offset by entry of new single-industry firms into manufacturing.

In manufacturing, all measures of diversification point to a strong relation between a manufacturing firm's primary industry and the extent to which it diversifies in manufacturing operations. (For example, firms primarily based in the electrical machinery industry diversified far more than those based in tobacco or food products.) On the other hand, the frequency with which manufacturing firms entered into *nonmanufacturing* activities was independent of their primary industries.

Size of firm played a somewhat surprising role in diversification. It was positively related to one measure of diversification—the number of industries in which companies maintained activities; however, it was not related to another measure, namely, the relative magnitude of nonprimary activities.[5] Size of firm showed little relation to measures of integration. Of importance also is the fact that the ratio of a company's administrative employees to its other employees was no greater for the larger than for the smaller firms. (Indeed, when certain statistical biases are considered, the data are not inconsistent with a hypothesis of a negative relation between size of firm and relative number of administrative employees.) This conflicts with a widely held belief that as a firm grows, it incurs diseconomies arising from increasing administrative costs.

[4] Large-seller dominance was measured by the proportion of total shipments contributed by the leading four producers.

[5] The relative magnitude of nonprimary activities was measured by the ratio of employment in these activities to that in the primary ones.

CHAPTER 2
Concepts and Methods

THIS chapter is concerned with developing definitions and measures of the concepts of diversification and integration, and with examining the technical characteristics of the data employed. It is written primarily for those interested in a close examination of the basis for conclusions reached in this study.

Concepts of Diversification

Diversification may be defined as an increase in the heterogeneity of *markets* served by an individual firm. Heterogeneity of *production* is distinct from diversification if it involves minor differences of essentially the same product, or if it takes the form of vertical integration. (The latter is discussed in a later section.)

In economic theory, it is usual to propose cross-elasticity of demand as a basis for identifying separate markets, and hence separate products for the purpose of measuring diversification. If cross-elasticity is high, the products are close substitutes and, hence, belong to the same market; if it is low, the products belong to separate markets. Unfortunately, there is little information on cross-elasticities of demand and, even were it available, one would still need to define the value of elasticity below which products may be considered as being separate—a definition that of necessity would be largely arbitrary.

Another solution to the problem is to identify separate markets on the basis of the immobility of productive resources. When resources can be shifted rapidly from one set of products to another, products may be deemed to fall in a common industry from the standpoint of the producer, though they are distinctly separate as seen by the consumer. Considerable mobility of resources leads to interdependence in supply for products. Changes in price (and hence in earnings) associated with one product lead to a shift in resources, and thus to changes in price and output of the other. Therefore, the phenomena of interdependence in prices, output, and earnings associated with high cross-elasticities of demand tend to be present also where a high degree of mobility of resources exists. Moreover, though there are many exceptions, the more common circumstances under which productive capacity can rapidly be diverted from one use to another are those involving products that are close substitutes. Thus the two sets of conditions may be considered complementary in identifying separable industries. Once again, however, progress in identifying diversification on the basis of interdependence in supply is constrained both by the absence of appropriate information and by a lack of clear-cut definitions of limits.

In summary, diversification may be defined as an increase in the heterogeneity of output from the point of view of the number of markets served by that output. Two products may be specified as belonging to separate markets if their cross-elasticities of demand are low and if, in the short run, the necessary resources employed in the production and distribution of one cannot readily be shifted to the other. An increase in the number of regional markets served by an enterprise may, under some circumstances, fit the above definition of diversification. However, except when transportation costs are high, manufacturing resources are likely to be highly mobile between the demands of different regions for substantially similar products. (Mobility here simply entails selling the manufactured product in another region rather than moving plant and equipment.) Since limited short-run mobility is specified as a condition for distinguishing between markets, diversification through regional heterogeneity of output is far less likely to occur in manufacturing than in the distributive and service trades. Two quite similar products at opposite extremes of the relevant price range may also be characterized by very low cross-elasticity of demand. Immobility of resources between the two is, however, considerably less likely, though not inconceivable. In any event, our study is concerned neither with this last type of diversification nor with regional heterogeneity.

For this study, products were identified as belonging to separate markets if they could be classified into separate industries on the basis of the 1945 Standard Industrial Classification Code. As a practical matter, there was little choice since most of the data available were cast in the mold of the Classification Code. The industry code was developed mainly from product classes widely in use and therefore is largely based on differences and similarities in products. However, industries are sometimes also distinguished on the basis of production processes and raw materials employed. In most instances all three criteria lead to the same classifications, but there are many exceptions to this. In consequence, the implications of diversification, as measured on the basis of industry distinctions made in the Code, will vary to some extent depending on the classification criteria that had been employed. Generally, similarities in products are associated with high cross-elasticities of demand, and similarities in production processes with mobility of resources.

Measures of Diversification

How may quantitative differences in the heterogeneity of markets served by a firm be measured so as to distinguish more and less diversified enterprises? The choice among the several measures developed depends to some extent upon the problems one chooses to examine. Thus, if the problem is to predict differences in the response of earnings or output to cyclical fluctuations or to long-term trends in demand for the primary product of an enterprise, what is needed is a measure of concentration of output in the primary industry. That is, one would wish to know the extent to which the operations of the total enterprise are dependent upon the demand for its most important product. Another measure of diversification might be designed to throw light on the extent to which an enterprise is likely to enter activities unrelated to its primary operations in response, for example, to high earnings or growth prospects in other industries. For this purpose, an appropriate measure may simply be a count of the number of industries in which the enterprise produces goods or services.

The ratio of primary industry output to total output for the enterprise yields a measure of homogeneity—and the complement of this ratio, a measure of diversification—that is relevant for projections of the earnings of firms.[1] A limitation of this measure may be illustrated by a simple example. Assume that two firms show an identical primary industry specialization, but the nonprimary output of one company is evenly divided between five industries, whereas in the second company it is concentrated in a single industry. If diversification is measured as the complement of the ratio of primary industry output to total output, no differences between the two firms would be revealed, though for most purposes the first may be considered the more diversified. This could be corrected, to some extent, by adding the second largest industry to the numerator of the ratio. However, as the number of industries in the numerator is increased, more of the diversification to be measured is concealed. Indeed, if a sufficient number of industries were grouped with the primary industry in the ratio, all firms would appear to have a homogeneous output.

On the other hand, a measure of diversification based upon a simple count of industries would give undue weight to a wide dispersion over the industrial spectrum of activities that, in the aggregate, account for only a small proportion of the firm's total operations. While both the above measures were used individually, a composite measure which employs both the primary industry ratio and the number of industries in which operations are to be found was also used in this study. It was derived by multiplying the complement of primary industry specialization by the

---

[1] The complement of the ratio gives the relationship of nonprimary industry to total output.

number of industries in which the enterprise showed operations. A simple alternative designed to serve the same objectives would be to count the number of industries that account for a specified percentage of the total output or employment of the enterprise. The larger the number, the more diversified the firm. This method, however, proved insufficiently sensitive for our data in that it generated a large number of tied ranks in the sample of 111 large companies, ranked on the above basis.

A satisfactory direct measure of output was not available for nonmanufacturing activities. As a result, primary industry specialization was in most instances measured on the basis of employment data. For our sample of 111 firms, measures of diversification restricted to *manufacturing* activities were based on manufacturing payrolls. Because of variations in wage rates and in the number of hours worked, payrolls tend to approximate output somewhat more closely than does employment. For this sample of 111 companies further refinements were possible. Specifically, it was possible to separate and exclude payrolls associated with integration from the denominator of the primary industry specialization ratio.[2] Thus differences between companies in integration did not appreciably affect our measures of diversification for this sample. Again, for the manufacturing activities of the 111 firms, in measures of diversification based on a count of activities an attempt was made to exclude those which might be considered trivial in relation to the total size of the firm. For this purpose, all manufacturing activities within the firm with less than 1 per cent of manufacturing employment were excluded from the count. A 2 per cent exclusion rule was also tested.

Another variation was introduced in the measure of diversification by the choice of level of industry detail in identifying the primary industry. Thus, 2-, 3-, and 4-digit levels of detail were used at various points in the study. In summary, several measures with varying refinements were used. Some comparisons of the results using the various measures are shown later in this chapter and in Chapter 3.

Concepts and Measures of Integration

Integration may be defined as the act of combining two or more separable stages of production under common ownership. But how may a stage be identified? Within every establishment, the same productive functions

---

[2] In measuring diversification, it is conceptually best to combine integration employment with that in the industry to which it is auxiliary. This, however, did not prove feasible, partly because of limited information and partly, also, because operations in a given industry may be auxiliary to several rather than to one activity.

may be conceived of as a continuous process or, alternatively, subdivided into a vast number of separate operations, each of which may be identified as a separate stage in production. While in all industries certain productive processes are commonly regarded as being separate from others, these distinctions follow no uniform principle among the various industries. Stages of production may be identified as being separable if the productive processes could be performed successfully under separate ownership. Thus activities may be considered separable if, in fact, some firms successfully engage in them independently of the other activities in question. Therefore, if a firm combines two sets of successive operations though these operations are not combined under one ownership by other firms, the former may be said to have combined separable stages of production. A classification system based on this concept would not identify processes that are always combined within single plants as separable stages of production. Less obviously, if some manufacturing activities are never performed except in conjunction with the ownership of supplies of requisite raw materials, the extractive and manufacturing operations, even though performed in separate establishments, will not, in accordance with the above definition, be regarded as separable stages.

Changes in integration associated with the combination of two or more stages under common ownership normally entail separate investment decisions. Usually they will be made after explicit consideration of the alternative of purchasing the needed product or service outside the firm. Thus integration decisions, as defined above, are generally separable from decisions to manufacture the other products of the firm.

There exists, of course, no classification system that will uniformly identify separable stages of production in all the sectors of the economy. Nevertheless, the industry classification system used in this study largely achieves this objective. Productive processes associated with separate 4-digit SIC industries will, with only a few exceptions, constitute the entire scope of operations for at least some firms. Accordingly, a firm that combines two or more 4-digit activities, all of which are component processes associated with a single final product, may be considered more integrated than another whose operations are restricted to a single industry.

The measure of integration chosen for this study was based on the ratio of employment in all auxiliary activities to aggregate employment for the firm. An auxiliary product or service may either be an input (or a component part) of the "major" product or service or, alternatively, may constitute an operation that occurs at a later point in the production process (for example, a marketing outlet for a firm primarily engaged in

12

manufacturing). The distinction between "major" and auxiliary within the context of this study rests exclusively upon which of the two is the larger for the individual firm, with size measured by employment. One productive activity may be auxiliary to more than one major operation and, conversely, several activities may be auxiliary to the same major product or service. The specific technique employed in identifying auxiliary activities involved first grouping for each firm all the activities associated with common products or services. Second, within each group the largest in terms of employment was defined as major and the others were classified as auxiliary.

The attempt to measure integration was restricted to the sample of 111 large manufacturing enterprises. Distinctions between integration and diversification were made on the basis of qualitative information derived for each company from public records. In addition, individuals with expert knowledge of particular industries were consulted in some instances. Notwithstanding the care taken, arbitrary judgment is doubtless present in some of the allocations of activities between the categories of diversification and integration.[3] This is especially true for products or services designed to serve both purposes. Thus a manufacturer may maintain retail outlets both for the distribution of his products and for the sale of complementary products of other firms. Similarly, manufacturers frequently produce component parts for an external market as well as for their own use. In these circumstances, allocations were made on the basis of estimates of which category of uses was the larger in terms of sales.

Employment associated with sales and central administrative offices was classified as "integration" employment in computing a measure of integration. The major parts of sales and central office activities probably do not constitute separable stages in the sense defined earlier, since they are essential components of the operations of the firm. Yet the scope of activities of both sales and central offices varies considerably among companies. In some companies, these establishments perform services that elsewhere are purchased outside the firm. Examples are research and new product development, advertising, and various legal and engineering services. Our objective in classifying sales and central office employment as integration was to allow our measure of integration to reflect these differences among companies.

Integration (the ratio of auxiliary to total employment) is measured

---

[3] This was particularly a problem for activities that were very small relative to total firm size. The amount of information available was greater for the more important activities and thus permitted more reliable allocations.

on the basis of plant rather than product data, and consequently does not purport to measure differences in intraplant integration. It has been found, however, that establishments characterized by high primary product specialization ratios do not show a materially different ratio of value added to shipments than do establishments in the same industries characterized by lower specialization ratios.[4] Generally, a higher value-added to shipments ratio indicates greater integration. This would suggest that plant heterogeneity is not strongly related to integration. Stated in another way, for manufacturing enterprises on the whole, auxiliary operations that fall into distinguishable industries are reflected primarily in the variety of plants under common ownership rather than in product heterogeneity of the plants themselves.

Types of Data Used

Four sets of data were used for this study. First, the magnitude of primary relative to nonprimary activities for industry aggregates was derived from published census tabulations at roughly a 3-digit level of industry detail.[5] Second, for the relations between company size and diversification and company size and central office activities, unpublished data were prepared in a special census tabulation for 721 enterprises falling in 19 2-digit industries. Of these, 595 fell into thirteen manufacturing categories and 126 into six nonmanufacturing industries. The basic data were drawn from the 1954 Economic Censuses and consisted primarily of employment records for establishments, classified by industry of establishment. All of the employment of the relevant enterprises was included in these data, though out-of-census-scope records (that is, employment falling outside of manufacturing, minerals, trade, and services) were somewhat less reliable than those for in-census-scope industries. The enterprises comprised all of the multiestablishment companies with 2,500 and over employees that fell, on the basis of their primary industries, into the 19 2-digit industry categories.[6]

A major part of this study is based on a sample of 111 large enterprises.[7] Our third and fourth body of data relate to these enterprises.

[4] U.S. Bureau of the Census, *Working Paper Number 2*, 1956, Table II (Part II).

[5] The source of these data was U.S. Bureau of the Census, *Company Statistics: 1954 Censuses of Business, Manufacturing, Mineral Industries*, Washington, 1958. The Standard Industrial Classification Code was modified for these tables, but approximated the 3-digit level of detail.

[6] A narrower classification would not have generated a sufficient number of companies within individual categories to permit analysis of differences between companies within industries. Industries that had a negligible number of enterprises with 2,500 and over employees were omitted from the tabulation.

[7] The composition of this sample is discussed in a separate section later in this chapter.

Substantially the same type of information, but with a few additional statistics, was developed for this sample of companies from the 1954 Census as for the 721 companies mentioned above. In addition, similar information, but restricted to manufacturing industries, was derived from the 1947 Census of Manufactures for these 111 firms. Finally, in addition to census data on company employment and payrolls classified by industry, information on the products of the 111 firms was obtained from public records.

The information from public records consisted of all the products and services produced by these companies in 1954 and the changes in product composition for the companies that occurred in the periods 1929–39, 1939–50, and 1950–54.[8] The sources for these data consisted of information for individual companies in Moody's *Industrials,* in corporate annual reports to stockholders, and in *Thomas' Register of American Manufactures.* Products reported in 1954, as well as changes in product composition in each of the three periods indicated above, were classified into 4-digit SIC industries. Apart from conceptual advantages (discussed at a later point), the use of a 4-digit level of classification for product data served to eliminate the effects of variations in the detail with which various companies reported their product structures; that is, all companies reported their products at not less than a 4-digit level of detail, even though the Code was probably not directly considered when the reporting method was chosen. Products that were added and abandoned within the same interval of time were not recorded. Therefore, only changes in product structures between the initial and terminal dates of each period were entered. When a company added several products in the same 4-digit class during any one of the three periods, it was credited with only one addition. However, since each period was analyzed separately, if a product new to the company was added within one of the three periods, it was counted as an addition even though the company may have had other operations within the same 4-digit industry at the outset of the period. This procedure avoided a possible bias originating in the fact that since the total number of industry classes is limited, the more a firm diversifies in an earlier period, the fewer are the industries which remain to be entered at a later time.

The initial year 1929 was chosen because listings of products in public records are considerably less complete before the late 1920's. Nineteen hundred and fifty-four was chosen as the terminal year of the study because

[8] The periods began and ended in December of the initial and terminal years of each period.

an economic census was taken for that year. The three periods which subdivide the interval covered by the study were selected partly with a view to distinguishing diversification in the 1930's, a time primarily of low-level economic activity, from that associated with the high levels of output and investment in the 1950's. Also, diversification within the 1939–50 period probably reflects the impact on product structures of mobilization for World War II. While 1947 would probably have been preferable to 1950 as a point at which to divide the post-1939 interval, information available for 1950 from the Federal Trade Commission enabled us to check the accuracy of our data at the time of their preparation.[9] Moreover, since the initial and terminal dates of our periods had to be chosen in advance of the preparation of data, they do not necessarily mark off the points at which trends in diversification show marked changes in the rate of change over time.

To test the completeness of our product record, comparisons were made for 1954 between the product composition of companies as derived from public sources of information with that derived from census data for estab-

TABLE 1

MANUFACTURING INDUSTRIES APPEARING IN 1954 CENSUS ESTABLISHMENT DATA BUT NOT SHOWN IN PUBLIC RECORDS, 111 COMPANIES

Primary Industry of Company	Number of Companies	Number of 4-Digit Industries Not Shown[a]	Average Ratio of Employment in Industries Not Shown to Total Manufacturing Employment[b]
Food products	12	6	.002
Tobacco manufactures	5	0	0
Textile mill products	4	1	.004
Paper products	8	0	0
Chemicals	14	10	.002
Petroleum	10	1	.002
Rubber products	5	0	0
Stone, clay, and glass products	7	1	.016
Primary metals	10	2	.001
Fabricated metal products	5	1	.002
Machinery	13	3	.015
Electrical machinery	5	2	.011
Transportation equipment	13	10	.007

SOURCE: Described in Chapter 2.

[a] The maximum number of 4-digit industries not shown for any one company was six.

[b] Unweighted average ratio for companies in each industry.

[9] Subsequently, however, when census data became available, the accuracy of information on products was checked against the latter source.

lishments. Since establishments frequently produce more than one product, it was to be expected that our product record would show a larger number of 4-digit industries than that revealed in census establishment data. The latter record only the primary product of an establishment. Though the degree of classification detail was the same for both, the 111 companies, in the aggregate, showed 1,709 manufacturing activities in the product record as compared with 1,073 in census establishment data. Of greater interest in testing the adequacy of the product record were instances in which census establishment data showed an industry that did not appear in the product record. These proved to be very few; for manufacturing activities there were only forty-seven such instances for the aggregate of 111 companies (as compared with 1,026 activities shown in census data which also appeared in our product record). Table 1 shows the distribution, by major industry of company, of instances in which industrial activities were revealed in the census but not in the public record. As may be seen from the table, in no industry group of companies was the unweighted average ratio of employment in omitted activities (those omitted from public records) to total manufacturing employment greater than 1.6 per cent. Employment in the omitted activities was measured on the basis of census establishment data. It is apparent that omissions of products that were primary to the operations of individual establishments proved to be of negligible importance.

For the purpose of all data in this study, an enterprise was defined as the combination of all properties (including all corporate subsidiaries) falling under common ownership or control. Control was deemed to be exercised where the parent company held 50 per cent or more of the voting stock of a subsidiary, or where a parent company reported effective control to the Census Bureau even though it held less than 50 per cent of the voting stock. For purposes of non-census data, an indication of effective control with less than 50 per cent voting stock ownership was, on occasion, found in public records.[10] In short, the definition of a company or enterprise was substantially the same for both census data and data derived from public records.

For companies that had undergone large mergers during the period studied, the antecedent company of a merged one was deemed to be the

[10] A few instances in which two companies each held 50 per cent of the voting stock were encountered. In these cases, effective control was determined on the basis of qualitative information as to which of the parent companies performed the main supervisory functions. Companies that were related only in the sense that the same stockholder had a decisive voice in their management (that is, companies subject to the same personal, as distinct from corporate, control) were not combined in the data used.

largest individual component company, in terms of total assets, at the time of the merger.

The geographical scope of census data was defined by the boundaries of the United States. For data secured from public records, however, operations in Canada as well as the United States were incorporated in the study, but not those of subsidiaries in other countries.

Characteristics of the Sample of 111 Large Enterprises

The 111 large companies, on which much of our analysis is focused, were drawn from thirteen 2-digit manufacturing industries primarily on the basis of asset size. Appendix Table A-1 shows, for each company individually, total assets in 1929, 1939, and 1954, and the ratio of net income to net worth for the period 1947-54. The classification of companies according to industry was based on a 1951 Federal Trade Commission report which, in turn, classified companies on the basis of "the manufacturing activity which accounted for the largest percentage of total receipts in the post-war period."[11] In several instances, however, the industry in which a company was classified was altered on the basis of information derived from annual reports on the composition of the companies' output in 1954. The primary basis for selecting companies was inclusion in the list of 200 largest manufacturing firms.[12] The resources available required that the total sample be limited to between 100 and 120 companies. Accordingly, to secure broader industrial representation, it was necessary to limit the number of companies in a relatively homogeneous industry such as petroleum to ten, and the number in the considerably more heterogeneous chemical industry to fourteen. This was achieved by selecting the largest ten and fourteen firms in each of the two industries, respectively. Similar constraints were imposed on the number of companies selected for some of the other major industries. In a few instances, on the other hand, it was necessary to go outside the list of the 200 largest manufacturing companies to secure more adequate representation for the industry. Some companies were excluded because their histories, or public information on them, did not extend back to 1929. Industries which were not represented in the list of 150 largest companies, or which had fewer than four firms among the largest 500, were omitted

---

[11] U.S. Federal Trade Commission, *A List of 1,000 Large Manufacturing Companies, Their Subsidiaries and Affiliates, 1948,* June 1951, p. 2.

[12] The ranking of firms on the basis of total assets was primarily derived from "Directory of the 500 Largest U.S. Industrial Corporations," *Fortune Magazine,* Supplement, July 1956.

TABLE 2
TOTAL ASSETS OF 111 ENTERPRISES AND OF ALL CORPORATIONS IN
THIRTEEN MAJOR INDUSTRIES, 1954

Primary Industry of Company	Number of Companies	Total Assets of Companies in Sample ($000)	Total Assets of All Companies in Industry ($000)	Ratio of Assets in Sample to Assets of All Companies in Industry (per cent)
Food products	12	4,004,399	17,026,767	23.5
Tobacco manufactures	5	2,323,650	2,896,230	80.2
Textile mill products	4	543,527	8,623,017	6.3
Paper products	8	1,816,366	7,184,262	25.3
Chemicals	14	7,582,514	16,628,583	45.6
Petroleum	10	20,595,927	28,812,881	71.5
Rubber products	5	2,357,369	2,912,388	80.9
Stone, clay, and glass products	7	1,501,790	5,456,300	27.5
Primary metals	10	10,429,045	17,781,799	58.6
Fabricated metal products	5	1,315,766	8,149,487	16.1
Machinery	13	4,147,000	16,018,734	25.9
Electrical machinery	5	4,029,695	9,352,591	43.1
Transportation equipment	13	11,088,443	18,715,954	59.2
Total	111	71,735,490	159,558,993	45.0

SOURCE: For total assets of sample of companies, Moody's *Industrials,* 1954; for total assets of all corporations in industry, U.S. Internal Revenue Service, *Statistics of Income,* Preliminary Report, 1954.

altogether in selecting the sample. Table 2 shows that, for most of the thirteen major industries, the companies in our sample accounted for a substantial proportion of the total assets of all corporations that can be classified in those industries. The aggregate assets of the 111 companies accounted for 45 per cent of the total assets of all corporations in the thirteen industries in 1954.

The selection of firms that were largest in their respective industries in 1954 may have introduced a small bias in our data. The firms that are largest on the terminal date of a fairly long interval of time are likely, as a group, to have grown faster than average in the course of the period. Since diversification is a form of growth, they are also likely to have diversified somewhat more than average. However, within the sample (as Appendix Tables A–2 and A–3 show) there was no significant concentration of rapidly growing companies in particular 2-digit industries. Appendix Table A–4 shows that companies in petroleum and in primary metals were, on the average, larger in 1954 than those in the sample as a whole, while companies in textile mill products, paper products, and stone, clay, and glass products tended to fall in the lower asset-size classes.

19

Conceptual Problems in the Data Used

An important problem arises from the use in this study of both product and plant data. When census (plant) data were used, *all* of the payrolls of an establishment were classified into the single largest (primary) industry irrespective of the product mix of the plant. The use of plant data opens the possibility that measures of diversification are biased to the extent that certain groups of enterprises have more homogeneous plants than others. For example, it is possible that larger plants will tend to be more heterogeneous than smaller ones, or that certain classes of enterprises tend to segregate varied industrial activities into separate plants while others combine varied activities in the same plants. Since the definition of an establishment itself contains a margin of ambiguity, the proportion of a company's activities falling within the scope of a single establishment is at times arbitrary. If it were true that companies with a larger variety of plants tended to have plants that internally were more homogeneous, measures of diversification based on plant data would be seriously inadequate.

Does internal homogeneity of plants systematically offset the greater diversity of plants owned by some firms? To resolve this problem, companies were divided into deciles on the basis of a measure of diversification (hereafter referred to as measure D_3) derived from establishment data. The measure was based on 1954 census information and consisted of the complement of the ratio of primary 4-digit industry payrolls to total company payrolls in all manufacturing activities, multiplied by the number of manufacturing industries in which the company maintained activities. The number of activities included only those which were not associated with integration and which accounted for at least 1 per cent of a company's total manufacturing employment. Manufacturing payrolls associated with integration were subtracted from the denominator of the ratio given above. For the group of companies in each decile, a ratio was computed of the total number of 4-digit manufacturing products produced in 1954 (derived from the product record described earlier in this chapter) to the sum of 4-digit manufacturing industries shown for the companies in the 1954 census establishment record. The higher the ratio, the greater the heterogeneity of products within plants, and the greater the tendency of establishment data to understate diversity of operations.

As may be seen in Table 3, the ratio of products to industries of establishments shows a reasonable degree of stability among companies grouped by the above measure of diversification. For eight of the deciles, the relevant ratio fell within the range of 1.4 to 1.7. Though the decile associated

TABLE 3
DIVERSIFICATION AND RATIO OF NUMBER OF INDUSTRIES BASED ON
PRODUCT RECORD TO THOSE BASED ON ESTABLISHMENT DATA

Diversification Decile[a] (ascending order)	Number of Companies[b]	Ratio of Number of 4-Digit Industries in Product Record to Those in Establishment Data[c]
1	13	3.1
2	10	1.7
3	11	1.5
4	11	1.4
5	11	1.7
6	11	1.5
7	11	1.7
8	11	1.6
9	11	2.1
10	11	1.4
All companies		1.6

SOURCE: Special census tabulation based on 1954 Census of Manufactures and product data for 1954 developed from public information by methods described in this chapter.

[a] The diversification measure was based on the 1954 Census of Manufactures and consisted of two components. First, the complement of the ratio of primary 4-digit-industry payrolls to manufacturing payrolls, minus manufacturing payrolls associated with integration, was computed. Second, the resultant statistic was multiplied by the number of manufacturing industries shown in census establishment data each of which accounted for at least 1 per cent of manufacturing employment for the company concerned. Activities characterized as integration were excluded.

[b] There are thirteen companies in the first decile because of tied ranks. Since ninety-eight companies remained for deciles 2–10, one decile was randomly selected to consist of ten companies.

[c] The product record was based on 1954 data developed from public records. Establishment data were derived from the 1954 Census of Manufactures.

with lowest diversification showed the highest ratio, there was no consistent tendency for companies that were more diversified on the basis of establishment data to show a lower ratio of number of products to number of industries of establishments. In short, the more diversified companies derived their greater diversity mainly from the greater heterogeneity of their establishments. These results tend to show that even had we, in later analysis, used a diversification measure based on product rather than on plant data, the resultant measures would have been substantially similar. Table 4 was developed as a further test of this conclusion. The table shows that when companies were grouped into deciles on the same basis as in Table 3, the average number of products per company was roughly thirty-seven for the highest decile as compared with only about ten for the lowest. Similarly, the average number of *manufacturing* products per company was roughly thirty for the highest decile and only five for the lowest. The table shows a relatively steady rise, from one decile to

TABLE 4

THE RELATION OF AVERAGE NUMBER OF PRODUCTS PER COMPANY TO DIVERSIFICATION
DECILES BASED ON MEASURE D_3 FOR 111 LARGE COMPANIES

Deciles on Basis of D_3	Number of Companies[a]	Average Number of Products per Company, 1954	Average Number of Products in Manufacturing Per Company, 1954
1	13	10.5	5.2
2	11	14.1	8.4
3	10	14.1	8.4
4	11	17.9	12.1
5	11	18.5	12.1
6	11	21.8	16.7
7	11	21.0	15.7
8	11	29.2	21.8
9	11	30.9	26.0
10	11	37.2	30.5

SOURCE: Number of products per company based on product record described in this chapter. D_3 based on census establishment data for 1954. The latter measure is defined on p. 58.

[a] The numbers of companies in the deciles were uneven because of tied ranks and uneven total number of companies.

the next, in the number of products that companies produced in 1954.

Several qualifications, however, need to be appended. First, there appear to be differences in plant heterogeneity between industry groupings of companies, so that not all of the variations between individual companies are random. Second, as compared with the cross-section of products in 1954, a somewhat larger proportion of products added since 1939 were produced in plants classified in industries other than those of the added products. Thus recent increases in diversification tend to be understated in census plant data. This results from the lesser likelihood that new activities, which have not as yet attained maturity, will account for the major part of the output of multiproduct plants. In addition, the Standard Industrial Classification Code (the industry classification system used for the study) is unlikely to incorporate industries of very recent origin (such as nuclear products). Under these circumstances, products that fall into the newest industries tend to be classified into previously existing categories and thus may not contribute to a measure of change in diversification. To the extent that these factors are present, there will be a relative understatement in the measure of diversification in 1954 for firms that have diversified more recently.

Some might also raise the question whether the directions of diversification (that is, the types of industries into which firms most frequently diversify), as reflected in plant data, are the same as those revealed in product data. On this point, however, the answer given in Chapter 7 is decisively in the affirmative.

Another possible bias arising from the nature of the data may be found in some other unsatisfactory aspects of the Classification Code. The division between industries in the Code does contain elements of arbitrary judgment, and industries are not equidistant from each other either in terms of substitution or mobility of resources between products. Nevertheless, if the errors in the Code as judged by an ideally designed classification system are generally random with respect to both the dependent variable (diversification) and the explanatory variables, these errors need not do much violence to broad generalizations.

Because the Code has been developed at several levels of industry detail, its use necessitates selection of the most appropriate level. The problem is made more difficult by the fact that if our objective is to segregate groupings of products defined by market boundaries, the most appropriate level given in the Code is not uniform for all industries. In general, the 4-digit level of detail represents the best compromise between, on the one hand, arbitrary breakdowns between close substitute products and, on the other, common classifications for heterogeneous products. Nevertheless, we have tried wherever possible to analyze the results at more than one level of industry detail. To the extent that varying classifications lead to substantially similar findings, the problem of choosing among the several alternatives becomes less critical.

The Relation Among Diversification Measures

Because of the variety of diversification measures used in this study, it is well to recapitulate them before analyzing further how much the use of one, rather than another, affects the findings. Fundamentally, three types were used: first, those based on primary industry concentration; second, those based on number of products produced or number of industries in which the firm was producing; third, measures that were composites of these two. In addition, the above measures were used at differing levels of industry detail, with as well as without adjustment for integration, and on the basis of differing bodies of data. The following is a summary of the measures used and tested.

$$D_1 \quad = \quad 1 - \quad \frac{P_r}{M_r - I_r}$$

$$D_2 \quad = \quad 1 - \quad \frac{P_r + S_r}{M_r - I_r}$$

$$D_3 \quad = \quad N_1 \left(1 - \frac{P_r}{M_r - I_r} \right)$$

$$D_4 \quad = \quad 1 - \frac{G_e}{V_e - A_e}$$

$$D_5 \quad = \quad N_2 \left(1 - \frac{G_e}{V_e - A_e} \right)$$

$$D_6 \quad = \quad 1 - \frac{P_e}{M_e}$$

$$D_7 \quad = \quad 1 - \frac{L_e}{V_e}$$

$$D_8 \quad = \quad N_3$$

P_r = primary 4-digit industry payrolls; M_r = total manufacturing payrolls; I_r = manufacturing payrolls associated with integration; S_r = manufacturing payrolls in the second largest 4-digit industry; N_1 = number of 4-digit manufacturing industries, excluding those which account for less than 1 per cent of manufacturing employment and those classified as integration; N_2 = the total number of 2-digit industries; G_e = employment in the primary 2-digit industry; V_e = total company employment; A_e = employment in 2-digit activities associated primarily with integration; P_e = primary 4-digit industry employment; M_e = total company employment in manufacturing; L_e = primary industry employment at the modified 3-digit level of detail; and N_3 = number of 3-digit industries.[13]

The first five measures were used exclusively for the sample of 111 firms because the requisite information was not available for the other sets of data. The only difference between measures D_1 and D_2 is the addition in the latter of the second largest activity in the numerator of the ratio. The Spearman coefficient of rank correlation between these two measures

[13] The modified 3-digit level of detail was that employed in *Company Statistics*.

was .94. Measures D_1 and D_3 differ in the addition to the latter, as a multiplier, of number of industries engaged in. The correlation here was also .94. Measures D_4 and D_5 are the same as D_1 and D_3 except that they employ the 2-digit level of detail and include nonmanufacturing activities; they were also highly correlated (.85). High correlation for the three sets of measures was, of course, to be expected since in each case one of the two measures being correlated is a component of the other.

To determine the effect of changing the level of industry detail, rank correlation coefficients were computed between measures D_1, D_2, and D_3, on the one hand, and D_4 and D_5, on the other. The results were as follows: the Spearman coefficient of rank correlation for diversification measures D_1 and D_4 was .62, for measures D_2 and D_4 it was .66, and for measures D_3 and D_5 it was .75. Differences in the ranks assigned to companies on the basis of the 4- and 2-digit measures did not arise merely from differences in the level of industry detail. The 2-digit measures incorporated diversification in nonmanufacturing industries, whereas those at the 4-digit level were restricted to manufacturing activities. Further, the latter were based on data for payrolls, while the former were based on employment data (information on payrolls being unavailable for out-of-census-scope activities). Therefore, if both 2- and 4-digit measures had been computed on the same basis, the resultant rank correlations would very probably have been higher. In short, while differences obviously arise as one changes the level of industry detail, the coefficients were sufficiently high to indicate that the measures of diversification used were not merely the accidental results of a single arbitrary breakdown of industries.

Greater confidence can be placed in a measure of diversification that yields roughly similar results for several levels of industry detail than in one that is highly unstable with regard to the system of classification used. The greater stability of measure D_3 than of measure D_1 (when compared with similar measures at the 2-digit level) makes it preferable, on that basis, as a general measure of diversification. However, all measures were used to a degree, though some only for comparative purposes.

Measures D_6 and D_7 were developed for the broader sample of 595 manufacturing enterprises in thirteen industry groups. The companies were ranked within each group on the basis of the two sets of ratios, and Spearman coefficients of rank correlation were computed for each group. As Table 5 shows, for nine of the thirteen groups the coefficients exceeded .8. Thus, once again, alternative levels of classification generate measures that lead to substantially similar rankings of companies.

TABLE 5

SPEARMAN COEFFICIENTS OF RANK CORRELATION FOR NONPRIMARY
EMPLOYMENT RATIOS AT TWO LEVELS OF INDUSTRY DETAIL[a]

Primary Industry of Company	Number of Companies	Rank Correlation[b]
Food products	78	.642
Textile mill products	66	.841
Paper products	39	.825
Chemicals	60	.810
Petroleum	27	.790
Rubber products	12	.934
Stone, clay, and glass products	22	.764
Primary metals	52	.649
Fabricated metal products	27	.858
Machinery	88	.866
Electrical machinery	52	.834
Transportation equipment	54	.899
Instruments	18	.944

SOURCE: Data used for computing correlations were derived from a special census tabulation based on the 1954 Censuses.

[a] The ratios correlated were nonprimary employment over *total manufacturing* employment at the 4-digit level and nonprimary employment over *total* employment at a modified three-digit level of detail.

[b] All coefficients were significant at the .01 level.

CHAPTER 3

Patterns and Trends in Diversification

How important are multi-industry firms in the American economy and how large are their nonprimary activities? In how many industries do large multiestablishment firms maintain production? The first part of this chapter is devoted to answering these questions. The second traces the trends in diversification since 1929 for large manufacturing companies. Most of the results in this part of the study are based on information for the 111-firm sample. The generalizations, therefore, apply primarily to large companies. Since, in terms of industry composition, the sample is not representative of the universe of large firms, measures of diversification for the sample as a whole cannot be taken as accurate estimates of average diversification for all large firms. However, they give a rough indication of the level of this average as well as a number of other characteristics of diversification for large companies in general.

The discussion in this chapter focuses primarily on the manufacturing activities of companies. Nonmanufacturing activities are discussed mainly in Chapter 6.

Summary

Firms that have establishments in more than one industry account for less than 1 per cent of the total number of firms in each of six sectors of the economy.[1] However, in 1954, in the six sectors combined they contributed roughly 38 per cent of the employment of all firms. Their role was largest in manufacturing and second in mineral extraction industries. Using the ratio of nonprimary to total employment as a measure of diversification, companies in manufacturing appear to be considerably more diversified than those in the other five sectors.

For the sample of 111 companies, the mean value of the ratio of payrolls in nonprimary manufacturing activities to total manufacturing payrolls was 39.2 per cent (using the 4-digit definition of primary industry). It declined moderately to 36.0 per cent when activities characterized as integration were excluded. Another measure of diversification is the number of industries in which firms maintain operations. The 111 firms produced goods and services in an average of 15.6 manufacturing industries, or 20.4 if nonmanufacturing activities are included.[2] They maintained

---

[1] The six sectors were those covered in the 1954 Economic Census and consisted of manufacturing; extraction of minerals; wholesale, retail, and service trades; and public warehousing.

[2] Once again, the 4-digit level of industry detail was employed.

separate establishments in an average of 9.7 manufacturing industries. A rather surprising fact was the large proportion of activities that were of relatively minor importance to individual companies. In the manufacturing operations of the 111 companies, 45.3 per cent of the separate industrial activities accounted individually for less than 2 per cent of the manufacturing employment of their companies.

The current widespread interest in diversification might suggest the phenomenon is of recent origin. The evidence, however, points to a contrary conclusion. The annual rate of product additions for the group of 111 companies was higher in the 1929–39 period than it was in 1939–50, though for either of the above periods it was substantially less than the rate in 1950–54. Further, although one might normally expect that suspension of activities would be more frequent in periods of low economic activity (particularly when suspension does not necessitate the sale of a plant), the annual rate of product abandonments rose over time and was roughly three times as high in the 1950's as in the 1930's. In consequence, the decline from the first to the second period was more marked, and the rise in the third period less pronounced, when measured by net than by gross product additions.

If an increase in diversification is measured by the decline in the relative importance of a firm's primary activities, a majority of the 111 companies showed an increase in diversification for the period 1947–54. However, the average decline for the 111 companies was relatively modest, being 5 percentage points or 7.2 per cent (a drop from 69.0 per cent to 64.0 per cent for the ratio of primary industry payrolls to total company payrolls in manufacturing).

When a separate activity is recorded only if it is primary to at least one plant, the number of manufacturing activities for the 111 companies combined increased from 823 in 1947 to 1,073 in 1954. However, in 1954, a considerable proportion of the new activities were still relatively small as compared with the size of their companies.

With companies grouped by primary industry, the same groupings tended to show the highest frequencies of product additions in successive periods. Thus some groups of companies appear to have consistently diversified more than others, and, in consequence, differences among companies in degree of diversification must have increased over the 1929–54 period. Another important characteristic of the trends in diversification has been that new activities have tended increasingly to be in industries less closely related to the primary ones in terms of production processes employed or the final uses of products.

Multiestablishment Enterprises

Multiestablishment firms, that is, firms operating more than one plant or establishment, represent a larger proportion of all firms in the higher than in the lower size classes of companies. Therefore, they play a much greater role in the economy than their relative numbers would suggest. In each of the six broad sectors of the economy covered in the 1954 Census, the number of multi- as compared with single-establishment companies was fairly small (Table 6). For the aggregate of the six sectors, they accounted for only 2.45 per cent of all companies reporting in the Census.[3]

TABLE 6

The Role of Multiunit and Multi-Industry Companies in 1954

	All Indus- tries	Min- erals	Manu- factur- ing	Whole- sale	Retail	Selected Service	Public Ware- houses
Multiunit companies as percentage of all companies	2.45	6.67	3.07	4.64	2.53	1.35	3.68
Multi-industry companies as per- centage of all companies	.246	1.25	1.30	.555	.098	.067	.016
Multi-industry companies as per- centage of multiunit companies	10.04	18.73	42.29	11.97	3.87	4.96	4.47
Multiunit employment as percent- age of employment for all companies[a]	52.03	57.12	64.41	26.75	38.67	23.38	24.18
Multi-industry employment as per- centage of employment for all companies[a]	38.37	35.01	53.02	11.31	20.84	9.82	2.20
Multi-industry employment as percentage of multiunit employment[a]	73.74	61.29	82.32	42.29	53.89	42.00	9.09

Source: Based on data in *Company Statistics*, Table C.

[a] The classification of employment according to industry categories was based on the industry of the parent company rather than of the establishment.

Yet, as Table 6 shows, multiunit companies accounted for roughly 52 per cent of the employment of all companies in the six sectors combined. The highest ratios were those for manufacturing and minerals extraction, for which they were 64.4 per cent and 57.1 per cent, respectively. The importance of multiunit firms is likely to be greater in industries with a relatively high average size of firm since company size is positively related to the

[3] Multi-industry companies, that is, those that operated establishments in more than one industry, were, of course, an even smaller proportion of the total number of firms in the six sectors, accounting for only a fraction of 1 per cent of the latter. "Industry" for this purpose was defined at the 4-digit level.

relative numbers of multi- as compared with single-establishment companies.[4]

Multi-industry companies accounted for roughly 38 per cent of total employment in the six sectors. Their relative roles within these sectors were, however, very unequal. In manufacturing, they contributed approximately 53 per cent to total employment, and for mineral industries 35 per cent. Though there were important differences, for five of the six divisions (all except public warehousing) a substantial percentage of the employment of multiunit firms was contributed by firms that maintained establishments in more than one industry. The differences among the various sectors are larger for the ratio of multi-industry to total employment than they are for the ratio of multi-industry to multiunit employment. Multi-industry companies contributed 82 per cent to the employment of multiunit companies in manufacturing and 61 per cent in mineral extraction industries. For the other sectors, the ratios were distinctly smaller. Thus if the relative importance of multi-industry companies is taken as a very rough measure of diversification, the latter appears to be strongest in manufacturing.

Multi-industry companies vary considerably in their relative importance among industry categories within each of the sectors of the economy, and particularly within the manufacturing sector. Generally, they are more important in industries in which average firm size is high.

The Magnitude of Nonprimary Activities in Aggregative Data

A primary industry is one that is associated with the largest individual activity of the firm. Differences in degree of specialization of operations in the primary activities of companies can be examined through aggregative industry data as well as on the basis of information for individual companies. In the former, the ratios of nonprimary to total employment can be based on information showing total employment of all companies classified in a particular industry and aggregate employment restricted to the primary industry of the same grouping of companies.[5]

[4] For seventy-one industries, the Spearman coefficient of rank correlation between the ratio of number of multi- to single-unit companies (based on data in U.S. Bureau of the Census, *Company Statistics: 1954 Censuses of Business, Manufacturing, Mineral Industries,* Washington, 1958, Table 2) and average size of firm in the industry (based on data described in Appendix D) was .77.

[5] These ratios give us a measure of specialization of activities in the primary industry that automatically gives greater weight to a large than to a small company. This may be distinguished from average ratios for particular industries, derived from data for individual companies, where the ratios are not weighted for differences in company size. Unweighted average ratios are better suited than aggregative data for the purpose of measuring the extent of diversification in a "typical" company. Census data for industry aggregates also

The ratios will vary depending on how *industry* is defined in each case. Thus, if industry is defined as one of the six broad sectors described earlier, the relevant percentage of nonprimary employment to total employment for each sector is as follows: manufacturing, 9.9 per cent; mining, 8.2 per cent; wholesale trade, 3.6 per cent; retail trade, 3.5 per cent; and services, 1.3 per cent. This measure, however, would not allow for the fact that an important proportion of activities outside the major division represents integration rather than diversification. Moreover, the activities to be found within the major division are highly heterogeneous. Indeed, diversification is to be found primarily in the heterogeneity of a firm's output within its primary division rather than outside it. Thus the above definition of industry is far too broad. Using the same six divisions in which to classify the enterprises, but substituting the previously described 3-digit definition of primary industry, the ratios of nonprimary to total employment were as follows: manufacturing, 21.4 per cent; minerals, 9.2 per cent; retail trade. 5.5 per cent; wholesale trade, 4.6 per cent; and services and public warehousing, less than 2 per cent.

Table 7 is a frequency distribution for eighty-six manufacturing and mining and thirty-four trade and service industries for the ratio of employment in nonprimary activities to employment in the primary industries of the companies concerned. Appendix Table D–6 shows the ratio in question for each of 120 industries. It is apparent from these tables that,

TABLE 7
NONPRIMARY INDUSTRY EMPLOYMENT AS
PERCENTAGE OF PRIMARY INDUSTRY EMPLOYMENT, 1954

| *Manufacturing and Mining* | | *Trade and Services* | |
Nonprimary as Percentage of Primary Employment	Number of Industries	Nonprimary as Percentage of Primary Employment	Number of Industries
.0– 4.9	17	0– .9	7
5.0– 9.9	18	1–1.9	12
10.0–14.9	10	2–2.9	3
15.0–19.9	8	3–3.9	5
20.0–24.9	9	4–4.9	3
25.0–29.9	7	5 and over	4
30.0–39.9	2		
40.0–49.9	7		
50.0 and over	8		
Total	86		34

SOURCE: *Company Statistics,* Table 2.

incorporate single-unit as well as multiunit companies. For this reason, they will show a relatively smaller volume of nonprimary activities than would be true for samples of companies restricted to multiunit enterprises.

on the basis of data for establishments,[6] in most industrial categories companies with highly homogeneous product structures predominate.

A rather interesting aspect of the aggregative ratios of nonprimary to primary employment for the eighty-six manufacturing and mining industries is that nonprimary activities appear relatively larger, compared with those in primary industries, on the basis of employment than on the basis of number of establishments. This was true for fifty-four of eighty-six industries. It implies that for the majority of industries the average size of establishments in nonprimary industries was larger than that for the primary ones—a conclusion opposite to that indicated at another point in the study for the sample of 111 large enterprises. This finding, however, can be explained by the fact that multi-industry companies tend to be larger and thus generally operate larger plants than do single-industry firms. Thus the establishments in nonprimary industries, as they are owned by the larger, multi-industry firms, tend to be larger than the average establishment in the primary industries. In short, if we exclude single-industry companies, and particularly the large numbers of single-establishment companies in most industry classes, aggregative data would probably point to the same conclusion as data for the 111 large companies.

Diversification Patterns for the 111-Firm Sample

For this sample, the data permitted a distinction to be made between activities associated with diversification and those characterized as integration. For the 111 companies, the mean value of the ratio of payrolls in the primary 4-digit industry to total *manufacturing* payrolls, excluding those associated with integration, was 64.0 per cent with a standard deviation of 28.7 percentage points.[7] When payrolls associated with integration activities were included in the denominator, the ratio dropped only slightly to 60.8 per cent, and the standard deviation to 24.8 percentage points. The inclusion of activities outside manufacturing in the analysis permitted the use of only a 2-digit level of industry detail for the above relationships. Further, the information was for employment rather than payrolls. The mean ratio of primary 2-digit employment to total employment (including that in nonmanufacturing) was 81.2 per cent when integration employment was subtracted from the denominator, and only

[6] Establishment data may be distinguished from data that would not classify *all* of the output or employment of a multiproduct establishment into a single industry.

[7] The average ratio for the 111 companies of primary plus secondary industry payrolls to total manufacturing payrolls (excluding those associated with integration) was 78.9 per cent. The secondary industry is defined as the second largest for the individual firm, not counting those classified as integration.

60.4 per cent when it was not excluded. The standard deviations were 18.8 and 20.5 percentage points, respectively. Thus it appears that exclusion of integration affects the ratios of primary to total employment far more when nonmanufacturing activities are included in the analysis. This stems from the fact that, for manufacturing enterprises, integration as compared with other activities is more important outside manufacturing than within it.

For the two ratios which include nonmanufacturing activities, the coefficient of variation was distinctly higher with integration employment included in the denominator: 33.9 per cent compared with 23.2 per cent if integration employment is excluded. This indicates a more stable relationship among the companies between primary employment and that part of nonprimary employment associated with diversification than be-

TABLE 8

AVERAGE RATIOS OF PRIMARY INDUSTRY EMPLOYMENT TO TOTAL EMPLOYMENT AND
PRIMARY INDUSTRY PAYROLLS TO TOTAL MANUFACTURING PAYROLLS,
111 LARGE ENTERPRISES, 1954

Primary Industry of Company	Number of Companies	Average Primary Two-Digit Ratio		Average Primary 4-Digit Ratio	
		Unadjusted Employment[a]	Adjusted Employment[b]	Unadjusted Employment[a]	Adjusted Manufacturing Payrolls[c]
Food products	12	.659	.933	.530	.783
Tobacco manufactures	5	.832	.999	.585	.726
Textile mill products	4	.651	.754	.444	.514
Paper products	8	.780	.893	.410	.576
Chemicals	14	.606	.752	.338	.478
Petroleum	10	.306	.886	.306	.927
Rubber products	5	.558	.697	.344	.477
Stone, clay, and glass products	7	.683	.833	.502	.637
Primary metals	10	.656	.831	.573	.723
Fabricated metal products	5	.586	.685	.524	.529
Machinery	13	.555	.807	.400	.609
Electrical machinery	5	.585	.667	.302	.365
Transportation equipment	13	.663	.728	.587	.682
Ratio of variances[d]		4.291	1.891	2.461	3.716

SOURCE: Special census tabulation.

[a] Ratio based on data for employment; employment associated with integration not subtracted from denominator.

[b] Ratio based on data for employment; employment associated with integration subtracted from denominator.

[c] Ratio based on data for payrolls restricted to manufacturing; payrolls associated with integration subtracted from denominator.

[d] For each column the ratio of the variance between industries to that within industry cells with $N_1 = 12$, $N_2 = 98$.

tween the former and *all* nonprimary employment (including integration).

In a majority of the thirteen industry groups of companies, average primary 4-digit employment was less than 50 per cent of total employment unadjusted for integration (Table 8). On the same basis, primary 2-digit employment was between 55 per cent and 70 per cent of total employment in ten of the thirteen industry groups. Because no adjustment was made for employment associated with integration, the ratios tend to understate the extent of specialization of operations in the company's primary industry. With the adjustment, the specialization of employment in the primary 2-digit industry exceeded 70 per cent in ten of the thirteen groups. On the adjusted basis also, and using data for payrolls for manufacturing operations, the primary 4-digit industry accounted for more than 50 per cent of total manufacturing payrolls in all but two of the thirteen industry categories. All four measures of primary industry specialization in Table 8 showed wide differences in average ratios between industry groupings of companies.[8]

TABLE 9

DISTRIBUTION OF COMPANIES BY NUMBER OF
PRODUCTS AND SERVICES PRODUCED IN 1954

Number of Products and Services[a]	*Number of Companies*	
	All Products and Services Counted	Only Manufacturing Products Counted
1– 5	9	17
6–10	10	30
11–15	16	19
16–20	23	18
21–25	25	9
26–30	9	10
31–35	5	3
36–40	7	1
40 and over	7	4

SOURCE: Product record described in Chapter 2.

[a] Products or services falling within the same 4-digit industry counted as one product or service.

As distinct from the relative magnitude of nonprimary activities measured by either payrolls or employment, one might wish to inquire into the number of separate products and services that the 111 firms produced in 1954. At the 4-digit level of detail, the arithmetic mean for the 111 companies was 15.6 excluding nonmanufacturing activities and 20.4 including the latter. Table 9 is a frequency distribution showing the number of companies falling into various classes based on number of activities in 1954.

[8] The variance between industry means was, in the case of all four ratios, significantly greater than that between companies within industry classes.

34

Table 10 shows the number of manufacturing industries in which the 111 enterprises maintained establishments in 1954. The nonprimary activities of *plants* did not enter into the count of industries. (In this respect Table 10 differs from Table 9.) The average number for the 111 companies was 9.7. The electrical machinery group accounted for the largest number per company (22.2) and petroleum for the lowest average number (3.9) of the thirteen groups.

Table 10 also shows the number of minor manufacturing activities in which the 111 firms were engaged—that is, activities which account for a relatively small proportion of the company's manufacturing employment. The table indicates the proportion of activities that contributed more than 2 per cent and more than 1 per cent of total manufacturing employment for the companies in question.[9] It is rather surprising to find that for a majority of the 111 large enterprises, minor activities accounted for a substantial proportion of the total number of industrial activities in which the companies were engaged. In six of the thirteen industry groups, at least one-third of the manufacturing activities individually contributed not more than 1 per cent to the manufacturing employment of their companies. When the boundary between minor and nonminor activities is set at 2 per cent, a third or more of the activities were minor in eleven of the thirteen industry groups. For the 111 companies combined, 45.3 per cent of all manufacturing activities fell below the 2 per cent boundary and 32.4 per cent fell below the 1 per cent boundary. This seems to indicate that, for large enterprises, a considerable proportion of the individual manufacturing operations in which companies are engaged are not crucial and, probably, not even important to the success of the enterprise as a whole. A reason for the existence of a large number of relatively minor activities is that many of them are new to companies and have not had time to attain the size intended for them in long-term plans. This, however, is likely to explain only a part of the phenomenon.

An increase in the number of minor activities in which a firm is engaged may reduce the effectiveness of central controls over a firm's operations. However, from the point of view of an investor in the firm, the hazards associated with new and risky ventures are smaller when these activities account for a small proportion of the total employment (and investment) of the firm.[10]

[9] The 1 per cent and 2 per cent boundaries for minor activities are, perforce, somewhat arbitrary. Thus, it is interesting to see to what extent the results are affected by changing the boundary.

[10] While the hazards of unfavorable surprises are likely to be smaller, so are the effects of favorable ones.

TABLE 10

NUMBER OF 4-DIGIT MANUFACTURING INDUSTRIES FOR 111 LARGE ENTERPRISES, 1954

Primary Industry of Company	Number of Companies	Total Number of Industries	Average Number per Company	Number with over 2 Per Cent of Total Manufacturing Employment	Percentage of Total Number[a]	Number with over 1 Per Cent of Total Manufacturing Employment	Percentage of Total Number[b]
Food products	12	132	11.0	60	45.4	81	61.4
Tobacco manufactures	5	22	4.4	17	77.3	18	81.8
Textile mill products	4	30	7.5	20	66.7	23	76.7
Paper products	8	68	8.5	45	66.2	52	76.5
Chemicals	14	173	12.4	99	57.2	116	67.0
Petroleum	10	39	3.9	22	56.4	24	61.5
Rubber products	5	62	12.4	36	58.1	45	72.6
Stone, clay, and glass products	7	61	8.7	35	57.4	50	82.0
Primary metals	10	110	11.0	46	41.8	57	51.8
Fabricated metal products	5	55	11.0	36	65.4	44	80.0
Machinery	13	89	6.8	66	74.2	76	85.4
Electrical machinery	5	111	22.2	44	39.6	60	54.0
Transportation equipment	13	121	9.3	61	50.4	79	65.3
Total	111	1,073	9.7	587	54.7	725	67.6

SOURCE: Special census tabulation.

[a] Those with over 2 per cent of manufacturing employment as a percentage of all activities.

[b] Those with over 1 per cent of manufacturing employment as a percentage of all activities.

TABLE 11

TOTAL NUMBER OF ESTABLISHMENTS AND PROPORTION IN
PRIMARY INDUSTRIES, 111 LARGE ENTERPRISES, 1954

Primary Industry of Company	Number of Companies	Total Number of Establishments	Average Number per Company	Percentage of Establishments in Primary 4-Digit Industry
Food products	12	1,149	95.7	43.0
Tobacco manufactures	5	57	11.4	33.9
Textile mill products	4	74	18.5	29.0
Paper products	8	276	34.5	30.6
Chemicals	14	656	46.8	24.6
Petroleum	10	157	15.7	62.0
Rubber products	5	225	45.0	18.9
Stone, clay, and glass products	7	211	30.1	43.6
Primary metals	10	464	46.0	32.7
Fabricated metal products	5	212	42.4	37.0
Machinery	13	163	12.5	28.2
Electrical machinery	5	358	71.6	24.0
Transportation equipment	13	341	26.2	52.6

SOURCE: Special census tabulation.

TABLE 12

RATIO OF NUMBER OF MANUFACTURING PRODUCTS TO NUMBER OF 4-DIGIT
MANUFACTURING INDUSTRIES, 111 LARGE ENTERPRISES, 1954[a]

Primary Industry of Company	Ratio
Food products	1.18
Tobacco manufactures	1.18
Textile mill products	1.30
Paper products	1.72
Chemicals	1.63
Petroleum	2.15
Rubber products	2.47
Stone, clay, and glass products	1.51
Primary metals	1.39
Fabricated metal products	1.58
Machinery	2.01
Electrical machinery	1.61
Transportation equipment	1.69
All companies	1.61

SOURCE: Product record for 1954 described in Chapter 2, and special census tabulation.
[a] Number of products based on data from public records. Number of industries is that shown in census establishment data.

Industries of Products	Industries of Companies					
	Food (12)	Tobacco (5)	Textiles (4)	Paper (8)	Chemicals (14)	Petroleum (10)
Ordnance					7	
Food products	85				4	
Tobacco manufactures		18				
Textile mill products	2	2	16	3	8	
Apparel			6			
Lumber and wood[b]	2	1		11	5	
Furniture				1	1	
Paper products	5	1	1	39	4	
Printing and publishing	2	1		5	2	
Chemicals	47	1	6	22	161	57
Petroleum and coal products				1	9	17
Rubber products			1	1	1	
Leather	3					
Stone, clay, and glass products	1		5	8	7	
Primary metals					17	2
Fabricated metal products	3	2	1	1	9	2
Machinery[c]	4		1	17	23	2
Electrical machinery				2	6	
Transportation equipment	1				3	
Instruments[d]				3	2	1
Misc. manuf. industries	1		2	3	7	3
Total	156	26	39	117	280	84
Average per company	13.0	5.2	9.7	14.6	20.0	8.4

For the thirteen industry groups, there was no correlation between the relative numbers of minor and nonminor activities and average diversification in each industry, as measured by the D_3 measure of diversification. This indicates that the large role of minor activities noted above is not a characteristic peculiar to highly diversified companies.

Differences among the thirteen industry groups in the extent to which manufacturing activities were concentrated in the primary 4-digit industry followed roughly the same pattern when measured on the basis of the distribution of establishments among industries as they did on the basis of payroll data. On the average, however, primary industry specialization *and Number of Products*[a]

Rubber (5)	Stone, Clay, and Glass (7)	Primary Metals (10)	Fabricated Metal Products (5)	Machinery (13)	Electrical Machinery (5)	Transportation Equipment (13)	Total (111)	Total Less Primary Industry Additions
8	1	1	1	3	2	15	38	38
				1			90	5
							18	0
20	2			1	2		56	40
6							12	12
2	3	1	1	1	2	1	30	30
3	2	2	1	5	4	1	20	20
2	9		8	4	2	1	76	37
		1	2	4	2	1	20	20
29	19	9		1	14	8	374	213
1	1	7		1		1	38	21
17	1		1			3	25	8
2							5	5
7	35	6	4	2	12	6	93	58
3		49	10	18	18	26	143	94
10	5	42	20	7	21	26	149	129
8	4	19	23	74	30	43	248	174
8	2	8	4	17	53	21	121	68
13		4	6	9	7	44	87	43
3	4		3	8	6	6	36	36
11	4	4	3	3	4	1	46	46
153	92	153	87	159	179	204	1,729	
30.4	13.1	15.3	17.4	12.2	35.8	15.7	15.6	

SOURCE: Product record described in Chapter 2.

[a] Numbers in parentheses refer to number of companies in the specified industry.

[b] Except furniture.

[c] Except electrical.

[d] Professional, scientific, and controlling instruments, photographic and optical goods, watches and clocks.

based on data for numbers of establishments (Table 11) was lower than that based on payrolls. This reflects the fact that, for the 111 companies, plants associated with primary industries are larger as well as more numerous than those associated with nonprimary manufacturing activities.

The thirteen industry groups of companies differ also in the degree of product homogeneity which characterizes their plants. Table 12 shows the ratios of number of manufactured products (based on public records) to number of manufacturing industries (based on census plant data). The average ratio for the 111 companies was 1.61. The plants of companies in the petroleum, rubber products, and machinery industries tended to be more heterogeneous than those of other companies, while those of companies in food, tobacco, and textile mill products were more homogeneous than average for the establishments of all companies in the sample. Product data compiled for 1954 is also revealing with respect to the composition of industrial activities to be found under common ownership. Table 13 shows the 1954 product patterns for the 111 companies at the 2-digit level of industry detail. On the basis of the average number of manufactured products per company in 1954, the more diversified companies fell in the electrical machinery, rubber products, chemicals, and fabricated metal products industries, while companies with the most homogeneous product structures were to be found in the tobacco and petroleum industries. Of interest also is the composition of activities under common ownership. For roughly half of the thirteen industrial categories into which companies were classified, chemical industries accounted for the largest number of nonprimary products. (Nonprimary is defined here as falling outside the primary 2-digit industry.) Frequency of activity in chemical industries was especially striking for companies in the paper; petroleum; rubber products; stone, clay, and glass; and food products industry groups. For textile mill products companies, the apparel and chemical industries accounted for the largest number of nonprimary products. For companies classified in the machinery industry, primary metals contributed the largest number of products outside the primary industry. Tobacco companies revealed no concentration of activities outside of tobacco manufacturing, and the remaining categories of companies —namely, transportation equipment, electrical machinery, fabricated metal products, primary metals, and chemicals—had the largest number of their nonprimary manufacturing activities in the machinery industry. Besides chemicals and machinery, other nonprimary activities frequently engaged in by the 111 companies were primary metals, fabricated metal products, electrical machinery, and ordnance.[11]

An indication of the heterogeneity of ventures within nonprimary industries may be obtained from an examination of the activities of food products companies in the chemical industries. Seven of the twelve companies in the sample produced drugs or toilet preparations or both. These products included, among others, soaps, epsom salts, vitamin-mineral fortifiers, and drugs for liver disorders and for arthritis. One meat-packing firm produced a purified form of ACTH, and an alcoholic beverage

[11] A somewhat more detailed breakdown in the Code for some industries, e.g., chemicals, may have exerted a moderate influence on the results in that two or more nonprimary products are less likely to fall in the same 4-digit industry (and thus be counted only once) when the industry breakdown is more detailed.

company manufactured hydrogen peroxide and perfume bases. Apart from drugs and toilet preparations, cleaning compounds were produced by four companies, fatty acids and adhesives each by three companies, and fertilizers, sulphuric acid, and products for paint manufacturing each by two companies. The wide range of industrial chemicals produced by the companies is exemplified by the meat-packing firm that produced chemicals used in the separation of nonmetallic ores, the dairy products company that manufactured plastic molding compounds, and the alcoholic beverage company that produced butyl acetate and liquefied propane and butane.

Appendix Table B–2 shows the number of companies in the 111-firm sample that maintained production in the twenty-one 2-digit manufacturing industries. There were fifty-three companies with nonprimary operations in machinery, forty-eight in fabricated metal products, and forty-seven in chemicals. Of the remaining eighteen 2-digit industries, nonprimary activity counts ranged from zero to thirty-three. Only tobacco, of the twenty-one categories, showed zero operations emanating from nontobacco companies. The next lowest were food products and leather products, with four companies each (once again excluding companies with primary operations in the industries).

The Measurement of Trends

The magnitude of a movement toward diversification can be measured in ways similar to those by which diversification at a point in time was measured, namely, both in terms of the number of products added to a firm's product structure and in terms of the change in the relative importance of a firm's primary industry. Most of our data on changes over time were derived from public sources of information for which data on volume of sales or output of individual products were not available. Therefore, the data consist primarily of frequencies of product additions between successive points in time, recorded at the 4-digit level of industry detail.[12] Negative changes in heterogeneity, that is, product abandonments, were measured in the same way as additions. Information on trends was restricted to the 111-firm sample. The average frequencies of additions for this group of companies do not necessarily approximate an average for the universe of large firms. However, the changes over time in number of additions and abandonments and, to a large extent,

[12] In using the 4-digit SIC Code for counting the number of product additions, several products added within a specified interval of time and falling within the same 4-digit industry were counted as one addition in that period. The reason for this procedure is explained in Chapter 2.

Industries of Companies

Industries of Product Additions	Food (12)	Tobacco (5)	Textiles (4)	Paper (8)	Chemicals (14)	Petroleum (10)	Rubber (5)
Ordnance					2		
Food products	38						
Tobacco manufactures		1					
Textile mill products			2		1		5
Apparel			4				
Lumber and wood[b]	1						1
Furniture							1
Paper products	1		1	22			2
Printing and publishing							
Chemicals	11		2	5	53	9	7
Petroleum and coal						10	
Rubber products			1	1	1		5
Leather							
Stone, clay, and glass products			4	2	3		3
Primary metals					3		
Fabricated metal products		1	1		1	1	2
Machinery[c]	1		1		3	2	2
Electrical machinery							3
Transportation equipment					1		4
Instruments[d]					1	1	2
Miscellaneous			2	1	2	1	2
Total additions	52	2	18	31	71	24	39
Primary industry additions	38	1	2	22	53	10	5
Total less primary industry additions	14	1	16	9	18	14	34

the industries most frequently entered, are likely to be similar for the sample and for large firms in general. In a later section of this study (Chapter 7) it is shown that the characteristics of industries that attract diversifying entry proved substantially the same on the basis of aggregative data as for the 111-firm group.

For reasons discussed in Chapter 2, the 1929–54 period was divided into three shorter intervals of time: 1929–39, 1939–50, and 1950–54. The

and Number of Additions[a]

Stone, Clay, and Glass (7)	Primary Metals (10)	Fabricated Metal Products (5)	Machinery (13)	Electrical Machinery (5)	Transportation Equipment (13)	Total Additions	Primary Industry Additions	Total Less Primary Industry Additions
				1	2	5	0	5
						38	38	0
						1	1	0
				1		9	2	7
						4	0	4
	1					3	0	3
	3	1	2	2		9	0	9
4		1		1		32	22	10
1		1		1		3	0	3
9					5	101	53	48
1						11	10	1
					1	9	5	4
				2		2	0	2
13	1	1		1	1	29	13	16
	12	1		5	4	25	12	13
5	21	1	1	8	12	54	1	53
2	2	3	20	11	15	62	20	42
	1		9	20	9	42	20	22
				1	10	16	10	6
		1	1	4	4	14	0	14
2			2	3		15	0	15
37	41	10	35	61	63	484		
13	12	1	20	20	10		207	
24	29	9	15	41	53			277

SOURCE: Product record described in Chapter 2.

[a] Numbers in parentheses refer to number of companies in the specified industry.

[b] Except furniture.

[c] Except electrical.

[d] Professional, scientific, and controlling instruments, photographic and optical goods, watches and clocks.

availability of additional data from the Census of Manufactures for the years 1947 and 1954 led us to examine also the changes that occurred in the 1947–54 interval. For this period, it was also possible to examine one aspect of change in the composition of output not necessarily related to diversification, namely, the relative importance in 1947 and 1954 of the firms' largest activities in 1947. Changes in the importance of the initial year's primary industries can occur to a marked degree without net in-

Industries of Companies

Industries of Product Additions	Food (12)	Tobacco (5)	Textiles (4)	Paper (8)	Chemicals (14)	Petroleum (10)	Rubber (5)
Ordnance					2		6
Food products	21				1		
Tobacco manufactures							
Textile mill products			7		3		6
Apparel			2				
Lumber and wood[b]	2						
Furniture							1
Paper products			1	12	1		
Printing and publishing	1			1			
Chemicals	10	1	4	8	48	30	11
Petroleum and coal				1	1	4	
Rubber products				1			5
Leather							1
Stone, clay, and glass products			2	3	1		2
Primary metals					2	2	2
Fabricated metal products	1				1	1	3
Machinery[c]			1	6	12		2
Electrical machinery				2	1		1
Transportation equipment					1		9
Instruments[d]				2	1		1
Miscellaneous				2	1		3
Total additions	36	1	17	38	76	37	53
Primary industry additions	21	0	7	12	48	4	5
Total less primary industry additions	15	1	10	26	28	33	48

creases or declines in diversification, since new primary industries can supplant former ones, leaving the degree of specialization in the primary industry unchanged.

Trends in Diversification

In the period 1929–54 the 111 large companies added 1,389 products in manufacturing activities. These product additions appear to account for

and Number of Additions[a]

Stone, Clay, and Glass (7)	Primary Metals (10)	Fabricated Metal Products (5)	Machinery (13)	Electrical Machinery (5)	Transportation Equipment (13)	Total Additions	Primary Industry Additions	Total Less Primary Industry Additions
		1	3	3	4	19	0	19
						22	21	1
						0	0	0
						16	7	9
						2	0	2
1			1			4	0	4
2				3		6	0	6
3		4				21	12	9
			1	1		4	0	4
6	1	1		6		126	48	78
1					1	8	4	4
1					1	8	5	3
						1	0	1
10				2	4	24	10	14
	5		3	4	4	22	5	17
	3	3	2	7	9	30	3	27
		6	14	7	12	60	14	46
		3	6	21	7	41	21	20
			1	4	16	32	16	16
1			5	2	5	17	0	17
		3		2		11	0	11
25	9	21	36	62	63	474		
10	5	3	14	21	16		166	
15	4	18	22	41	47			308

SOURCE: Product record described in Chapter 2.

[a] Numbers in parentheses refer to number of companies in the specified industry.

[b] Except furniture.

[c] Except electrical.

[d] Professional, scientific, and controlling instruments, photographic and optical goods, watches and clocks.

well over half of the separate industrial activities in which the firms were engaged in 1954. Table 14 shows, for the 1929–39 period, the number of products added in each 2-digit manufacturing industry by the various industry groupings of companies. Tables 15 and 16 give the same information for 1939–50 and 1950–54, respectively. Table 17 is a frequency distribution for each period showing the number of companies falling into various classes based on number of product additions.

Industries of Companies

Industries of Product Additions	Food (12)	Tobacco (5)	Textiles (4)	Paper (8)	Chemicals (14)	Petroleum (10)	Rubber (5)
Ordnance					3		4
Food products	11				2		
Tobacco manufactures							
Textile mill products			1	3	3		11
Apparel							3
Lumber and wood[b]				4	2		1
Furniture				1	1		1
Paper products	1			11	1		
Printing and publishing				1	1		
Chemicals	17		1	11	40	15	4
Petroleum and coal					2	4	1
Rubber products				1			6
Leather							1
Stone, clay, and glass products				2	1		
Primary metals					4		
Fabricated metal products					3		3
Machinery[c]				3	11		2
Electrical machinery					1		3
Transportation equipment					2	1	8
Instruments[d]					1	1	2
Miscellaneous			1	1	5		4
Total additions	29	0	3	38	83	21	54
Primary industry additions	11	0	1	11	40	4	6
Total less primary industry additions	18	0	2	27	43	17	48

There were 484 products added by the 111 firms in 1929–39, 474 in 1939–50, and 431 in 1950–54. Since the three periods are unequal in duration, a more meaningful comparison may be derived from the annual rates—namely, 48.4, 43.1 and 107.8 for 1929–39, 1939–50, and 1950–54, respectively. In short, the annual rate of product additions for the group of companies was higher in 1929–39 than in 1939–50, though clearly less than in 1950–54. The addition of products normally entails expenditures

and Number of Additions[a]

Stone, Clay, and Glass (7)	Pri- mary Metals (10)	Fabricated Metal Products (5)	Machinery (13)	Electrical Machinery (5)	Transpor- tation Equip- ment (13)	Total Addi- tions	Primary Industry Addi- tions	Total Less Primary Industry Addi- tions
1	1				11	20	0	20
						13	11	2
						0	0	0
2						20	1	19
						3	0	3
				2		9	0	9
			1		1	5	0	5
1		1				15	11	4
		1				3	0	3
2	1		1	3	2	97	40	57
						7	4	3
		1				8	6	2
						1	0	1
5	2			1		11	5	6
	5	1	1	3	4	18	5	13
	3	2		2	6	19	2	17
	5	1	18	11	24	75	11	64
1	2	2	3	12	7	31	12	19
	1	4	5	2	22	45	22	23
3			2	1	2	12	0	12
1	2	1	2	1	1	19	0	19
16	22	14	33	38	80	431		
5	5	2	18	12	22		137	
11	17	12	15	26	58			294

Sᴏᴜʀᴄᴇ: Product record described in Chapter 2.
[a] Numbers in parentheses refer to number of companies in the specified industry.
[b] Except furniture.
[c] Except electrical.
[d] Professional, scientific, and controlling instruments, photographic and optical goods, watches and clocks.

on plant and equipment, research, and product promotion, so that comparisons of frequency of product additions with capital expenditure rates are of some interest. In the 1950–54 period, capital expenditures for the 111 companies, even after adjustment for price changes, proceeded at an annual rate considerably greater than twice that of 1929–39. Thus, on this basis, the movement toward diversification in the earlier as compared with the later period appears to have been strong. The moderate decline

TABLE 17

111 LARGE ENTERPRISES DISTRIBUTED BY NUMBER OF PRODUCTS AND
SERVICES ADDED, 1929–54

Number of Products and Services Added[a]	Number of Companies			Number of Products Added in Manufacturing	Number of Companies		
	1929–39	1939–50	1950–54		1929–39	1939–50	1950–54
0	12	17	17	0	17	17	22
1–2	23	27	30	1–2	29	38	32
3–4	25	23	26	3–4	27	20	26
5–6	17	8	15	5–6	14	9	13
7–8	10	15	8	7–8	8	10	6
9–10	7	5	4	9–10	5	6	3
11–14	8	9	5	11–14	6	6	4
15–17	5	4	3	15–17	2	3	2
18 and over	4	3	3	18 and over	3	2	3

SOURCE: Product record described in Chapter 2.
[a] Includes nonmanufacturing as well as manufacturing products and services.

in the rate of product additions from the 1929–39 to the 1939–50 period also shows that diversification does not closely follow cyclical fluctuations in general business activity. This stems at least partly from the fact that diversification is at times a defensive measure intended to counteract declines in demand for the primary activities of companies. Further, it can frequently be accomplished through merger, or by shifting productive capacity from other uses, rather than by capital outlays.

Changes in the product structures of firms followed a variety of paths, though, as will be shown in Chapter 7, there was considerable similarity in the economic characteristics of entered industries. An example of differing patterns for similar companies is that of two firms whose primary activity consisted in manufacturing railroad cars and related equipment. Both were faced with a demand that showed little prospect of growth, if not a likelihood of secular decline. Both chose to diversify, but in sharply differing ways. In the 1929–39 period, one began producing tanks (ordnance) while the other chose to operate a bank. The first acquired a large subsidiary in the 1939–50 period which was engaged in the construction of petroleum refineries and general chemical processing plants. The subsidiary also produced plastics, refractory products, utility-power piping systems, and metal panels for buildings. Through another acquisition in the same period, it also began producing earth-moving equipment. On the other hand, the parent company was legally obliged to divest itself of the maintenance and operation of railroad passenger cars. In the 1950–54 period, the company withdrew from production of earth-moving equipment but, through the acquisition of still another subsidiary, began

48

producing highway truck trailers. It also entered into the production of rocket motors for guided missiles and the manufacture of alloy steels.

The second firm added only one category of manufactured products, namely, pressed-steel products, in the 1939–50 period. In the same interval, it disposed of property used in producing motor-driven rail cars, trucks and buses, snow sweepers, and gas engines; it closed a shipyard and facilities used in producing interior woodwork. In 1950–54, however, it acquired facilities to produce tools and sheet metalworking equipment, computers and electronic components for data-processing equipment, radar equipment, air-frame components, aircraft ordnance, fire-control systems, and navigational instruments.

Examples of dissimilar companies entering the same industries are also abundant. Thus in 1929 one firm produced only incandescent lamps and vacuum tubes for radio receiving sets. Another, though it could be classified in the same 2-digit industry, produced a large variety of electrical machinery for public utility systems and a considerable number of electric home appliances, lamps, scientific instruments, passenger and freight elevators, insulating materials, and numerous other products. Although their lists of product additions were not identical, in the 1929–54 interval both firms began producing fluorescent lighting fixtures, radio and television receiving sets, special tubes for military and industrial uses, X-ray equipment, electronic equipment for industrial uses, and nuclear reactor equipment. In 1954 both also maintained research laboratories for missile systems and for atomic energy.

The most common pattern—namely, that of similar companies diversifying (and also, integrating) in similar ways—may be illustrated by two rubber-tire manufacturers. In the 1929–54 period, both began producing synthetic rubber and a variety of rubber products, such as rubber athletic goods and synthetic fibers for tires. Both also began producing plastic materials and products, aviation equipment, and components for guided missiles. Of course, no two companies that have actively diversified their product structures will have followed identical paths. For example, one of the two tire manufacturers also began producing internal combustion and underwater engines—the other did not. In the category of plastic products, one produced seat covers; the other manufactured plastic tiles. In the category of aviation equipment, one produced jet-assist take-off units and aircraft wheels; the other manufactured airplane assemblies and flight trainers. The essential similarity of the patterns is, however, unmistakable.

As may be judged from Tables 14, 15, and 16, when only additions outside the primary 2-digit industries of companies are considered, the manufacturing industries entered most frequently by the 111 companies in the 1929–39 period were those falling into the chemicals and fabricated metal products industries. Among the industry classes with very few non-primary additions were: food products, tobacco, and petroleum and coal products. (The counts for the first two were zero and for the third the count was one.) In the 1939–50 and 1950–54 periods, industry classes accounting for the largest number of nonprimary additions were chemicals and machinery. Among those with few or zero instances of entry were once again the food products, tobacco, and petroleum and coal products categories. Appendix Tables B–7 through B–9 show the *number of companies* that added products in each of the twenty-one 2-digit manufacturing industries in the three periods studied. The tables show that, even after primary product additions are excluded, a substantial percentage of companies entered the chemicals and machinery categories in each of the three periods, and the fabricated metal products group in the first two of the three periods. The reasons for the frequent choice of these industries for diversification are discussed in Chapter 7.

It would appear from the above that, in the three periods, roughly the same 2-digit industries tended to remain the most attractive as measured by the frequency with which companies added products in these industries. This impression is supported by more formal tests. The correlation was .93 between number of products added in 1929–39 and 1939–50 in each of the twenty-one 2-digit manufacturing industries. For 1939–50 and 1950–54 the correlation was .94. Since the number of companies with primary activities in each of various manufacturing industries differed considerably, a better indication of degree of continuity in the choice of industries for diversification may be secured by examining those additions that fell outside the primary industries of companies. This reduces the bias in frequencies of additions that stems from the composition of our sample. On the latter basis, the correlation coefficient for frequencies in the 1929–39 and 1939–50 periods was .84—that is, only slightly lower than the degree of correlation present when additions in primary groups are included. For the frequencies in the 1939–50 and 1950–54 periods, excluding those in primary industries, the correlation was .90.

Product abandonments display a somewhat surprising pattern. As Tables 18 through 20 show, the period of highest annual frequency of abandonments was 1950–54 (16.8 per year), followed by 1939–50 (12.6 per year), with 1929–39 showing the lowest annual rate (5.7 per year). An abandonment most frequently takes the form of discontinuance in production rather than the sale of a business. Consequently, if abandonments responded strongly to cyclical influences, one would expect a high rate of abandonments when economic activity is at an ebb and both demand and earnings are relatively low. This is the reverse of the observed pattern. It is obvious, however, that the total number of products that can be abandoned by a firm is limited by the number of separate industrial activities in which it is engaged. In the two later periods, the 111 enterprises were engaged in a larger number of activities and this increased the number of possible product abandonments. Another source of the change might be related to the trend of diversification away from similar or related production processes and products (discussed in detail in a later section); possibly this introduces increased risks, and consequently a greater frequency of product abandonments. Certainly the lower rate of abandonments in 1929–39 as compared with 1950–54, coupled with the relatively high rate of additions in the former period, clearly indicates that the movement toward product heterogeneity is not of recent origin.

Viewed in terms of the industries into which product abandonments fall, the pattern resembles that for product additions. This is to be expected to some degree, since industries which account for a large proportion both of additions and of the total number of a firm's activities offer the largest opportunities, in a statistical sense, for deletions of products. It is clear that the number of abandonments in a given industry is limited by the number of activities to be found therein, and that a positive relation between number of activities and frequency of abandonments is to be expected in the absence of offsetting factors. Appendix Tables B–10 through B–12 show the *number of companies* that abandoned activities in each of the twenty-one 2-digit manufacturing industries in the 1929–39, 1939–50, and 1950–54 periods.

Variability Among Companies in Diversification Movements

In each of the three periods studied, there was a pronounced tendency for the same companies to show the highest frequencies of additions. Two tests were applied to establish this conclusion. First, the frequencies of additions in successive periods were compared for companies grouped by number of additions in one of the periods. Second, companies were grouped by primary industry, and the groups were then ranked by frequency of product additions in each period. The rankings for successive periods were then compared.[13]

[13] Individual companies, as distinct from groups of companies, were not ranked on the basis of number of product additions because of the very large number of tied ranks that would have been generated.

Industries of Companies

Industries of *Product Abandonments*	Food (12)	Tobacco (5)	Textiles (4)	Paper (8)	Chemicals (14)	Petroleum (10)
Ordnance						
Food products	2					
Tobacco manufactures						
Textile mill products			1			
Apparel						
Lumber and wood[b]						
Furniture						
Paper products				2	1	
Printing and publishing					1	
Chemicals					4	1
Petroleum and coal						3
Rubber products						
Leather						
Stone, clay, and glass products					1	
Primary metals						
Fabricated metal products		1			1	4
Machinery[c]						
Electrical machinery						
Transportation equipment						
Instruments[d]						
Miscellaneous						
Total abandonments	2	1	1	2	8	8
Primary industry abandonments	2	0	1	2	4	3
Total less primary industry abandonments	0	1	0	0	4	5

Differences between groups of companies remained relatively stable when frequencies of product additions in successive periods were examined. Table 21 shows that when companies were grouped into five classes by number of manufactured products added in the period 1929–39, the frequency with which products were added in the 1939–50 period was substantially higher for companies falling in the upper classes with respect to 1929–39 product additions. Substantially the same results may be observed for the 1950–54 product additions when companies are grouped *and Number of Abandonments*[a]

Rubber (5)	Stone, Clay, and Glass (7)	Primary Metals (10)	Fabricated Metal Products (5)	Machinery (13)	Electrical Machinery (5)	Transportation Equipment (13)	Total Abandonments	Total Less Primary Industry Abandonments
							0	0
							2	0
							0	0
2							3	2
							0	0
						1	1	1
							0	0
							3	1
							1	1
1	1	1				1	9	5
						1	4	1
1							1	0
1							1	1
	1				1	1	4	3
		4					4	0
					1	1	8	8
			1	2	1		4	2
					1	1	2	1
		1	1	1		5	8	3
1							1	1
					1		1	1
6	2	6	2	3	4	12	57	
1	1	4	0	2	1	5		
5	1	2	2	1	3	7		31

Source: Product record described in Chapter 2.

[a] Numbers in parentheses refer to number of companies in the specified industry.

[b] Excluding furniture.

[c] Excluding electrical.

[d] Professional, scientific, and controlling instruments, photographic and optical goods, watches and clocks.

by number of products added in 1939–50.[14] Generally speaking, the

[14] Companies at the extremes of the distribution in one period may be expected to move toward the center in a subsequent period. Thus it is not surprising that the range of variations between classes of companies is smaller when the classes are defined by frequency of product additions in an earlier period rather than in the current period. Despite this tendency, the ranking of groups of companies in terms of number of products added remained unchanged for the two sets of successive periods. This conclusion would have been equally supported by a table which grouped companies by frequency of product additions in the later period and then showed, for the resulting groups, the number of additions in an antecedent period. A table of this type can be readily derived from the data in Appendix B.

Industries of Companies

Industries of Product Abandonments	Food (12)	Tobacco (5)	Textiles (4)	Paper (8)	Chemicals (14)	Petroleum (10)
Ordnance						
Food products	11					
Tobacco manufactures						
Textile mill products		1	4			
Apparel						
Lumber and wood[b]	1			1		1
Furniture						
Paper products	1	2		9		
Printing and publishing						
Chemicals	1			2	12	4
Petroleum and coal						1
Rubber products						
Leather						
Stone, clay, and glass products					2	
Primary metals					5	
Fabricated metal products					1	2
Machinery[c]	1					1
Electrical machinery						
Transportation equipment					1	
Instruments[d]				1		1
Miscellaneous						1
Total abandonments	15	3	4	13	21	11
Primary industry abandonments	11	0	4	9	12	1
Total less primary industry abandonments	4	3	0	4	9	10

companies that added most products in 1929–39 also showed the largest number of additions in 1939–50. Similarly, the companies that diversified most, as judged by number of additions in 1939–50, showed the highest change toward diversification in 1950–54. As a result, absolute differences between companies in number of separate activities are likely to have been substantially greater in 1954 than they were in 1929.[15]

[15] The data necessary for a measure of variability among companies in diversification in 1929 were not developed.

and Number of Abandonments[a]

Rubber (5)	Stone, Clay, and Glass (7)	Primary Metals (10)	Fabricated Metal Products (5)	Machinery (13)	Electrical Machinery (5)	Transportation Equipment (13)	Total Abandonments	Total Less Primary Industry Abandonments
							0	0
							11	0
							0	0
							5	1
							0	0
			3			2	8	8
	1						1	1
			1				13	4
							0	0
	4	1				2	26	14
		1	1				3	2
							0	0
					2		2	2
	1	1					4	3
		2	2			1	10	8
	2	3	1			1	10	9
	1	2		10		6	21	11
2				1	1	3	7	6
1		2		1	1	3	9	6
2						2	6	6
1					1		3	3
6	8	13	8	12	5	20	139	
0	1	2	1	10	1	3		
6	7	11	7	2	4	17		84

Source: Product record described in Chapter 2.
[a] Numbers in parentheses refer to number of companies in the specified industry.
[b] Excluding furniture.
[c] Excluding electrical.
[d] Professional, scientific, and controlling instruments, photographic and optical goods, watches and clocks.

With companies grouped by primary industry (Tables 14, 15, and 16), the results were substantially similar. When the thirteen industry groups were ranked by number of product additions per company in manufacturing for each of the three periods, rank correlation for the 1929–39 and 1939–50 rankings was .69; for 1939–50 and 1950–54, it was .80. Once again, the results point to an increase in absolute differences among companies in number of separate activities.

Continuity in patterns between successive periods was revealed not

					Industries of Companies	
Industries of Product Abandonments	Food (12)	Tobacco (5)	Textiles (4)	Paper (8)	Chemicals (14)	Petroleum (10)
Ordnance						
Food products	6					
Tobacco manufactures						
Textile mill products			2		1	
Apparel	1					
Lumber and wood[b]						
Furniture						
Paper products						
Printing and publishing					1	
Chemicals	6		1		5	1
Petroleum and coal					1	
Rubber products				1		
Leather	1					
Stone, clay, and glass products			1	1		
Primary metals					1	
Fabricated metal products					2	1
Machinery[c]					1	
Electrical machinery						
Transportation equipment						
Instruments[d]						
Miscellaneous					2	
Total abandonments	14	0	4	2	14	2
Primary industry abandonments	6	0	2	0	5	0
Total less primary industry abandonments	8	0	2	2	9	2

only through a tendency for the same companies to show the highest rates of product additions but in the extent of variation among companies in frequencies of additions. For the 111 companies, the coefficients of variation for number of additions of manufactured products in the 1929–39, 1939–50, and 1950–54 periods were 120 per cent, 107 per cent, and 126 per cent, respectively.

E 20

LARGE ENTERPRISES, BY INDUSTRY, 1950–54

and Number of Abandonments[a]

Rubber (5)	Stone, Clay, and Glass (7)	Primary Metals (10)	Fabricated Metal Products (5)	Machinery (13)	Electrical Machinery (5)	Transportation Equipment (13)	Total Abandonments	Total Less Primary Industry Abandonments
							0	0
							6	0
							0	0
1							4	2
							1	1
						1	1	1
							0	0
							0	0
	1						2	2
	2		1				16	11
							1	1
1						1	3	2
							1	1
	2					1	5	3
			1				2	2
			1			1	5	4
1				2		4	8	6
				1	1		2	1
1						2	3	1
						1	1	1
	1	2	1				6	6
4	6	2	4	3	1	11	67	
1	2	0	1	2	1	2		
3	4	2	3	1	0	9		45

SOURCE: Product record described in Chapter 2.

[a] Numbers in parentheses refer to number of companies in the specified industry.

[b] Excluding furniture.

[c] Excluding electrical.

[d] Professional, scientific, and controlling instruments, photographic and optical goods, watches and clocks.

The Role of Technical Propinquity

Technical propinquity between products may be visualized in at least two ways. Type 1 propinquity refers to one or more of the following: similar or complementary uses of products, similar production processes, and the use of common raw materials for the products. In short, it concerns relations between the physical characteristics of products. In Type 2

TABLE 21
NUMBER OF PRODUCTS ADDED IN SUCCESSIVE PERIODS BY CLASSES OF
COMPANIES

	Classes on Basis of Number of Products Added[a]					
	0	1–2	3–4	5–8	9–25	Total
Number of companies in each class (based on 1929–39 additions)	17	29	27	23	15	111
Products added, 1929–39	0	43	92	148	201	484
Average per company, 1929–39	0	1.5	3.4	6.4	13.4	4.4
Products added, 1939–50	25	83	121	114	131	474
Average per company, 1939–50	1.5	2.9	4.0	5.0	8.7	4.3
Number of companies in each class (based on 1939–50 additions)	17	38	20	19	17	111
Products added, 1939–50	0	59	69	124	222	474
Average per company, 1939–50	0	1.6	3.5	6.5	13.1	4.3
Products added, 1950–54	27	90	64	105	145	431
Average per company, 1950–54	1.6	1.3	3.2	5.5	8.5	3.9

SOURCE: Product record described in Chapter 2.

[a] The classes were selected with a view to approximating an equal number of companies in each class.

propinquity, resources other than "material" that are useful in producing one product are also useful in producing another. These resources may consist of research and development staffs, the availability of experienced salesmen, the requirement of common managerial skills for two or more products, and others. While the presence of Type 1 propinquity renders the presence of Type 2 propinquity more likely, the two types of technical relations between products can be usefully distinguished for analytic purposes.

The Standard Industrial Classification Code is generally based on Type 1 propinquity. Therefore, the greater the number of product additions in the primary 2-digit industry of a company as compared with those outside it, the greater is the relative influence of Type 1 propinquity. When relative frequencies of additions within and outside of primary 2-digit industries are examined, a distinct decline is shown in the proportion of total manufacturing additions contributed by the primary industries. Primary industry additions accounted for 42.8 per cent of total additions in 1929–39, 35.0 per cent in 1939–50, and only 31.8 per cent in 1950–54.[16] Thus the importance of Type 1 propinquity appears to have declined.

[16] The proportion of abandonments of manufactured products that fell within the primary 2-digit industry of companies was similar to that for product additions. In 1929–39 the ratio of primary industry to total abandonments was 43.9 per cent compared with 38.8 per cent for 1939–50 and only 33.8 per cent in 1950–54. For reasons indicated earlier, the pattern of abandonments is likely to resemble that for additions.

There were wide differences among companies in the proportion of their additions that fell in the primary 2-digit industries.[17] Prior to 1950, there appears to be no systematic relation between the number of additions that companies made within and outside their primary 2-digit class. As a test, the 111 companies were grouped in thirteen 2-digit industries by primary activity, and the resulting groups were ranked first by number of products added within primary 2-digit industries, and second by number added outside the primary industries. The coefficient of rank correlation (Spearman's) for the two rankings for 1950–54 additions was .66. However, for the two sets of rankings in the two earlier periods, namely, 1929–39 and 1939–50, the coefficients were only .01 and .19, respectively. The presence of correlation in the 1950–54 period between frequency of additions within and outside the primary industry of companies suggests that the ability to diversify in any direction may be increasingly governed by the characteristics of the diversifying firm. In particular, the ability of a firm's employees to deal with the complex technologies of industries that attract diversification may be of decisive importance.

Trends after 1947

For the 1947–54 period, information was available from the Censuses of Manufactures that shows the relative magnitude of each manufacturing activity for an individual company. Thus, for example, the change in importance to the firm of its primary activity could be traced. Census data, however, classify all of the payrolls or employment of a plant in its primary industry and thus tend to understate increases in diversification. As noted in an earlier section, recently commenced activities are frequently too small to account for the major activity of a plant. Moreover, the Classification Code tends to classify products in the newest industries into previously existing categories.

Notwithstanding these limitations, census data show that substantially more companies increased than decreased the number of their activities from 1947 to 1954. The increase in diversification is also revealed in a decline, for the majority of firms, in the ratio of payrolls in the primary

[17] The primary industry of companies was determined on the basis of employment data for 1954. Some of the companies probably altered their primary 2-digit industry in the course of the 1929–54 interval of time. This introduces an element of error in comparisons of primary and nonprimary additions. Since, however, the overwhelming majority of companies in the group of 111 did not change primary 2-digit industries in the course of the 1929–54 period, the error is not likely to be large.

industry to total manufacturing payrolls for the firms.[18] The magnitude of this decline, however, was not very large—a fact which may be attributed at least partly to the limitations of the data, noted above.[19]

Based on establishment data, the number of 4-digit manufacturing activities in which the 111 large enterprises were engaged increased from 823 to 1,073 in the period 1947–54—a rise of 30.4 per cent. If activities that are of relatively minor importance[20] to individual companies are excluded, the rise from 1947 to 1954 is considerably smaller. This is to be expected, since new products added by means other than merger cannot immediately be produced in large volume. It is necessary to develop markets and to overcome numerous delays associated with acquisition of plant and equipment, raw materials, and skilled personnel before production can commence on a large scale. None of the new activities referred to above had had a life of more than seven years, and some doubtless were introduced in the terminal year of the period. In consequence, if we exclude minor activities, the residual number shows an increase from 625 to 725 in the 1947–54 period—a rise of only 16.0 per cent. When companies are grouped by industry, all groups except those in food products, tobacco, and primary metals categories showed an increase from 1947 to 1954 in number of 4-digit activities (Table 22). When minor manufacturing activities are again excluded, the food products and tobacco groups show a slight increase rather than a decline, but the decline for primary metals is considerably sharper.

Table 23 shows that in ten of thirteen industry groups of companies, the ratio of primary 4-digit industry payrolls to total manufacturing payrolls (excluding those associated with integration) showed a decline from 1947 to 1954. Thus, on the basis of the relative importance of non-primary activities, diversification increased in most industry categories. For the ten groups of companies which show a decline in the average ratio, the average drop was eight percentage points or 11.7 per cent. For all 111 companies combined, the average decline was five percentage points or 7.2 per cent. The average ratio rose for companies in food products, tobacco, and primary metals. The sharpest declines were for rubber products and chemicals. As suggested earlier, when a rapid increase takes place in the number of activities in which firms are engaged, the rise in

---

[18] Primary industry specialization may, of course, change as the result of uneven growth of *existing* activities and not only as the result of acquisition of new ones.

[19] For example, a new product might have been added to a plant classified in the primary industry.

[20] Minor activities are here defined as those which individually account for less than 1 per cent of a firm's manufacturing employment.

TABLE 22
NUMBER OF MANUFACTURING ACTIVITIES, 111 LARGE ENTERPRISES,
1947 and 1954

Primary Industry of Company	Number of Companies	Number of Four-Digit Manufacturing Activities			
		1947	1947[a]	1954	1954[a]
Food products	12	144	78	132	81
Tobacco manufactures	5	23	17	22	18
Textile mill products	4	25	19	30	23
Paper products	8	42	38	68	52
Chemicals	14	130	90	173	116
Petroleum	10	39	22	39	24
Rubber products	5	45	27	62	45
Stone, clay, and glass products	7	52	44	61	50
Primary metals	10	113	70	110	57
Fabricated metal products	5	52	35	55	44
Machinery	13	72	65	89	76
Electrical machinery	5	98	57	111	60
Transportation equipment	13	88	63	121	78
Total	111	823	625	1073	725

SOURCE: Special census tabulation.
[a] Excluding activities that account for less than 1 per cent of a company's manufacturing employment.

TABLE 23
AVERAGE PRIMARY INDUSTRY SPECIALIZATION,
111 LARGE ENTERPRISES, 1947 AND 1954

Primary Industry of Company	Number of Companies	Average Ratio of Primary Four-Digit Industry Payrolls to Total Manufacturing Payrolls[a]	
		1947	1954
Food products	12	.763	.783
Tobacco manufactures	5	.596	.726
Textile mill products	4	.536	.514
Paper products	8	.626	.576
Chemicals	14	.607	.478
Petroleum	10	.967	.927
Rubber products	5	.718	.477
Stone, clay, and glass products	7	.727	.637
Primary metals	10	.689	.723
Fabricated metal products	5	.598	.529
Machinery	13	.681	.609
Electrical machinery	5	.380	.365
Transportation equipment	13	.745	.682
All companies	111	.690	.640

SOURCE: Special census tabulation.
[a] Payrolls associated with integration excluded from the measure of total manufacturing payrolls.

the ratio of nonprimary payrolls to total payrolls is likely to be greater in the long than in the short run. This follows from the fact that activities undertaken in the recent past through means other than merger will not have had time in the short run to attain their intended ultimate share in total operations. It contributes to explaining the small decline in primary industry specialization compared with the percentage increase in number of activities.

Excluding payrolls associated with integration from the denominator of the ratio, sixty-four of the 111 companies showed a decline in primary industry specialization from 1947 to 1954, forty showed a rise in the ratio, and seven remained unchanged (Table 24). In the same interval of time, fifty-seven of the 111 companies showed an increase in number of 4-digit manufacturing activities, thirty-two showed a decline, and twenty-two remained unchanged. When both minor activities and those associated with integration were excluded, the number of companies showing no change in number of activities increased from twenty-two to thirty-six, primarily at the expense of the group that showed a decline. Using the binomial distribution, the number of companies which show a rise in

TABLE 24

CHANGES IN PRIMARY INDUSTRY SPECIALIZATION AND IN NUMBER OF
ACTIVITIES, 111 LARGE ENTERPRISES, 1947–54

	Number of Companies with Increases	Number of Companies with Decreases	Number of Companies with No Change
A. Primary industry specialization (excluding integration payrolls from denominator of ratio)	40	64	7
B. Primary industry specialization (including integration payrolls in denominator of ratio)	41	65	5
C. Total number of four-digit manufacturing industries	57	32	22
D. Number of four-digit manufacturing industries (excluding those with less than than 1 per cent of company employment)	62	24	25
E. Number of four-digit manufacturing industries (excluding those with less than 1 per cent of company employment and those associated with integration)	53	22	36

NOTE: At 4-digit level of industry detail. The denominators of measures of concentration were restricted to manufacturing payrolls.

SOURCE: Special census tabulation.

the count of 4-digit activities exceed significantly at the 1 per cent level the number that show a decline. This was true counting (1) all 4-digit activities, (2) all nonminor ones, and (3) all those that were neither minor nor associated with integration. On the basis of the same test, the number of companies with a decline in primary industry specialization exceeded significantly at the 5 per cent level the number which showed a rise (both when integration payrolls were excluded from denominators of the ratios and when they were not).

The above results indicate a clear preponderance in the number of companies which became more diversified in the 1947–54 period. Substantially the same conclusions may be reached from Table 25. The latter shows an increase from 1947 to 1954 in the number of companies associated with relatively low primary industry specialization and a decline for those associated with high specialization. Thus, in 1954, thirty-eight of the 111 companies reveal primary industry specialization of less than 50 per cent compared with twenty-eight in 1947. Conversely, thirty-three companies were associated with a concentration of 80 per cent or more in 1954 compared with forty-two in 1947.

TABLE 25

DISTRIBUTION OF 111 COMPANIES BY PRIMARY AND BY PRIMARY PLUS
SECONDARY INDUSTRY SPECIALIZATION, 1947 AND 1954

Primary Industry Specialization[a] (per cent)	Number of Companies		Primary and Secondary Industry Specialization[b] (per cent)	Number of Companies	
	1947	1954		1947	1954
0–29.9	6	10	0–49.9	4	9
30–39.9	9	14	50–59.9	10	10
40–49.9	13	14	60–69.9	12	12
50–59.9	12	10	70–79.9	17	23
60–69.9	16	18	80–89.9	21	16
70–79.9	13	12	90–99.9	26	22
80–89.9	13	9	100	23	19
90–99.9	17	12			
100	12	12			

SOURCE: Special census tabulation.

[a] Payrolls in primary 4-digit industry as percentage of total company payrolls in manufacturing activities. Payrolls for activities associated with integration excluded from measure of total company payrolls.

[b] Payrolls in primary plus secondary (second largest for the firm) 4-digit industry as percentage of total company payrolls in manufacturing activities. Payrolls for activities associated with integration excluded from the measure of total payrolls. If the secondary activity was associated with integration, it was not incorporated in the measure of primary plus secondary payrolls. Instead the second largest activity characterized as diversification (if one existed) was used.

As distinct from measures of change in diversification, an indication of *turnover* in output composition may be secured from changes in the rank of particular activities within the output structures of individual firms. Thus, for sixteen of the 111 companies, the primary industry in 1954 was different from that in 1947. For sixteen companies, also, the activity that was second largest in 1947 had been eliminated completely by 1954. In all, for fifty-nine of the 111 companies, the industry that was second largest in 1947 had either been downgraded by 1954 or, alternatively, (in a few instances) had become primary. However, a considerable number of the instances of change in rank for the activity that was second largest in 1947 involved merely an interchange in rank between the second and third largest activity.

The Role of Regulation

Regulation has doubtless affected the diversification patterns of individual companies. Since this subject is largely outside the scope of the present study, one or two examples will suffice to illustrate the relation. For example, a consent decree in 1920 has directly limited the scope of activities of meat-packing firms. The Motor Carriers Act of 1935 imposed minimum rate regulation on common and contract carriers and may have thus stimulated the acquisition of trucking fleets by manufacturing firms. The antimerger legislation of 1950 has probably had a broad range of effects, though the period covered by our study ends too early to assess them. In general, however, most changes in product structure did not take place through merger—a circumstance that has limited the effects of merger regulation on diversification patterns.

CHAPTER 4

Diversification and the Size, Growth, and Profit Rate of Companies

THIS chapter discusses certain characteristics of diversifying firms, namely, their size, growth, and profit rate. The relation of diversification to size of firm was studied primarily on the basis of data for the large sample of 721 multiestablishment firms, while that between diversification and growth and profit rates was based on the 111-firm sample.

Summary

For the 721-firm sample it was found that, as of 1954, size of firm showed a strong positive association with number of industries in which companies maintained establishments. However, it was not clearly related to the ratio of nonprimary to primary employment. This means that as company size increases, the share in a firm's total output contributed by the primary activity does not change materially, but the average share contributed by *individual* nonprimary activities tends to decline.

The relation of diversification to company growth is a consequence of reciprocal influences, but not all of them lead to a positive association. Generally, it may be expected that companies will try to select the more rapidly growing industries in which to diversify. Moreover, diversification is also a form of investment, and hence contributes to company growth. On the other hand, unfavorable prospects in the primary industries of companies may spur diversification as a defensive measure. This would tend to offset a positive association between the latter and company growth. For the 111 firms, the relation of growth to diversification did not suggest a clear-cut pattern. However, after 1939 there appeared to be a mild positive relation between the two variables when the latter is measured by frequency of product additions.

For the 111 companies, profit rates in 1947–54 were neither correlated with diversification, measured as of 1954, nor with change in diversification from 1947 to 1954. Similarly, the distribution of company earnings between income retentions and dividend payments was not correlated with diversification.

The Relation of Company Size to Diversification

It was shown earlier that there is a strong positive relation between the average size of firm for an industry and the relative numbers of multi- and single-industry firms therein. This result is attributable in part to the fact that single-establishment firms are on the average smaller than multi-establishment firms; therefore they are likely to be relatively more numerous in industries with smaller average firm size. (Single establishment firms were, by definition, subsumed in the category of single-industry companies.) The question now asked is whether, within the universe of multiestablishment firms, size of firm is related to diversification.

A priori, there are several reasons to expect a positive relation between diversification and size of firm. If a firm has entered a number of industries on a scale sufficient to be reasonably efficient, it will usually have a fairly large aggregate size. Stated in another way, diversification is a form of investment, and as such contributes to the total size of a firm.

Another reason for expecting a positive relation between the two variables is the likelihood that as the size of a firm increases, its ability to raise investment funds in substantial amounts is enhanced.[1] This advantage may be further reinforced by the possible presence of economies of scale in research and development. As is shown in Chapter 7, the industries which have proved most attractive as investment outlets for diversifying firms are associated generally with heavy capital requirements and high rates of employment of technical and scientific personnel.

It will be recalled that substantial differences were observed among industries in the extent to which the output of firms was heterogeneous. In consequence, the relation between size of firm and diversification is best examined through data for companies within the same industry, rather than for firms falling into diverse industries. In this way, the relation between size and diversification can be more effectively isolated from the other factors that generate interindustry differences in measures of diversification. Accordingly, for this purpose, all multiestablishment companies with 2,500 and over employees were segregated into broad industry categories.[2]

Two measures of diversification—the number of industries in which firms maintain establishments and the relative magnitude of nonprimary employment—were studied. The first was examined by grouping companies into size classes within each of the nineteen industry classes. The choice of size class was to some extent arbitrary, being constrained by census rules regarding nondisclosure of individual company information.

---

[1] However, beyond some point further increments to firm size are likely to have a diminishing effect on command over capital funds.

[2] The companies comprise the sample of 721 firms described in Chapter 2. Information for a few companies, however, was subsequently omitted to avoid disclosure of individual company information. While the firms are segregated into nineteen 2-digit industries, their separate activities were identified at roughly the 3-digit level of detail.

The number of size classes varied considerably among the nineteen industries and the terminal class differed with respect to the number of companies included in it.[3] Average employment per company in each size class is shown for the nineteen industry categories in Appendix Table C–1.

The number of industries in which multiunit companies maintained establishments showed a strong positive relation to company size in fifteen of the eighteen industry categories in Table 26. The table shows a fairly regular decline in number of industries, as we move to successively lower size classes, in most of the categories of companies. As a further indication of the strong relation between company size and number of industries per company, for almost all categories the highest size class was associated with the largest average number of industries.

For the smaller sample of 111 large enterprises, information on frequency of product additions does not show a clear association between the latter and company size. Table 27 shows the relation between asset size and frequency of product additions for these firms. For companies segregated into five classes based on total assets in 1939, the higher size classes did not show a greater rate of product additions per company in 1939–54 than did the lower ones. For product additions in 1929–39, however, companies with total assets in 1929 of $250 million and over showed a higher frequency of additions than those with assets of less than $250 million, but a consistent rise in additions as one moves to successively higher asset classes is not in evidence.

The difference in conclusions to which the findings in Tables 26 and 27 seem to point can be explained by the difference in the composition of the two samples. The group of 111 enterprises was restricted to very large companies. Thus variations in size within the group were narrower than for the larger sample of multiestablishment firms. Moreover, it seems plausible that, beyond some level, economies of scale are exhausted and size ceases to exert a positive influence on diversification. Still another

---

[3] The first class consisted of the four largest companies in terms of employment in each industry group. The second was comprised of those companies having ranks 5 through 8. The third consisted of companies with ranks 9 through 20, and all subsequent classes were comprised of successive groups of ten companies, when ranked on the basis of employment size. For the first three classes the breakdown was determined by the fact that data showing the proportion of an industry's output contributed by the four, eight, and twenty largest firms in the industry had previously been published by the Bureau of the Census, thus generating possible "disclosure" problems if a different breakdown were adopted.

For "merchant wholesalers" there was only one class since information for the second class had to be suppressed. Thus comparisons of number of industrial activities for various size classes of companies could only be made for eighteen industries.

The lowest size class was eliminated in industries in which the residual number of companies falling into the class was smaller than four.

TABLE 26

AVERAGE NUMBER OF INDUSTRIES PER COMPANY IN RELATION TO EMPLOYMENT SIZE
CLASS OF COMPANY, EIGHTEEN INDUSTRY CATEGORIES

Industries of Companies	Average Number in Each Size Class[a]										Industry Mean
	(4)	(4)	(12)	(10)	(10)	(10)	(10)	(10)	(10)	(10)	
Mining	9	4	3(10)								5
Food	15	10	4	5	4	3	3	2	3(8)		5
Textiles	6	7	4	3	3	3	2	2(6)			3
Paper	9	6	4	3	3(9)						4
Petroleum and coal products	10	10	6	6(7)							7
Rubber	13	8	3(4)								8
Stone, clay, and glass	9	4	4								5
Primary metals	18	17	9	5	3	3					7
Fabricated metal products	9	5	5	3(7)							5
Machinery[b]	8	5	5	5	2	4	3	2	2	3(8)	4
Electrical machinery	20	7	3	2	3	2					4
Transportation equipment	15	3	6	6	3	3	3(4)				5
Instruments[c]	9	2	3(10)								4
Chemicals	19	11	7	4	5	4	4				6
Retail grocers	9	5	3								4
Other retail	7	3	2	2	2	2	2				2
Drug and variety stores	2	2	2(8)								2
Restaurants and bars	4	2	3(6)								3

SOURCE: Special census tabulation.

[a] Based on data for all multiestablishment companies in the specified industries with 2,500 and over employees, except for several for which data could not be shown because of disclosure problems. Numbers in parentheses indicate the number of companies represented in the class. The first class consists of the largest four, the second, the next four, etc. Numbers in parentheses in the body of the table show the number of companies in a cell where the numbers differ from those in the column head.

[b] Except electrical.

[c] Professional, scientific, and controlling instruments, photographic and optical goods, watches and clocks.

factor is that variation between firms in number of product additions depends partly on the companies' primary industries. This relation may be sufficiently strong to obscure others, such as that between diversification and firm size.[4]

For the 721-firm sample, the relation of firm size to diversification was examined with the latter again measured by relative magnitude of nonprimary employment. The method of analysis was to determine the shape

[4] Although data for the larger sample were segregated by industry, the sample of 111 companies was not sufficiently large to permit both industry and size breakdowns.

TABLE 27
COMPANY SIZE AND FREQUENCY OF PRODUCT ADDITIONS

Asset Size[a] (millions of dollars)	Number of Companies[b]	Total Number of Product Additions	Average per Company
		1929–39	
1929			
Under 50	31	159	5.1
50 and under 125	27	136	5.0
125 and under 250	20	102	5.1
250 and under 500	14	115	8.2
500 and over	13	93	7.1
Total	105	605	
		1939–54	
1939			
Under 50	29	353	12.2
50 and under 125	33	247	7.5
125 and under 250	25	245	9.8
250 and under 500	9	105	11.7
500 and over	13	129	9.9
Total	109	1079	

SOURCE: Product record described in Chapter 2 and data for total assets from Moody's *Industrials.*
[a] Size measured on the basis of total assets.
[b] Asset data were not available in 1929 for six companies, which accounted for fourteen product additions during the 1929–39 period; and for two companies in 1939, which accounted for ten additions during 1939–54.

of the curve that relates nonprimary to primary employment.[5] This relation was examined without reference to industry—that is, the observations were not segregated by industry class. The data used consisted of average values for nonprimary and for primary employment for the various size groupings of companies discussed in connection with Table 26.[6]

[5] For companies grouped by industry and by size, as in Table 26, the ratio of non-primary to primary employment did not vary consistently between successive size groups within the industries. However, this method of analysis gives a biased indication of the relation of nonprimary to primary employment as firm size changes. This is because company size is measured by total employment and, hence, both the numerator and denominator of the above ratio are components of the measure of firm size. To avoid this problem, the method of analysis described in the text was employed.
[6] For reasons of Census Bureau rules on nondisclosure of individual company information, it was not possible to use information for individual companies. The groupings of firms were such that only those within the same 2-digit industries were combined. This increased the homogeneity of companies within groups and thus reduced the disadvantage of using information for groups of companies rather than for individual firms. Data for nonprimary employment are shown in Appendix Table C–3. Those for primary employment were obtained by subtracting nonprimary from total employment (the latter in Appendix Table C–1).

CHART 1A
Relation of Number of Primary to Nonprimary
Employees, 90 Groups of Companies

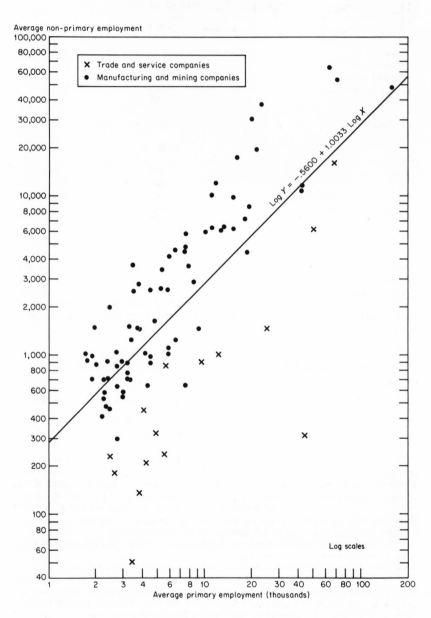

When the original observations are converted to logarithms, the following equation, as may be judged from Chart 1A, fits the observations quite well.[7]

(1) $$\log_{10} Y = -.5600 + 1.0033 \log_{10} X, \quad r = .691$$
$$(.1118)$$

Y denotes nonprimary employment and X is total employment.

The fact that the regression coefficient in the equation approximates unity points to a constant ratio of Y to X in original observations.[8]

Chart 1B shows the scatter around the estimated values when both a straight line and a second degree polynomial are fitted to the observations.[9] The equations, once again with Y denoting nonprimary employment and X primary employment, appear below.

(2) $$Y = 706.8 + .3918X, \qquad\qquad r = .749$$
(3) $$Y = -792.2 + .6002X - 10^{-6} \times 1.7632X^2$$

It is clear that the straight line does not fit the observations well at both tails of the distribution and, hence, must be rejected as a description of the relation of Y to X. Equation 3 gives a somewhat better fit than the straight line, and, though the residual variance in Y is reduced only modestly from 43.9 per cent to 40.5 per cent, the coefficient of X^2 was statistically significant. Equation 3 points to only moderate variations in the ratio Y/X for companies in the medium to large size range, and in this respect tends to support the conclusion reached on the basis of Equation 1.[10]

As still another test of the relation between the relative importance of nonprimary employment and company size, data for the sample of 111 large enterprises were analyzed. These companies were ranked on the

[7] Companies in trade and service industries (indicated by crosses in the Chart) fairly consistently show a lower than estimated volume of nonprimary employment. This accords with data shown earlier for industry aggregates, which point to a lower ratio of nonprimary to total employment for trade and service industries compared with manufacturing and mining. The total number of observations was ninety. That is, analysis was based on ninety groups of companies drawn from eighteen 2-digit industries and encompassing 684 individual companies. Information for petroleum companies was not used because most of the nonprimary employment of these firms was associated with integration rather than diversification.

[8] If $\log Y = a + \log X$, then $\log Y - \log X = a$, or $\log \left(\dfrac{Y}{X}\right) = a$. Hence $\dfrac{Y}{X}$ is constant.

[9] As in Chart 1A, there were ninety observations. Chart 1B, panel I, shows the scatter for the lower values of X, while panel II shows the same information, but on a different scale, for the upper values of X. The rectangle in panel II shows the area covered by panel I.

[10] Equation 3 indicates that the ratio is at a maximum for a firm with roughly 21,000 primary industry employees, but varies only within the range of .41 and .53 for companies having from 5,000 to 100,000 primary industry employees. (The ratios were .433, .525, and .416 when X was 5,000, 20,000 and 100,000, respectively.)

71

CHART 1B

Relation of Number of Primary to Nonprimary
Employees, 90 Groups of Companies

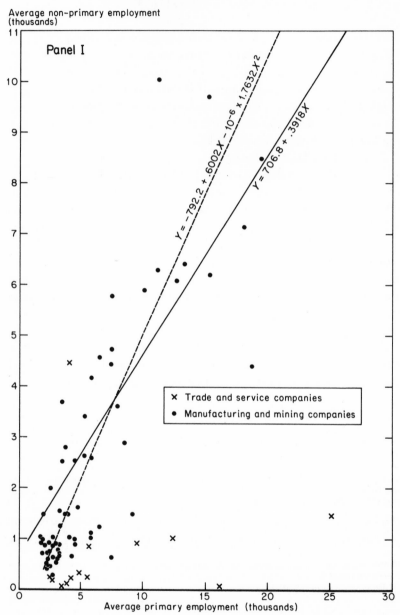

Average non-primary employment
(thousands)

Panel I

$Y = -792.2 + .6002X - 10^{-6} \times 1.7632X^2$

$Y = 706.8 + .3918X$

× Trade and service companies
• Manufacturing and mining companies

Average primary employment (thousands)

CHART 1B (concluded)

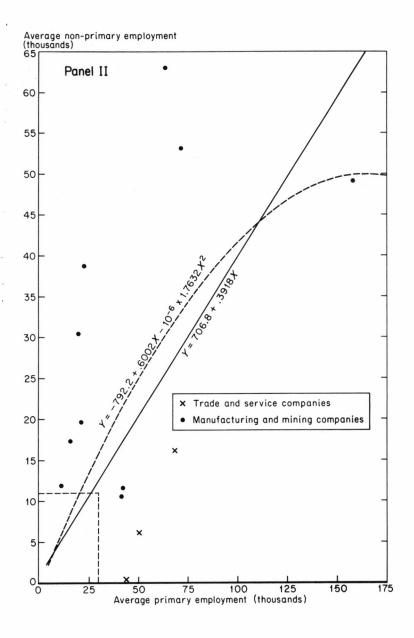

Average non-primary employment (thousands)

Panel II

$Y = -792.2 + .6002X - 10^{-6} \times 1.7632X^2$

$Y = 706.8 + .3918X$

× Trade and service companies
● Manufacturing and mining companies

Average primary employment (thousands)

basis of total assets in 1954 and the ratio of nonprimary to total employment. The Spearman coefficient of rank correlation for the two variables was only .14.

It is clear from the preceding discussion that the ratio of nonprimary to primary employment does not show the pronounced positive association with company size which characterizes the relation between the latter and *number* of nonprimary activities (at least as revealed by data for the larger sample of multiestablishment firms). In consequence, it must follow that nonprimary employment increases with company size less than proportionately to number of nonprimary activities. Thus the *average* nonprimary activity accounts for a greater proportion of the firm's total employment in a smaller than in a larger firm.

There are plausible reasons for this phenomenon. It is difficult to envisage a new activity that would, initially at least, account for a large proportion of the total employment of a leading steel or automobile producer. On the other hand, when a small firm diversifies, the new activity is likely to contribute a significant proportion of the firm's total employment. This is especially true if there are sizable economies of scale and if the new venture is initiated on a scale sufficiently large to permit reasonably efficient operation. In short, when the minimum efficient size of establishments in a newly entered industry is relatively high, for a firm of moderate size successful entry will necessarily produce a high ratio of nonprimary to primary employment. This is consistent with a wide dispersion that is present in the ratio of nonprimary to primary employment for the smaller firms among those with 2,500 and over employees. With companies grouped as in Table 26, the groups representing the smaller firms generally contained both firms with zero nonprimary employment and those with very high ratios of nonprimary to primary employment (though frequently the latter had but a single nonprimary activity).

Diversification and Company Growth and Profit Rates

Since no historical information was available for the 721 multiunit companies, analysis of the relation of diversification to growth and profitability was necessarily restricted to the 111 large enterprises.[11]

The direction of causation in the relation between diversification and company growth is by no means clear. On the one hand, diversification is a form of growth. In consequence, firms that have diversified should, in the absence of offsetting factors such as slower growth in the primary

---

[11] Information on growth was, however, available for 109 rather than all 111 companies.

industry, have grown more on the average than those whose output has remained homogeneous. Conversely, a rapidly growing, and hence more successful, company is under some circumstances likely to diversify more. For example, faster growth may be associated with higher rates of return and, thus, a larger volume of investment funds generated from earnings. This facilitates diversification. Faster growth may also reflect more aggressive managerial policy and, consequently, a greater likelihood that investment opportunities in industries new to the company will be discovered and exploited. Offsetting these two influences leading to a positive relation between growth and diversification is the fact that the rate of growth of a firm is partly dependent upon the rate of growth in demand in its primary industry. Faster growth in primary industry demand will increase the attractiveness of investment opportunities within the existing industrial scope of a firm's output relative to those elsewhere in the economy. Assuming scarcity of managerial, capital, and other resources, this leads to a negative relation between growth and diversification. Alternatively, some low-growth or low-profit-rate firms may undertake to diversify their output as a defensive measure, thus offsetting the positive relation that might otherwise have been present.

To ascertain the association between company growth and diversification, two tests were employed. In the first, growth was measured by the ratio of total assets in 1954 to total assets in 1939. This ratio was then correlated with the composite D_3 diversification measure. For 109 companies, the coefficient of rank correlation (Spearman's) was only .16.

In the second test, the 111 companies were grouped by deciles on the basis of growth in total assets for the 1929–39 and 1939–54 periods. The frequency of product additions in the various deciles in the two periods was then examined. Companies associated with higher growth deciles did not reveal greater frequencies of product additions in 1929–39 than did those in the lower deciles (Table 28). For the 1939–54 period, there is indication of a positive relation between growth and frequency of additions, at least starting with the third decile. The decline in frequencies from the first to the third decile suggests, though inconclusively, a U-shaped curve. Generally, data for the 1939–54 period would seem to support the conclusion of a moderate positive relation between diversification and company growth, with exceptions arising from companies that embark upon diversification because of decline or slow growth in demand for their primary products.

The absence of relation in the first test may be explained, perhaps, by

TABLE 28

COMPANY GROWTH IN TOTAL ASSETS AND FREQUENCY OF PRODUCT ADDITIONS

Growth Deciles and Median Growth in Assets[a]		Number of Companies[b]	Number of Product Additions	Average per Company[c]
		1929–39		
1.	−45.03%	11	76	6.9
2.	−25.75	11	75	6.8
3.	−13.75	10	68	6.8
4.	−5.82	10	38	3.8
5.	4.62	10	34	3.4
6.	8.51	11	52	4.7
7.	15.29	11	65	5.9
8.	28.90	10	74	7.4
9.	62.20	10	60	6.0
10.	156.75	10	54	5.4
All companies	7.02	104	596	5.4
		1939–54		
1.	55.34%	11	102	9.3
2.	115.07	10	76	7.6
3.	150.68	11	51	4.6
4.	182.22	11	88	8.0
5.	209.07	11	101	9.2
6.	249.52	11	104	9.4
7.	279.95	11	100	9.1
8.	421.28	11	137	12.4
9.	587.29	11	106	9.6
10.	1,633.24	11	214	19.4
All companies	230.02	109	1079	9.7

SOURCE: Product record described in Chapter 2 and data on total assets from Moody's *Industrials*.

[a] Deciles are in ascending order in terms of growth. Median growth is expressed as a percentage of initial-year assets.

[b] Seven companies for which asset data were not available accounted for twenty-three product additions during the 1929–39 period, and two for ten additions during 1939–54.

[c] The value of F was significant for the 1939–54 period at the .05 level ($F = 2.0624$, with $N_1 = 9$, $N_2 = 99$). That is, the variance between classes was significantly greater than the variance within growth classes.

deficiencies in the data used. Data for total assets were not adjusted for changes in price, with the result that the measure of growth for individual companies was affected by the price level at which tangible assets were acquired. Thus a relatively mild relation between growth and diversification could easily have been concealed by variations in the time at which assets were acquired by different companies. In addition, the measure D_3 was based on data for a single point in time, namely, 1954. It is possible that growth rates and the changes in diversification that produced the 1954 pattern do not relate to the same periods in time; in the second test, on the other hand, both additions and growth were measured for the same interval of time.

The rate of return which companies experience is even more volatile over time than company growth rates. Consequently, when diversification is measured as of one point in time, statements about its relation to profitability must be strongly qualified. Although it is not known when the events that led to the 1954 values of measure D_3 occurred, one can still ask if the more diversified companies experienced a higher rate of return. Using data for 110 companies,[12] average net income after taxes for the period 1947–54 was expressed as a ratio to average net worth for the same interval of time.[13] The data were not adjusted for price changes and consequently are subject to the same limitations indicated for growth measured on the basis of total assets. The coefficient of rank correlation (Spearman's) for the indicated measure of rate of return and D_3 was − .04. This result must not be interpreted to mean that diversification exerted no influence upon the profitability of firms. Obviously the profit experience of the 110 companies depended largely upon that for their primary activities. Absence of breakdowns of earnings according to products or divisions renders it difficult to determine the net contribution of diversification to the profitability of companies. Moreover, numerous factors unrelated to diversification influence the rate of return in both the primary and the non-primary industries. The results, however, point to a conclusion that the influence of diversification upon profits is not, alone, sufficient to overcome other sources of variation in rates of return.

To remedy the deficiency of measuring diversification at a single point in time, the measure D_3 was computed for 1947, as well as for 1954, and the 110 companies were ranked on the basis of the change in D_3 between the two dates. This ranking and one based on average rate of return on net worth in 1947–54 led to a rank correlation (Spearman's) of only .09. Thus the result is substantially the same as that based on diversification measured at one point in time.

It is sometimes alleged that diversification is undertaken with the objective of reinvesting corporate income which, if distributed as dividends, would be subject to high marginal tax rates under the federal personal income tax. To test this hypothesis, the ratio of dividends to after-tax income in the 1947–54 period was computed for each of the 110

---

[12] Data on income were not available for one of the companies in our sample of 111.

[13] Net worth was defined as the balance sheet value of preferred and common stock, earned and capital surpluses, and reserves for contingencies.

companies and then correlated, first, with measure D_3 for 1947; and second, with change in D_3 from 1947 to 1954. The Spearman coefficients of rank correlation were $-$ .19 and .00, respectively. Thus it is clear that diversification did not produce unusually high rates of income retention, though of course it is still possible that retentions for some companies would have been lower in the absence of diversification.

CHAPTER 5
Integration

How much integration is there in the product structures of large enterprises? Within the universe of multiestablishment manufacturing firms, is size of firm related to integration? Does integration exert a positive influence upon diversification or do the two forms of growth represent competing demands on scarce resources, with the result that one tends to increase at the expense of the other? These and related questions are examined in the present chapter.

Summary

In 1954, employment associated with integration averaged 25.2 per cent of total employment for the sample of 111 large enterprises. In the same year, 21 per cent of the manufacturing activities in which the firms maintained one or more plants were classified as integration. One hundred and three of the companies maintained establishments in more than one manufacturing industry. For this group, the second largest activity in terms of payrolls could be classified as integration in roughly 23 per cent of the cases.

For the 111 firms, integration was positively related to size of firm, but only to a moderate degree. For a larger sample of 589 multiestablishment manufacturing firms,[1] integration could only be roughly approximated by the ratio of "value added" to shipments or sales. A higher ratio of value added to shipments generally signifies greater integration. The ratio of value added to shipments did not appear to be related to company size. This, therefore, tends to support the conclusion, reached on the basis of the 111-firm sample, that there is no strong positive relation between size of firm and integration.

There are indications that greater integration is achieved at the expense of diversification—that is, that the two tend to be primarily competing rather than mutually reinforcing forms of growth. In 1954, among the 111 firms, those that were characterized by greater integration generally seemed to have fewer diversifying activities.

Variations in the magnitude of administrative activities as firm size changes indicate the presence of administrative economies or diseconomies of scale. It is frequently alleged that the volume of administra-

---

[1] The 589 firms were drawn from the sample of 595 multiestablishment manufacturing companies which, in turn, were part of the 721 firm sample described in Chapter 2. For six of the 595 companies, information had to be suppressed.

tive activities rises more than proportionately to the size of an enterprise as size increases. The data, however, notwithstanding a statistical bias that should have operated in favor of this hypothesis, offered no support for it. Generally speaking, increases in the size of multiestablishment firms did not lead to materially higher ratios of central office to other employees. Thus the evidence is consistent with the hypothesis that as a firm increases in size, it incurs at most only proportionate increases in administrative costs.

Differences in Integration Among Industries

Integration was defined in Chapter 2 as the combination under single ownership of several stages in the production and distribution of a common product or service. Two or more productive processes associated with a common final product were deemed to be separate stages in production if they were identified with separate 4-digit industry classes. When a firm was engaged in production at two or more stages, the largest of the stages in terms of the firm's employment was deemed a "major" activity, while the other stages were identified as "auxiliary." A diversified firm would, by definition, have more than one major activity; but to be considered integrated as well, at least one of its major activities must be associated with auxiliary stages within the output structure of the firm. Integration was measured by the ratio of employment in auxiliary activities to total employment for the firm. Table 29, based on the sample of 111 companies, shows average ratios of auxiliary to total employees for each of thirteen industry groups. The lowest average ratio was 9.7 per cent for transportation equipment companies, and the highest was 67.3 per cent for petroleum companies.[2]

Within industry classes, variability in degree of integration differs considerably among the thirteen groups of firms. Somewhat surprisingly, the coefficients of variation for the 2-digit industry groupings of firms were not closely related to whether the groups were composed of companies with the same primary 4-digit industries. For example, relatively high coefficients of variation were associated with such comparatively homogeneous industry groups as primary metals and textile mill products, as well as with the heterogeneous groupings represented by transportation

[2] The ratio for petroleum companies would have been lower had the measure for all of the companies in this group been computed in accordance with the above definition of auxiliary employment. The difficulty in measurement arose from the fact that the major industry for the companies was specified as petroleum refining, even though for some of them employment in the production of crude petroleum exceeded that associated with manufacturing activities.

TABLE 29

THE RELATION OF INTEGRATION EMPLOYMENT TO TOTAL EMPLOYMENT
FOR 111 LARGE ENTERPRISES, 1954

Primary Industry of Company	Number of Companies	Integration Employment as Percentage of Total Employment	
		Mean	Coefficient of Variation
Food products	12	30.3%	33%
Tobacco manufactures	5	16.7	55
Textile mill products	4	16.1	89
Paper products	8	27.1	50
Chemicals	14	19.6	79
Petroleum	10	67.3	8
Rubber products	5	18.6	43
Stone, clay, and glass products	7	19.3	69
Primary metals	10	21.2	67
Fabricated metal products	5	15.0	27
Machinery	13	30.5	50
Electrical machinery	5	12.8	72
Transportation equipment	13	9.7	98

SOURCE: Special census tabulation.

equipment and chemicals. Conversely, relatively low coefficients of variation were associated with both the heterogeneous food products group and the highly homogeneous petroleum group.

In contrast to the concept of integration implicit in the ratio of auxiliary to total employment, one might wish to measure the "intensiveness" of production within a single firm. This is measured by the ratio of value added to sales or shipments. Every intermediate productive process that is incorporated in a firm's activities necessarily increases the ratio of value added to sales. However, not all changes that combine separable stages of production under common ownership exert an equal influence on this ratio. If a stage associated with an intermediate product is added, in most instances the numerator of the ratio will rise without an increase in the denominator. On the other hand, if a new activity is added at a later point in the productive process than the older ones of the firm, both the numerator and the denominator of the value-added to sales ratio will usually rise equally. In short, when integration is measured by this ratio, both change in integration over time and differences among firms at a single point in time will depend upon the stage in the productive process at which auxiliary operations occur.

Another though related bias of the value-added to sales ratio as a measure of integration arises from the effect of differences in the value of purchased materials. Thus, if two firms produce at successive stages of a given final product (for example, a manufacturer of automobile parts and one primarily engaged in assembly of the automobile), the value of the sales of one will be incorporated in the prices and sales totals of the other. If the two firms are characterized by roughly the same degree of integration (as measured, for instance, by the ratio of auxiliary to total employment), the one that produces at the earlier stages will necessarily show a higher value-added to sales ratio. This means that the value-added to sales ratio will, generally speaking, tend to be higher for firms producing raw materials or semifinished goods than for those engaged primarily in the production of consumer goods.

There is still a third characteristic that distinguishes the value-added to sales ratio from that of auxiliary to total employment. Value added may rise as the result of an increase in the amount of capital or labor employed in the primary activity. If the increase in inputs is directed towards producing a more valuable product rather than a larger quantity of the same product, the ratio of value added to sales would rise, though no rise will have taken place in the volume of auxiliary employment; in fact, the ratio of auxiliary to total employment will have declined.

Data showing the ratio of value added to shipments in 1954 were developed for the manufacturing establishments of 589 manufacturing companies in thirteen 2-digit industries.[3] Table 30 shows that the mean ratio of value added to shipments for the thirteen industry groupings varied only moderately. Nine of the thirteen mean ratios fell within the range of .4 and .6, and only in one case—petroleum—did the ratio fall far outside this range. Considering the heterogeneity of firms in the same industry groupings, it is perhaps also surprising that for nine of the thirteen groupings the coefficient of variation fell below 26 per cent.

The Relation of Integration to Size of Firm

When the 111 companies were ranked on the basis of the 1954 ratio of auxiliary to total employment, the Spearman coefficient of rank correlation for this ranking and one based on total asset size in 1954 was .37. Though statistically significant, the coefficient was relatively low inasmuch as investment in integration must contribute to the asset size of a firm. Moreover, the coefficient would have been even lower if, for some of the

---

[3] The sample is described in note 1 of this chapter and in Chapter 2. Census data on value added were available only for manufacturing and mining establishments. Our data, however, are restricted further to manufacturing establishments.

TABLE 30

RATIOS OF VALUE ADDED TO SHIPMENTS, 589 MANUFACTURING COMPANIES GROUPED ON THE BASIS OF INDUSTRY AND EMPLOYMENT SIZE, 1954

Primary Industry of Company	Ratios for Size Classes[a]										Industry Mean	Coefficient of Variation (per cent)
	(4)	(4)	(12)	(10)	(10)	(10)	(10)	(10)	(10)	(10)		
Food products	.209	.356	.309	.349	.404	.422	.377	.419	.342(8)		.364	43.1
Textile mill products	.339	.395	.386	.406	.455	.346	.402	.447(6)			.399	25.8
Paper products	.452	.367	.379	.435	.405(9)						.406	23.4
Chemicals	.553	.513	.496	.488	.529	.512	.404				.492	30.1
Petroleum and coal	.179	.145	.239	.147(7)							.193	56.5
Rubber products	.434	.468	.440(4)								.447	17.7
Stone, clay, and glass products	.617	.583	.577								.586	16.2
Primary metals	.370	.359	.338	.512	.481	.492					.436	28.2
Fabricated metal products	.446	.497	.554	.503(7)							.516	20.7
Machinery[b]	.479	.551	.554	.562	.572	.561	.654	.611	.580	.763(8)	.594	21.5
Electrical machinery	.535	.526	.445	.565	.571	.516					.522	23.4
Transportation equipment	.339	.529	.508	.475	.492	.476	.492(4)				.481	24.3
Instruments	.583	.582	.659(10)								.625	16.6

SOURCE: Special census tabulation.

[a] Included are all multiestablishment companies in the specified industries with total employment of 2,500 and over, except for six companies for which data could not be shown for reasons of disclosure of individual company information. Numbers in parentheses indicate the number of companies represented in the class. The first class consists of the largest four, the second, the next four, etc. Numbers in parentheses in the body of the table show the number of companies in a cell where the numbers differ from those in the column head.

[b] Except electrical.

petroleum companies, the "major" as distinct from auxiliary industry had been identified as crude petroleum production.[4]

Absence of a strong relation between size of firm and integration was further supported by examination of the ratios of value added to shipments. Table 30 does not show a positive relation between size of firm (measured on the basis of total manufacturing employment) and the ratio of value added to shipments. Indeed, in eight of the thirteen industry groupings, the highest size class was associated with a ratio that fell below the mean for the group. This may be attributable to a statistical bias in the value-added to shipments ratio noted earlier; namely, that firms whose auxiliary activities occur at an earlier point in the production process will, other things being equal, tend to show higher ratios of value added to shipments. Thus, if the larger firms are more active in producing final consumer goods and the smaller firms, in raw materials or semi-finished products, the value-added to sales ratio would be reduced for larger firms relative to that for the smaller ones. Nevertheless, if two companies have equal shipments, the one which shows a higher ratio of value added to shipments will necessarily be the larger of the two in terms of total inputs of resources. In most instances, it will also be the larger in terms of employment size. Accordingly, the absence of a positive relation between employment size and this ratio must be attributed to factors that offset the effect of greater integration (as measured by the ratio) upon company size.

Absence of a strong association between size of firm and integration, notwithstanding the positive effect that investment in integration must exert upon size, deserves further examination. The most plausible reason for the results is that investment in integration competes for scarce capital and managerial resources with both investment in diversification and in the primary activity of firms. This leads to a substitution of one form of investment for another.[5] Thus firms that are less integrated need not, on the average, be smaller in aggregate size.

The Relation of Integration to Diversification

The hypothesis that integration is related negatively to diversification is

[4] See note 2. This had the effect of increasing the ratio in question for a few companies. Since petroleum companies were among the largest in the sample, the effect of raising the ratio of integration to total employment had the effect of increasing the correlation.

[5] Of some relevance in this connection is the fact that the ranking of companies on the basis of the auxiliary to total employment ratio in 1954 appears to be negatively correlated, though only to a mild degree, with rankings of the same companies on the basis of growth in total assets in the period 1939–54. The Spearman coefficient of rank correlation was —.22. It was significant at the .05 level.

examined next. To test the relation between the two variables directly, the 111 companies were first grouped into deciles on the basis of the ratio of auxiliary to total employment. For each of the ten groups of companies, the number of industrial activities at the 4-digit level of industry detail was recorded (Table 31).[6] As may be judged from Table 31, the largest number

TABLE 31

RELATION OF INTEGRATION TO NUMBER OF MANUFACTURING PRODUCTS, 1954

Deciles Based on Ranking of Auxiliary to Total Employment Ratio[a]	Number of Companies	Number of Products in Manufacturing Industries	Average Per Company[b]
1	11	128	11.6
2	11	162	14.7
3	10	212	21.2
4	11	169	15.4
5	11	234	21.3
6	11	236	21.4
7	11	193	17.5
8	11	166	15.1
9	12	126	10.5
10	12	103	8.6
		1729	

SOURCE: 1954 product record and special census tabulation.

[a] The deciles are in ascending order with respect to the ratio.

[b] The ratio of the variance between classes to the variance within the class (decile) cells was 1.880 with $N_1 = 9$, $N_2 = 101$.

of industrial activities is to be found in deciles 5 and 6, with a fairly pronounced decline in number at both ends of the distribution.[7] These results lend support to the conclusion that, at least for the most highly integrated companies, there has been a tendency to substitute integration for diversification.

[6] Operations associated with integration were not removed from the list of 1,729 manufacturing activities of the companies in the sample. However, the pattern of variation among deciles in number of activities would probably not have been materially altered had integration activities been removed, since the overwhelming majority of products were associated with diversification. In these data, the ratio of activities associated with integration to those associated with diversification is likely to be of roughly the same magnitude as that observed on the basis of census data for manufacturing activities, namely, .21.

[7] When analysis of variance was applied, the high degree of variability in the number of activities associated with companies falling within the same integration deciles produced an F ratio (the variance between deciles to that within the deciles) that was significant at only the .10 level.

Activities of Manufacturing Companies in Distributive Trades

Manufacturing companies sell a large proportion of their products through separate sales offices. Some of them also employ their own wholesale and retail establishments for this purpose. A wholesale establishment, as defined in the Standard Industrial Classification Code, differs from a sales office in that it must either be a part of a subsidiary separately incorporated from the parent firm or else must sell primarily the products of other firms. A retail establishment, as defined in the Code, may be devoted wholly, partially, or not at all to the sale of the firm's own products. Thus some wholesale and retail establishments offer services that are substitutes for those of sales offices in that they participate in the sale of their owner's products. In the same way, they may perform marketing services that might otherwise be procured outside the firm. Consequently, the wholesale and retail activities of manufacturing firms in part represent integration.[8] This is also true of the latter's activities in the service trades.

The data available for the sample of 111 firms showed the activities of each firm in the wholesale, retail, and service trades on a combined basis, but gave information for sales offices separately. Ratios of employment in sales offices to total employment and of employment in wholesale, retail, and service trades to total employment were developed for the sample of 111 large manufacturing companies. Table 32 shows that substantial differences between industry groups of firms characterized both sets of ratios. Petroleum companies show a smaller ratio of sales office to total employment than any of the other companies, and a markedly higher ratio of employment in wholesale, retail, and service trades to total employment.[9]

Generally speaking, the variability within industry groups appeared to be higher for the wholesale, retail, and service trades ratios than that for sales offices. This was, of course, to be expected since a large proportion of sales office activities consists of operations that are essential to all firms. Variability within industry groups in sales office ratios was, however, too high to be explained satisfactorily by differences between companies in the character of their products. It is likely that companies vary considerably in the extent to which sales personnel are attached to separate

[8] The sense in which sales office activities represent integration was discussed in Chapter 2.

[9] The low level of the ratio of sales office to total employment for petroleum companies may indicate that central administrative offices attached to petroleum bulk stations were performing largely a sales function. The ratio of central administrative office employment to total employment for petroleum companies, as tabulated in the 1954 Census, was unusually high. A large proportion of central office employment for petroleum companies emanated from offices attached to bulk stations.

TABLE 32

MAGNITUDE OF EMPLOYMENT IN SALES OFFICES AND WHOLESALE, RETAIL, AND
SERVICE TRADES, 111 LARGE ENTERPRISES, 1954

Primary Industry of Company	Number of Companies	Sales Office Employment as Percentage of Total Employment[a]		Employment in Wholesale, Retail, and Services Trades as Percentage of Total Employment[a]	
		Mean	Coefficient of Variation (per cent)	Mean	Coefficient of Variation (per cent)
Food products	12	11.0–16.6	59	2.0–2.5	166
Tobacco manufactures	5	6.5– 8.0	72	0–2.0	b
Textile mill products	4	4.0– 6.5	174	6.5–8.0	157
Paper products	8	4.0– 6.5	147	2.0–2.5	207
Chemicals	14	6.5– 8.0	77	1.5–2.0	355
Petroleum	10	0– 2.5	2	18.1	36
Rubber products	5	4.0– 6.5	40	6.5–8.0	74
Stone, clay, and glass products	7	11.0–16.6	80	0–2.0	b
Primary metals	10	1.5– 3.0	65	0–2.0	115
Fabricated metal products	5	4.0– 6.5	93	0–2.0	b
Machinery	13	11.0–16.6	72	3.0–3.5	327
Electrical machinery	5	1.5– 3.0	139	3.0–3.5	98
Transportation equipment	13	2.5– 4.0	217	0–2.0	253

SOURCE: Special census tabulation.

[a] Expressed as percentage range to avoid possible disclosure of individual company data.

[b] Not computed in order to avoid possible disclosure of individual company data.

establishments identified as sales offices. Sales personnel affiliated with either general administrative offices or manufacturing plants were not reflected in data for sales office employment.

Size of company, as measured by total assets, was not significantly related to either of the above two sets of ratios. When companies were divided into two classes, those with total assets of over a billion dollars and those with assets of a billion dollars or less, the former class did show a lower ratio for sales office employment and a higher ratio for employment in wholesale, retail, and service trades. This, however, was wholly attributable to the effect of the petroleum companies in the sample, most of which had assets of a billion dollars and over in 1954.

The Relation of Employment in Central Administrative Offices to Company Size

An important subject in the study of integration is the relative size of central administrative office employment. Most central office activities are essential complements of the other processes of production for which they perform the supervisory, planning, and record-keeping functions. Unless these services are purchased outside the firm, it is probable that the size and scope of most central office functions cannot be materially altered without complementary changes in the volume or composition of the firm's output.[10] Accordingly, if smaller companies require relatively fewer administrative employees, this would indicate the presence of diseconomies of scale with respect to the cost of administrative services. The converse would, of course, be true if large companies had relatively fewer administrative employees. It has been frequently argued that as the size of a firm increases, the number of supervisory functions needed increases more than proportionately; that is, the number of administrative employees increases relative to the number of "production workers" as the firm becomes larger, with a consequent diseconomy offsetting whatever technical efficiencies may result from larger size. Our data do not support this hypothesis.

An attempt to establish the nature of the relation between employment size of company and central office employment was made on the basis of data for 684 companies[11] grouped by 2-digit industries and by employment size class.[12] These groupings, and the average employment in each group, are shown in Appendix Table C–1; average central administrative office employment in each group is shown in Table C–4.

The relation between central administrative office employment and *all other* employment is specified by the following equation, where Y denotes central office employment and X total employment minus central office employment:

$$(1) \qquad Y = -77.4 + .0671X, \quad r = .869$$
$$(115.5) \quad (.0013)$$

The standard error (indicated in parentheses) for the regression coefficient was very small. That for the negative constant, however, was high and the latter was not significantly less than zero. A zero constant would indicate a ratio of Y to X that does not vary with company size. The equation explains roughly 75 per cent of the variance in Y.

---

[10] However, while the functions cannot be modified easily, these functions can frequently be performed within manufacturing establishments as well as within separate central offices. This leads to a bias in the data, discussed at a later point.

[11] Data for petroleum companies were excluded because information on their central office employment was, for reasons indicated earlier, probably defective.

[12] The size classes were the following: the first consisted of the four largest firms; the second, the next four largest; the third, the next twelve; and all subsequent classes consisted of successive groups of ten. There were ninety groups of companies so that the relation was examined on the basis of ninety observations. The reasons for using group averages rather than individual company information, and for the choice of groups, are indicated in Chapter 4 in the discussion of relation of firm size to magnitude of non-primary employment.

If a second degree polynomial is fitted to the data, the resultant curve, as may be judged from Chart 2, approximates a straight line.[13] The equation is:

(2) $$Y = -100.7 + .0697 X - 10^{-8} \times 1.7544X^2$$

The additional variance explained by equation 2 as compared with a straight line is negligible, the residual variance in Y being 24.525 per cent for equation 2 as compared with 24.544 per cent for equation 1.

When the data for petroleum companies were reintroduced and a straight line fitted to the logarithms of the values of Y and X, the resultant equation was as follows:

(3) $$\log_{10} Y = -1.9044 + 1.1430 \log_{10} X, \quad r = .810$$
$$(.0862)$$

The regression coefficient was not significantly greater than unity at the .05 level of significance. A coefficient of one would indicate a constant ratio of Y to X as X increases. In this respect, equation 3 tends to support the conclusion reached on the basis of equation 1.

In summary, equations 1 and 3 are consistent with the hypothesis that the ratio of central office to total noncentral office employment does not vary much over the observed range of values, while equation 2 points, at least, to a relatively constant incremental ratio.[14] However, it is probable that the data used understate the role of administrative employees in the smaller companies relative to that in larger ones. A smaller company is likely to have a smaller proportion of its administrative employees in separate establishments; that is, such employees are less likely to be numerous enough to justify a separate central office.[15] For this reason,

---

[13] Chart 2, panel III, shows the scatter on a different scale for the highest values of X. Chart 2, panel II, reproduces on a larger scale the observations for companies with low noncentral office employment. The rectangle in panel I indicates the area reproduced in panel II.

[14] Even if the negative constant in equation 1 is taken into account, the ratio does not vary materially over a wide range of company sizes. The equation gives an estimate of central office as a percentage of noncentral office employment of 5.9, 6.3, and 6.6 per cent for companies with respectively, 10,000, 20,000, and 50,000 noncentral office employees.

Equation 1 indicates that central office employment would be zero for a company with 1,153 noncentral office employees. While the negative constant was not significantly less than zero, very small companies would tend to show zero central office employment since they are unlikely to house their administrative employees in separate establishments. However, we do not know the nature of the relation between the two variables for small companies since our data are truncated.

[15] The variation in the ratio of central office to other employees was considerably greater for the smaller companies when companies were grouped by employment size. This seems to reflect the fact that the smaller firms in the sample differed considerably in their practices with respect to whether they housed their administrative employees in separate establishments.

CHART 2
Relation of Central Office Employment to Company Size, 90 Groups of Companies, 1954

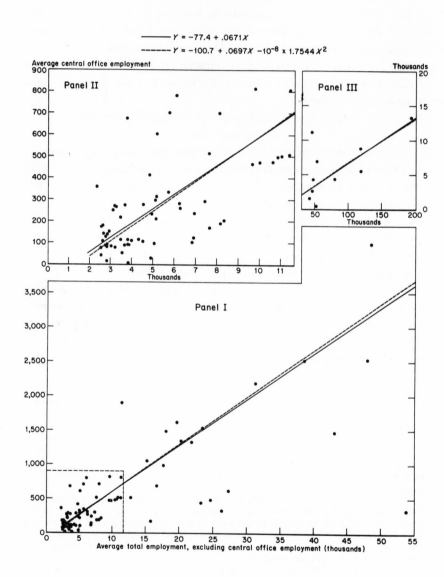

$Y = -77.4 + .0671X$

$Y = -100.7 + .0697X - 10^{-8} \times 1.7544 X^2$

the proportion of *all* administrative employees contributed by central offices probably increases with firm size. In consequence, since central office employment appeared to rise only proportionately to that outside central offices, one may infer that the share of a company's employment accounted by *all* administrative employees (including those that are not in central offices) is inversely related to firm size. This is a conclusion opposite to the one commonly assumed.

The hypothesis regarding administrative diseconomies arising from larger size does not depend exclusively upon the presence of a relatively larger number of employees engaged in administrative duties. It may well be that the effectiveness of central controls is reduced by larger size, thus leading to higher costs unrelated to the costs of administration. Nevertheless, one of the bases for the hypothesis that large firms incur administrative diseconomies appears to be inconsistent with our findings.

CHAPTER 6

Patterns and Trends in Nonmanufacturing Activities

THE focus of this chapter is on the nonmanufacturing activities of large manufacturing enterprises. It examines the extent to which significant patterns are present in the structure of nonmanufacturing activities at a single point in time, namely, 1954, and attempts to determine the trends that prevailed in the period 1929–54. Does entry of manufacturers into nonmanufacturing industries follow a definite pattern or is it merely the product of a wide array of random influences? How stable is the frequency of entry into nonmanufacturing activities as compared with that for manufacturing? What types of nonmanufacturing industries do companies commonly enter, and has the pattern changed over time? These questions are examined below on the basis of information for the 111-firm sample.

Summary

Analysis of the 111 companies' 1954 pattern of nonmanufacturing activities reveals that a large majority of these activities can be classified as integration. In particular, whenever a group of companies showed a bunching of activities within a nonmanufacturing industry class, it was usually associated with integration. Another conclusion based on the 1954 pattern was that backward integration into the extractive industries was a more frequent phenomenon than forward integration into retail trade.

An examination of trends in the 1929–54 period shows no consistency over time in the frequency with which particular groups of companies entered into nonmanufacturing activities. This is in sharp contrast to the pattern found for manufacturing product additions in that, for the latter, the frequency with which companies added products in one time interval was closely related to that for an antecedent or a succeeding interval. Moreover, once again in contrast to the pattern for manufacturing additions, the frequency of entry into nonmanufacturing operations was independent of the primary industries of companies. That is, companies classified in the same industry tended to differ markedly in the number of nonmanufacturing activities that they added.

For the 111 large companies, there was a tendency in the 1929–54 period for entry in nonmanufacturing industries to decline relative to that in the manufacturing sector. Thus for manufacturing firms the relative attractiveness of nonmanufacturing operations appears to be declining. Also, the frequency with which nonmanufacturing activities were abandoned was much higher, relative to their total number, than that for manufacturing operations. This fact could indicate that the risks of entry into nonmanufacturing industries are higher (at least for manufacturing firms) than those of entry into manufacturing. Besides the trends in the relative importance of manufacturing and nonmanufacturing additions, there were also changes in importance among various classes of additions *within* the latter category. Entry into the utility industries and the distributive trades tended to become less frequent relative to entry in the extractive industries and the service trades.

As is the case for all changes in product structure, the average rates of entry into nonmanufacturing industries need not be the same for the 111 companies as for the universe of large manufacturing firms. Moreover, since integration characterized a majority of entries into these industries, the specific activities that were added depended partly on the industry composition of the 111-firm sample. On the other hand, this sample was sufficiently broad to indicate the major trends for large manufacturing firms generally. For example, the observed changes in number of nonmanufacturing additions and abandonments, or the frequency of entry into and outside manufacturing industries, constitute broad tendencies that permit inferences applicable beyond the 111 companies.

The Pattern of Nonmanufacturing Activities in 1954

Table 33 shows the number of companies for the 111-firm sample that were engaged in various nonmanufacturing activities.[1] Companies in the petroleum and primary metals groups were most frequently active in nonmanufacturing industries, followed by those in the chemicals group. A large majority of the nonmanufacturing activities could be classified as integration, although a number constitute diversification and still others may initially have been auxiliary processes but have subsequently grown to encompass production intended for a market outside the firm. In particular, an examination of the nonmanufacturing operations in which a significant number of companies were engaged reveals the dominant role of integration in these activities. Thus, of the fifteen companies with operations in forestry, seven were paper manufacturers. Of the seventeen engaged in metal mining, ten were mainly producers of primary metals. A majority of the nineteen companies that produced crude petroleum were engaged in petroleum refining. Of the twenty-eight companies

---

[1] A number of instances of activities in wholesale trade are not shown in Table 33 because, on the basis of available information, they were difficult to distinguish from sales offices. Similarly, it was difficult to distinguish trucking and warehousing facilities associated with separable operations from those that were an integral part of the plant and equipment of the companies' other operations.

Number and Industries

	Food Products (12)	Tobacco Manufactures (5)	Textile Mill Products (4)	Paper Products (8)	Chemicals (14)
Farms	1	1	1		
Forestry	1			7	2
Fisheries	1				
Metal mining	1				3
Coal mining					
Petroleum and gas extraction	1				4
Nonmetallic minerals extraction	2		1	2	6
Building construction	1				
Other construction			1		1
Railroads	2			2	4
Water transportation	2			1	5
Air transportation					
Pipeline transportation					2
Services incidental to transportation				1	1
Telecommunications					
Utilities and sanitary services	2	1		6	3
Merchant wholesalers	5	1	3	3	1
Retail trade	3		1		2
Banking	1				1
Other credit agencies			1		1
Insurance	2				1
Real estate	1	1		2	7
Holding and investment companies			1		1
Hotels		1			
Miscellaneous business services	2		2	2	5
Automobile repair services and garages					
Miscellaneous repair services	1				
Radio and television broadcasting					1
Motion pictures					1
Amusement and recreation services	1				
Medical and health services					
Educational services				2	
Automotive dealers and gasoline stations					
Average per company	2.70	1.0	2.75	3.50	3.71

engaged in the mining of minerals nineteen fell into primary metals, chemicals, and stone, clay, and glass groups, once again reflecting the dominant role of integration in the combination of activities. There were twenty-eight companies that maintained railroads and twenty-seven *of Companies*[a]

Petroleum (10)	Rubber Products (5)	Stone, Clay, and Glass Products (7)	Primary Metals (10)	Fabricated Metal Products (5)	Machinery (13)	Electrical Machinery (5)	Trans- portation Equip- ment (13)	Total (111)
	1							4
		2	2		1			15
								1
		1	10		2			17
		1	7		1			9
10		3	1					19
2		4	9	1	1			28
			5					6
		1	4		2		1	10
7		1	8		1	2	1	28
9		2	7		1		2	29
1								1
10		2	1					15
1			2				3	8
3						1	1	5
3	1	1	5		2	1	2	27
								13
	4	2	6		2			20
					1			3
	1		1	1	3	2	5	15
4	1		2				2	12
9	2	3	7	1	6	2	2	43
2		1	2		1	1	2	11
								1
		1			5		5	22
	1						1	2
				2	1	1	4	9
	1					2		4
								1
						1	1	3
						1		1
						1	2	5
10	1							11
7.10	2.60	3.57	7.90	1.0	2.31	3.0	2.62	3.59

SOURCE: Product record for 111 companies described in Chapter 2.

[a] Numbers in parentheses refer to number of companies in the specified industry.

that operated utilities, but almost all for their own uses; only a few offered services outside the firm. Twenty-nine companies maintained water transport facilities, but once again these facilities were maintained primarily to transport raw material for the companies' own uses. Of the activities in real estate, a considerable number were maintained for the acquisition of property to be used in connection with the firms' manufacturing or extractive activities.

In contrast to the reasonably high frequency of operations in the production of raw materials, and of auxiliary services such as transportation and utilities, only thirteen companies were engaged in wholesale trade.[2] This is to be explained by the fact that sales at the wholesale level for the firms' own products were made in sales offices rather than in establishments which also sold the products of other firms. There were twenty companies engaged in retail trade, excluding the operation of automotive dealerships and gasoline service stations, and thirty if the latter are included. When separate activities at the 4-digit level of industry detail are counted, the number which the 111 companies maintained in the extractive industries was three times that in retail trade: 156 compared with only 53 (Appendix Table B–3).[3] This is somewhat surprising in view of the ease of entry into retail trade. It is partially explained by the fact that the manufactured products of a firm can frequently be sold through a single type of retail establishment. Thus, in contrast to activities in the extractive industries, the retail operations of a firm were usually shown as a single activity in the table. However, even if all extractive industries were combined into a single industry class, the number of firms with activities in this class would still prove considerably greater than that for operations in retail trade. A possible explanation for this fact is that ease of entry into retail trade produces a highly competitive industry structure. This, in turn, assures a manufacturer of a continued market for his products as long as there exists a sufficient demand from final consumers. Thus entry into retail trade as a defensive measure is rendered unnecessary. In contrast, supplies of raw materials are far less responsive to changes in demand than the supply of retail services, so that the former may be largely pre-empted by competing manufacturers who maintain their own activities in the extractive industries. Also, in periods of rising demand, the prices of raw materials are likely to rise rapidly. This, in turn, may offer an incentive for entry into raw-materials production as a defensive measure. However, the value of this step is offset by the fact that a manufacturer who produces his own raw materials loses the opportunity to

---

[2] This excludes the operation of sales offices for the firms' products.

[3] Appendix Table B–3, unlike Table 33, records the number of industrial activities at the 4-digit level of detail. Thus it allows for the fact that some companies were active in more than one 4-digit industry falling within the broader 2-digit nonmanufacturing categories. On this basis, the average number of activities was roughly 4.8 per company compared with 3.6 on the basis of Table 33.

acquire raw materials at low prices during periods of falling demand.

Companies engaged in the production of consumer goods (food, gasoline, tires) showed, as might be expected, a somewhat greater frequency of activities in retail trade than did the manufacturers of producer goods. Surprisingly, however, the difference was fairly small.

Additions and Abandonments of Products and Services

When the 111 large companies were grouped by their primary industry into thirteen industry categories, a ranking of industry groups based on average number (per company) of nonmanufacturing additions for the 1929–39 period, and one based on data for 1939–50, produced a coefficient of rank correlation (Spearman's) of only .12. For the 1939–50 and 1950–54 periods the coefficient was exactly zero. The lack of stability in the ranks over time may be contrasted to rankings based on average number of *manufacturing* product additions for each of the three periods. On the latter basis, as indicated in Chapter 3, rank correlation for the periods 1929–39 and 1939–50 was .69, and for 1939–50 and 1950–54 it was .80. In short, whereas for additions of manufacturing operations the same groups of

TABLE 34

AVERAGE NUMBER OF ADDITIONS PER COMPANY OF MANUFACTURING AND
NONMANUFACTURING PRODUCTS AND SERVICES, 111 LARGE ENTERPRISES,
GROUPED BY INDUSTRY, 1929–54

Primary Industry of Company	Nonmanufacturing 1929–39	1939–50	1950–54	Manufacturing 1929–39	1939–50	1950–54
Food products	1.75	1.17	.42	4.33	3.00	2.42
Tobacco manufactures	.20	.20	.40	.40	.20	0
Textile mill products	.75	1.25	.75	4.50	4.25	.75
Paper products	.63	1.50	.38	3.88	4.75	4.75
Chemicals	1.29	1.57	1.15	5.07	5.43	5.93
Petroleum	1.70	2.00	.20	2.40	3.70	2.10
Rubber products	.60	1.40	.60	7.80	10.60	10.80
Stone, clay, and glass products	1.71	.57	.43	5.29	3.57	2.29
Primary metals	1.80	1.50	1.00	4.10	.90	2.20
Fabricated metal products	.80	.20	.40	2.00	4.20	2.80
Machinery	.62	.46	.69	2.69	2.77	2.54
Electrical machinery	3.00	.20	.80	12.20	12.40	7.60
Transportation equipment	.77	.77	.38	4.85	4.85	6.15
All Companies	1.22	1.06	.59	4.36	4.27	3.88
Ratio of Variances[a]	1.76	1.25	.60	2.74	4.28	2.83

SOURCE: Product record described in Chapter 2.

[a] The ratio for each column of the variance between industry classes to the variance within industry cells, with $N_1 = 12$, $N_2 = 98$.

companies tend to be associated with the highest frequencies in successive periods, for nonmanufacturing activities there appears to be no such stable pattern. Thus, for example, the fact that food products companies may have had more additions of nonmanufacturing activities in a given period than did textile mill products companies offers no clue to the relative frequencies for the two groups in subsequent or preceding intervals of time.

Changes in the ranks assigned to industry groupings of companies for frequency of nonmanufacturing additions suggests an absence of a stable relation between the primary industry of a company and the firm's opportunities for integration or diversification by entry into nonmanufacturing activities. This conclusion is given further support by the substantial variability in the number of nonmanufacturing activities added in a given time period by companies in the same industry group. Table 34 shows substantial differences between the thirteen industry groups in mean frequencies of product additions, both for manufacturing and nonmanufacturing activities, and in each of the three periods. However, for nonmanufacturing additions, variations in frequencies between companies in the same industry groups were so wide that differences between in-

TABLE 35

TOTAL NUMBER OF ADDITIONS OF PRODUCTS AND SERVICES AND OF
NONMANUFACTURING PRODUCTS AND SERVICES, 111 LARGE
ENTERPRISES GROUPED BY INDUSTRY, 1929–54

Primary Industry of Company	Number of Companies	Total Additions			Nonmanufacturing Additions		
		1929–39	1939–50	1950–54	1929–39	1939–50	1950–54
Food products	12	73	50	34	21	14	5
Tobacco manufactures	5	3	2	2	1	1	2
Textile mill products	4	21	22	6	3	5	3
Paper products	8	36	50	41	5	12	3
Chemicals	14	89	98	98	18	22	15
Petroleum	10	41	57	23	17	20	2
Rubber products	5	42	60	57	3	7	3
Stone, clay, and glass products	7	49	29	19	12	4	3
Primary metals	10	59	24	32	18	15	10
Fabricated metal products	5	14	22	16	4	1	2
Machinery	13	43	42	42	8	6	9
Electrical machinery	5	76	63	42	15	1	4
Transportation equipment	13	73	73	85	10	10	5
Total	111	619	592	497	135	118	66
Percentage of total additions		100	100	100	21.8	19.9	13.3

SOURCE: Product record described in Chapter 2.

TABLE 36
TOTAL NUMBER OF ABANDONMENTS OF PRODUCTS AND SERVICES AND OF
NONMANUFACTURING PRODUCTS AND SERVICES, 111 LARGE
ENTERPRISES GROUPED BY INDUSTRY, 1929–54

Primary Industry of Company	Number of Companies	Total Abandonments			Nonmanufacturing Abandonments		
		1929–39	1939–50	1950–54	1929–39	1939–50	1950–54
Food products	12	5	27	22	3	12	8
Tobacco manufactures	5	1	3	0	0	0	0
Textile mill products	4	1	4	4	0	0	0
Paper products	8	2	15	2	0	2	0
Chemicals	14	11	30	17	3	9	3
Petroleum	10	8	16	9	0	5	7
Rubber products	5	10	9	8	4	3	3
Stone, clay, and glass products	7	4	12	7	2	4	1
Primary metals	10	14	34	11	8	21	9
Fabricated metal products	5	2	14	5	0	6	1
Machinery	13	5	15	4	2	3	1
Electrical machinery	5	4	12	1	0	3	0
Transportation equipment	13	24	29	13	12	9	2
Total	111	91	220	103	34	81	35
Percentage of total abandonments		100	100	100	37.4	36.8	34.0

SOURCE: Product record described in Chapter 2.

dustry means did not appear to be statistically significant when subjected to analysis of variance.[4] This appears to indicate that frequency of entry into nonmanufacturing activities is determined largely by conditions peculiar to individual firms rather than to the industries in which their main operations fall.

While for the 111 firms the number of nonmanufacturing activities grew in the 1929–54 period, the proportion of all additions that were outside manufacturing declined over this interval. In each of the three periods studied, additions of nonmanufacturing products or services exceeded abandonments (Tables 35 and 36). However, nonmanufacturing additions as a percentage of all additions declined, from 21.8 in 1929–39 to 19.9 in 1939–50, and more sharply to 13.3 in 1950–54. When net additions are computed by subtracting abandonments from gross additions, net nonmanufacturing as a percentage of net total additions declined from 19.1 in 1929–39 to 10.0 in 1939–50 and 7.9 in 1950–54.

For a manufacturing enterprise, the likelihood of survival in non-manufacturing operations appears to be distinctly less than in manu-

[4] Indeed, for the 1950–54 period, the variance within industry classes was greater than that between industry means.

TABLE 37

DISTRIBUTION OF NONMANUFACTURING ADDITIONS OF PRODUCTS AND SERVICES BY INDUSTRY,
111 COMPANIES GROUPED BY INDUSTRIES, 1929–39

	Number and Industries of Product Additions						
Industries of Companies[a]	Extractive Industries	Con- struction	Transpor- tation and Utilities	Retail and Wholesale Trade	Real Estate and Finance	Services	Total
Food products (12)	5	0	3	4	7	2	21
Tobacco manufactures (5)	0	0	0	0	0	1	1
Textile mill products (4)	1	0	0	1	1	0	3
Paper products (8)	2	0	3	0	0	0	5
Chemicals (14)	5	0	7	2	1	3	18
Petroleum (10)	4	0	6	1	4	2	17
Rubber products (5)	0	0	0	2	1	0	3
Stone, clay, and glass products (7)	5	0	3	2	1	1	12
Primary metals (10)	3	4	4	2	4	1	18
Fabricated metal products (5)	2	0	0	0	2	0	4
Machinery (13)	1	0	1	0	4	2	8
Electrical machinery (5)	1	0	6	0	2	6	15
Transportation equipment (13)	0	0	2	1	5	2	10
Total	29	4	35	15	32	20	135

SOURCE: Product record described in Chapter 2.

[a] Numbers in parentheses refer to number of companies in the specified industry.

facturing industries. In the three periods, nonmanufacturing abandonments ranged from 34.0 to 37.4 per cent of the aggregate number of abandonments for the 111 companies combined. This is distinctly greater than the percentage of all products and services of these companies contributed by nonmanufacturing activities, at least when measured as of the terminal data of the 1929–54 period.[5] The relatively high rate of abandonments for nonmanufacturing operations is even clearer when compared with the rate of additions. In manufacturing, the number of abandonments in the 1929–54 period as a whole equaled only 19.0 per cent of additions; for nonmanufacturing the comparable percentage was 47.0.

Nonmanufacturing Industries Entered by Large Enterprises

In this section, the discussion focuses on the types of industries most frequently entered. That is, given a number of broad nonmanufacturing sectors, how important is each as an integration or diversification outlet for our sample of firms?

[5] In 1954, at the 4-digit industry level, nonmanufacturing activities accounted for 18.6 per cent of all the activities of the 111 companies.

100

TABLE 38

DISTRIBUTION OF NONMANUFACTURING ADDITIONS OF PRODUCTS AND SERVICES BY INDUSTRY,
111 COMPANIES GROUPED BY INDUSTRY, 1939–50

Industries of Companies[a]	Extractive Industries	Con- struction	Transpor- tation and Utilities	Retail and Wholesale Trade	Real Estate and Finance	Services	Total
Food products (12)	3	1	4	3	2	1	14
Tobacco manufactures (5)	0	0	1	0	0	0	1
Textile mill products (4)	1	0	1	1	1	1	5
Paper products (8)	5	0	4	1	0	2	12
Chemicals (14)	7	2	9	2	0	2	22
Petroleum (10)	4	0	8	4	1	3	20
Rubber products (5)	0	0	1	3	0	3	7
Stone, clay, and glass products (7)	1	0	1	0	2	0	4
Primary metals (10)	4	1	6	0	4	0	15
Fabricated metal products (5)	0	0	0	0	1	0	1
Machinery (13)	0	0	1	1	1	3	6
Electrical machinery (5)	0	0	1	0	0	0	1
Transportation equipment (13)	0	1	1	1	3	4	10
Total	25	5	38	16	15	19	118

Number and Industries of Product Additions

SOURCE: Product record described in Chapter 2.
[a] Numbers in parentheses refer to number of companies in the specified industry.

An examination of the data in Tables 37, 38, and 39 reveals that important changes occurred in the choice of nonmanufacturing outlets for the period studied. In 1929–39, for the 111 companies additions in transportation and utilities accounted for 25.9 per cent of all nonmanufacturing additions. In 1939–50, the comparable percentage was 32.2. In 1950–54, however, it dropped to only 7.5. Similarly, in 1950–54, additions in wholesale and retail trade declined sharply as a percentage of total additions: the percentages were 11.1, 13.5, and 6.7 for the 1929–39, 1939–50, and 1950–54 periods, respectively. In contrast, additions in the extractive industries rose from roughly 21 per cent of all nonmanufacturing additions in the two earlier periods to roughly 33 per cent in 1950–54. For service industries, the relevant percentages were 14.9, 16.1, and 21.2 for the three successive periods. Thus, in the composition of their nonmanufacturing operations, large manufacturing enterprises appear to be moving away from transportation and utilities and wholesale and retail trade and toward services and the extractive industries. There was a substantial rise in the relative importance of real estate and finance in the

TABLE 39

DISTRIBUTION OF NONMANUFACTURING ADDITIONS OF PRODUCTS AND SERVICES BY INDUSTRY,
111 COMPANIES GROUPED BY INDUSTRY, 1950–54

	Number and Industries of Product Additions						
Industries of Companies[a]	Extractive Industries	Con- struction	Transpor- tation and Utilities	Retail and Wholesale Trade	Real Estate and Finance	Services	Total
Food products (12)	4	0	1	0	0	0	5
Tobacco manufactures (5)	0	0	0	0	2	0	2
Textile mill products (4)	0	1	0	1	1	0	3
Paper products (8)	0	0	0	0	0	3	3
Chemicals (14)	5	0	2	1	4	3	15
Petroleum (10)	0	0	1	0	1	0	2
Rubber products (5)	0	0	0	2	1	0	2
Stone, clay, and glass products (7)	2	0	1	0	0	0	3
Primary metals (10)	7	1	0	0	1	1	10
Fabricated metal products (5)	1	0	0	0	1	0	2
Machinery (13)	3	2	0	0	2	2	9
Electrical machinery (5)	0	0	0	0	2	2	4
Transportation equipment (13)	0	0	0	0	2	3	5
Total	22	4	5	4	17	14	66

SOURCE: Product record described in Chapter 2.

[a] Numbers in parentheses refer to number of companies in the specified industry.

terminal period as compared with 1939–50, but only a modest increase as compared with 1929–39.

Entry into the extractive industries was associated not only with integration—that is, production of raw materials for the firm's own manufacturing processes—but also with activity that can be classified as diversification. For example, there were instances of meat packers acquiring properties for the mining of minerals; and a number of companies, including a manufacturer of alcoholic beverages, entered into natural gas extraction.

In the finance sector, many of the additions consisted of finance companies whose primary function was to facilitate the financing of the companies' own sales. However, the firms also acquired a number of casualty insurance companies and banking facilities whose functions were not restricted to the internal needs of the acquiring firms.

The most frequent additions in transportation and utilities were of trucking fleets; a number of companies also acquired water transport and pipeline facilities. While some companies acquired railway and utility properties, the sale of railway equipment, waterworks, and electric power plants was not an infrequent occurrence.

102

CHAPTER 7
The Directions of Diversification

THIS section of the study explores the nature of the industries which firms enter when they diversify. It was reported earlier that diversifying firms enter some industries far more frequently than others. The discussion that follows examines which of the wide array of economic characteristics that distinguish one industry from another have a decisive role in attracting entrants.

First, several hypotheses are tested, using one explanatory variable at a time and data for number of product additions in each 4-digit industry. Second, they are tested using multiple regression analysis and data for frequency of additions in each 2-digit industry. Third, the hypotheses are re-examined, once again using multiple regression analysis, on the basis of aggregative data which show the proportion of total employment in each industry[1] contributed by firms whose primary activities are outside the industry. A final section of the chapter concerns the effects of diversification on changes in the composition of leading firms in the entered industries.

Summary

The manufacturing product additions of the 111-firm sample, when classified by 4-digit industry, were heavily concentrated in industries characterized by rapid growth, high increases in labor productivity, and a high ratio of technical[2] to all employees (hereafter referred to as the "technical personnel ratio"). For reasons given in this chapter, the latter two variables are rough indicators of the rate of technological change. The industries chosen for entry were not characterized by high cyclical stability in sales—a conclusion that raises doubt about the importance of short-run stability as a factor in diversification decisions. In choosing activities for diversification, the 111 companies showed no tendency to avoid industries in which the average investment per firm, as measured by average plant and firm size, was high. Thus relatively large capital requirements apparently were not a critical barrier to entry.

Analysis of additions by 2-digit industry showed that the number of products added was strongly correlated with the technical personnel ratio. Indeed, when the technical personnel ratio was used as an explanatory factor, additional variables contributed little toward explaining the

---

[1] The level of industry detail was the modified 3-digit level described in Chapter 2.

[2] In the data used, technical employees consisted of engineers, chemists, and surveyors.

variance in frequency of product additions. The results were substantially the same for each of the three periods examined, 1929–39, 1939–50, and 1950–54.

Employment in an industry contributed by firms whose primary activities are outside the industry is defined in this study as "external" employment. It measures approximately the volume of activity contributed by firms that have diversified into an industry. The ratio of external to total employment, therefore, indicates the attractiveness of an industry as a diversification outlet. This variable was also strongly correlated with the technical personnel ratio. In this respect the results based on data for frequency of product additions are confirmed.

In the 1929–39 interval, the 111-firm sample added 158 manufacturing products that, by 1954, were primary to at least one plant. Of these 158 additions, 60 led to the inclusion of the companies in the class of eight largest producers in 1954 in the industries in which the products were added. Of a similar list of 218 product additions in the 1939–54 period, 56 led to the inclusion of the companies in the group of eight largest producers in 1954. A substantial percentage of both the 60 and the 56 instances fell in industries in which the eight largest firms accounted for a relatively large fraction of total shipments. In these industries, a new entrant which captures enough of the market to become a leading producer will, in the process, materially affect competitive relations among sellers. Consequently, diversification has probably altered significantly the competitive position of firms in a number of industries.

Analytical Framework

A firm can be expected to undertake new activities rather than grow within the scope of its existing product structure if the former alternative promises a higher prospective return. The prospective return on investment (whether for diversification or for homogeneous growth) is, in turn, generally a function of growth in demand and technological change, for without these forces net investment would tend to reduce the prevailing rate of return. Another purpose of diversification may be that of reducing the variability of earnings—an objective best served by entering cyclically stable industries. Cyclical stability can thus affect the attractiveness of an industry as a diversification outlet. The role of the above influences on diversification, as well as that of possible barriers to entry, is examined more fully below.

Diversification, except insofar as it is achieved by shifting existing resources from one use to another, is a form of growth. Growth may be sought because it leads to greater earnings, or as an end in itself (an objective which could stem from the personal ambitions of managers to direct large enterprises). Both purposes, however, are best served by entering a rapidly growing industry; one, because rapid growth permits an earlier attainment of large size, and the other, because an industry characterized by rapid growth in demand, and hence in output, is one which may normally be expected to show a higher profit rate than that for the economy as a whole. Indeed, the relatively higher profit rate provides an inducement to capital formation which, in turn, generates growth in output. In consequence, the growth rate of an industry should be positively correlated with the frequency with which firms diversify into it.

Another variable that indirectly affects expectations of earnings from diversification is the rate at which technology changes. First, industries with rapidly changing technologies are likely to be growing rapidly. Second, some time will normally elapse between the introduction of new products or lower-cost production processes and the adjustment of supply, and hence price, to the new conditions—a circumstance that leads to higher than average profit rates. Third, when technology changes rapidly there will tend to be significant modifications of existing products. This leads to a greater variety of products within an industry and thus to a larger number of specialized submarkets in which competition, at least initially, is likely to be less intense than in the broader markets. Fourth, a rapidly changing technology generally affords greater opportunity for a new firm to overcome the competitive disadvantage of later entry and thereby to encroach upon the market of an older firm in the industry. A changing technology generates either new and superior products or lower-cost productive processes, but in either case, the innovator in the industry may be an established firm or a new entrant. Assuming, however, that random forces partly influence which firm will discover a new process or product, it is unlikely that the innovator will always be the established firm. To the extent an entering firm succeeds in adopting new products or production processes earlier than the older firms in the industry, it experiences a competitive advantage it would not have with a stable technology. In short, industries with rapidly changing technologies offer strong inducements to entry in the form of opportunities for gains to innovating firms.

Technological change does not lend itself readily to direct measurement. An indirect measure consists of the ratio of technical to all employees to be found in an industry (the technical personnel ratio). Although a substantial proportion of technical employees perform routine administrative functions, and most are not engaged in research and development, the number so engaged is likely to vary with the total number employed. It seems highly plausible that the rate at which technology changes is related to the volume of resources employed in producing the change. Conversely, the number of technical employees engaged in an industry is likely to reflect opportunities for technological change as determined by advances in the underlying sciences. A more intensive use of technical staffs frequently results from a more rapid development in the sciences that have direct application to an industry, even when such developments are generated outside the industry.

Another measure of technological change is the rate of change in labor productivity. Labor productivity indexes are related to a broad range of technological factors and reflect both changes in total unit costs and the substitution of capital for labor. From the standpoint of measures relevant for our hypothesis, they suffer from the defect that they are not designed to gauge technological change which takes the form of new and improved products.

Another frequently offered reason for diversification is the desire to stabilize earnings and sales. Since a wide range of random influences affects the sales and earnings from particular products, increases in the number of industries in which a company operates will, by diversifying risks, tend to reduce the chance of sharp declines in total company earnings arising from unpredictable changes in the economy. However, cyclical as distinct from random sources of instability lend themselves to prediction. Thus a mere increase in the number of activities without reference to their cyclical patterns is not an effective method of reducing cyclical instability. Indeed, for firms in industries with a relatively stable demand, the addition of a product for which demand is volatile may serve to destabilize total earnings and sales.

The addition of products even in cyclically unstable industries may stabilize aggregate sales for the company if the timing of peaks and troughs in demand for the newly added products tends to offset fluctuations in the older ones of the firm. To an extent, this advantage of diversification is present even for randomly selected products since diverse industries are unlikely to have perfectly synchronous peaks and troughs. A systematic selection of industries for offsetting fluctuations is, however, usually an unpromising course to follow, as the sequence of expansions and contractions in demand for particular industries is usually not sufficiently stable for this purpose. A far more effective indicator of the contribution of a new product to cyclical stability is the amplitude and frequency of fluctuations in its demand. Therefore, if cyclical considerations were decisive in diversification decisions, one would expect to find relatively high frequencies of entry in the cyclically stable industries.

Direct information on economies of scale is not, at present, available for most industries. Accordingly, two indirect measures—average size of plant and average size of firm in the industry—were used. Assuming both the presence of competition and gradual, as distinct from drastic, changes in technology, an industry with a larger average size of plant or firm is one which will normally be associated with a larger optimum size. This follows from competitive pressures to adjust the size of a plant or a firm to its most efficient scale.[3] Thus, in the long run, a tendency will exist for the most efficient size of plant or firm to expand in relative importance in its industry and for average size to change in the direction of optimum size. These relationships, of course, are likely to exist only as broad tendencies. Competitive forces may be restricted or technological change too rapid to allow time for adjustment of average to optimum size. The analysis presumes, however, that a strong positive relation exists between the two for a large majority of industries.

An industry which is associated with large economies of scale with respect to firm or plant size is commonly regarded as having high barriers to entry. These barriers result from the high capital requirements needed by the new entrant to compete successfully with other firms. Moreover, if large economies of scale are present, an important segment of the total market may have to be captured to enable operations at an efficient level of output. Rapid growth in demand, however, makes it easier to achieve a sufficient output without significant encroachment upon the markets of the older firms in the industry, thus reducing the importance of the barrier.

The industry characteristics which serve as barriers to entry for most firms may actually prove to be inducements to entry for some. Barriers to entry resulting from large capital requirements may, by reducing the number of actual and potential rivals, reduce the intensity of competition for firms which can raise capital on favorable terms. Hence high economies of scale in an industry may operate as inducements to entry for large firms.

The proportion of total sales accounted for by the leading producers in an industry is sometimes regarded as an indicator of barriers to entry. Once again, however, the implicit barriers may be more severe for small than for large firms. The role of leading producers in an industry was

[3] By efficiency, any advantage associated with scale is meant, whether related to marketing, financing, production, and so on.

measured by the proportion of industry shipments contributed by the four largest producers (the concentration ratio).

How does technical propinquity between primary industries and those into which firms diversify affect the directions of diversification? Earlier in the study, two types of technical propinquity were distinguished. Type 1 referred primarily to similar products or production processes and generally characterized activities within the same 2-digit industry categories.[4] Type 2 referred to similarities in the nonphysical resources employed— that is, similarities in managerial and technical skills. The two types of propinquity, however, frequently overlap in that the presence of Type 1 renders the presence of Type 2 more likely.

Obviously, when faced with a choice among activities that would be equally attractive if they were technologically equidistant from the primary one, a firm will usually undertake those for which technical propinquity to the primary activity is greatest. First, when prospective new products are similar to those already produced, the managers are far more likely to be aware of the attractiveness of such products as diversification outlets. Second, the managers' prior experience should give the firm an advantage in the new activities over firms in other sectors of the economy. Third, when old and new products are technologically related, existing plant, equipment, and personnel may be sufficient to produce the new ones. As an aspect of this, firms may wish to diversify in order to utilize excess capacity. Even entry in a declining industry can prove attractive if it makes possible the use of excess capacity or raw materials otherwise wasted. It is not surprising, therefore, that a substantial percentage of product additions made by the companies in our sample were characterized by Type 1 propinquity to the primary activities of the firms. In Chapter 3, it was shown that product additions falling within the primary 2-digit industries of the 111 companies contributed, depending upon the period selected for study, from 32 to 43 per cent of all manufacturing additions made by these companies.

The fact that technical propinquity was present in a large proportion of product additions does not, however, mean that it was decisive in determining the industries entered by diversifying firms. Except for joint products or by-products, where incremental cost approaches zero, no firm would choose to diversify simply because technological relations were present between its primary activity and others that could be initiated.

---

[4] Two-digit categories are, however, fairly broad, so that activities within the same categories often are only loosely related technologically. Conversely, Type 1 propinquity sometimes crosses 2-digit boundaries.

Indeed, all industries are adjacent to the primary activities of some firms, yet the frequency with which they serve as diversification outlets has been shown to differ markedly. Conversely, the primary activities of diversifying firms are technologically related to a vast range of products, yet these firms undertake to produce only a small fraction of this range. Clearly, influences other than technical propinquity must be at work. In this connection, the economic characteristics (e.g., growth, technological change) of the entered 4-digit industries were substantially the same whether or not they fell in the 2-digit categories of the firms' primary activities (that is, whether or not they were closely related in technology to the primary activities).[5] Thus it appears that technical propinquity did not materially affect the character of the industries chosen for diversification. The existence of technological relations between primary activities and those into which firms diversify reflects rather the role of technical propinquity in determining *which* firms diversify. Firms with primary operations technologically related to the industries that are intrinsically attractive as diversification outlets tend to diversify more than other firms in the economy. This is confirmed by evidence presented in Chapter 8.

Data and Methods

Analysis of the character of changes in product composition was based primarily on the record of additions and abandonments of products in the 1929–54 period. This part of our study was restricted to manufacturing activities. Added and abandoned products were classified into industries and measures for these industries were developed for the several variables discussed in the summary section of this chapter.[6] Table 40 indicates the periods for which estimates were made of the variables used to analyze product additions and abandonments in 1929–39, 1939–50, and 1950–54.

A priori, it seems plausible that the relation between frequencies of additions and the character of industries is multivariate. Hence multiple regression analysis is especially suited to the problem. The characteristics of data at the 4-digit level, however, did not permit this approach. Because of limitations of sample size, the frequencies of additions were too thin at the 4-digit level of detail to yield reliable estimates of the distribution of additions by 4-digit industry for the universe of firms.

For this reason, regression analysis with frequency of product additions

---

[5] As shown in the tables that follow, activities outside primary 2-digit industries displayed the same characteristics as all product additions, including those within the primary 2-digit groups.

[6] Sources and methods used in estimating the explanatory variables are indicated in Appendix D.

TABLE 40

PERIODS FOR WHICH ESTIMATES OF EXPLANATORY VARIABLES WERE DEVELOPED

Variable	Used with Product Changes in:		
	1929–39	1939–50	1950–54
Growth[a]	1929–39	1939–54	1939–54
Productivity change	1929–37	1937–53	1937–53
Cyclical variability (amplitude)	1923–41	1947–55	1947–55
Technical personnel ratio	1930	1940	1950
Concentration ratio	[b]	1947	1947
Size of plant	1935	1947	1947
Size of firm[c]	—	1947	1947
Cyclical variability (frequency of turning points)	1923–41	1923–41	1923–41

[a] Data on growth at the two-digit level of industry detail were for the periods 1929–37 and 1937–53.

[b] For the 1929–39 period, 1947 ratios were again used as the primary source of information. However, in some instances, 1935 ratios were used for those industries for which 1935 data had been reconciled to a 1947 Standard Industrial Classification Code basis.

[c] At the 2-digit level of detail, firm size was measured on the basis of total assets for the years 1938 and 1948, the former year being used to study product changes in 1929–39 and the latter in 1939–50 and 1950–54.

as the dependent variable was carried out only for nineteen manufacturing industries at the 2-digit level of detail. Use of 2-digit data has the disadvantage that measures for the relevant explanatory variables do not accurately represent the characteristics of specific activities in which individual product additions fall. The problem increases as the degree of industry detail is reduced. On the other hand, use of 2-digit data largely eliminates another difficulty present in 4-digit data, namely, that at the latter level frequencies of product additions are sometimes nonindependent. That is, entry into one 4-digit industry increases the likelihood of entry in adjacent industries. This problem is far smaller for data at the 2-digit level.

The discussion first deals with the relation between frequencies of additions and other variables, taken one at a time, at the higher level of detail. It then proceeds with multiple regression analysis at the 2-digit level. In the first part of the analysis, each industry for which data on explanatory variables were available was classified by deciles, based on the value for the industry of each variable.[7] This permitted the computation of frequencies with which our sample of companies added or

[7] The industries that were so classified were not restricted to those in which our sample of companies added or deleted products, but also included those for which the frequency of additions or abandonments was zero.

abandoned products in each decile and for each of the variables.[8] Information for frequencies of additions and abandonments on the basis of these deciles is presented in Appendix Table E–1. To simplify the analysis, the data were then compressed into three classes.[9] Thus, in each period, the frequencies in deciles 1 through 3, 4 through 7, and 8 through 10 were summed to form three classes for each variable; expected frequencies on the null hypothesis were then computed for the three classes.[10] Actual frequencies were compared with expected frequencies. The analysis was carried out on two bases: first for all product additions, and second for all additions outside the primary 2-digit industries of the companies. Generally, the results developed on the basis of three classes show substantially the same patterns of product additions as those indicated on the basis of deciles.

The median values of the explanatory variables differed markedly among the three classes of industries (lower 30 per cent, middle 40 per cent, and upper 30 per cent) for all the variables and in each period (with the possible exception of growth in 1929–39). Thus absence of differences among frequencies of additions in the three classes could not be attributed to an absence of significant variations in the explanatory variables. The range of variation in these variables can be readily derived from the tables in Appendix D and from other tables to which reference is made in this appendix.

Product Additions and Characteristics of Industries: 4-Digit Industry Data

Patterns of product additions with respect to individual variables were examined at the 4-digit level of detail. Since a number of the explanatory variables are interrelated, one cannot assess, on the basis of the analysis that follows, the net contribution of a given variable toward explaining the variance in frequencies of product additions. Nevertheless, the association of frequency of product additions with individual variables is of considerable interest. For example, a conclusion that firms diversify largely into high-growth industries suggests that the process of diversification, by increasing the supply of resources in rapidly growing industries, con-

---

[8] Since information was not available for all of the industries in which companies added or deleted products, for each variable a limited but differing set of industries had to be left out of the analysis.

[9] Since the data were originally prepared on the basis of deciles, it was not possible, for example, to use quartiles without extensive recomputation.

[10] The null hypothesis assumes that the likelihood of a product being added is unrelated to the explanatory variables.

tributes to the latter's growth. If entry is frequent in industries characterized by high concentration ratios, diversification may be an important source of potential competition in these industries. A conclusion that companies diversify into cyclically stable industries would suggest that diversification generally reduces cyclical instability in the total sales of companies. All these inferences are not affected by the presence of correlation between the several variables used to analyze product additions. For this reason, analysis with one variable at a time contributes to our understanding of the consequences of diversification. Moreover, should the results point to absence of relationship between product additions and particular variables, one would normally be justified in concluding that the latter do not exert a strong influence on diversification.

Tables 41 through 48 show for each of three periods the frequency with which product additions (first for all manufacturing additions, and second for all those that were outside the primary 2-digit industries) fell within each of three classes on the basis of the relevant variables. The tables show theoretical frequencies based on the null hypothesis and, also, the corresponding chi-squares.[11]

As Table 41 indicates, the frequency of additions in the highest growth class (Class III) was in all three periods greatly in excess of that which could be expected in the absence of association between growth and entry. Both Class I and Class II, covering the lower 70 per cent of industries as measured by growth, showed frequencies of additions considerably smaller than those expected on the null hypothesis. The results were essentially similar, and only moderately less striking, when product additions outside the primary 2-digit industries were examined. Consequently, the high concentration of product additions in high-growth industries cannot be explained by the growth rate of activities technologically adjacent to the companies' primary activities. The pattern is somewhat more pronounced in the two post-1939 periods as compared with the pre-1939 period, particularly for additions outside the primary 2-digit industries. In short, growth, while significantly related to product additions in all three periods, was less closely related to the latter during the 1930's. Taking all additions and combining the three periods under analysis, 602 additions fell in the top 30 per cent of industries in terms of growth, while only 433 fell in the lower 70 per cent.

In the analysis two measures of technological change were used. In-

---

[11] Theoretical frequencies were computed by multiplying total actual frequencies of additions for our sample of companies by the proportion of all industries that fall into each of the three classes. (E.g., 30 per cent would be expected to fall in a class consisting of three deciles.)

TABLE 41

RELATION OF FREQUENCY OF PRODUCT ADDITIONS TO INDUSTRY GROWTH

INDUSTRY CLASS[b]	AGGREGATE ADDITIONS Frequencies			ADDITIONS IN NONPRIMARY INDUSTRY GROUP[a] Frequencies		
	Actual	Theoretical	Chi-square[c]	Actual	Theoretical	Chi-square[c]
			1929–39			
I	56	104.1		36	54.9	
II	112	138.8		72	73.2	
III	179	104.1		75	54.9	
			81.291			13.886
Total	347			183		
			1939–50			
I	41	109.5		25	67.5	
II	100	146.0		51	90.0	
III	224	109.5		149	67.5	
			177.073			142.063
Total	365			225		
			1950–54			
I	28	96.9		23	60.3	
II	96	129.2		51	80.2	
III	199	96.9		127	60.3	
			165.101			107.483
Total	323			201		

SOURCE: Described in text.

[a] Outside of primary 2-digit group of company.

[b] Class I comprises deciles 1–3, Class II deciles 4–7, and Class III deciles 8–10 on the basis of growth. Class III represents highest growth.

[c] All chi-squares are significant at .01 level.

dustries were classified, first, by the ratio of technical to all employees; second, by the change in labor productivity indexes. Tables 42 and 43 reveal a strong relation between the frequency with which products were added in particular industries and both of these variables. However, while the technical personnel ratio was positively related to the frequency of product additions in all three periods, labor productivity showed a strong positive relation only in the two post-1939 periods, the 1929–39 interval showing some concentration of frequencies around the center rather than at the extremes with respect to the measure of change in productivity.[12] Product additions outside the primary 2-digit industries reveal

[12] However, when only product additions that could be classified according to productivity change at the 3- or 4-digit level were considered (that is, when information that was only available at the 2-digit level was ignored), the concentration of frequencies in the highest productivity-change class showed up markedly for the 1929–39 period. On this basis, the pattern for 1939–50 showed a more strongly positive relation than that indicated in Table 43.

TABLE 42

RELATION OF FREQUENCY OF PRODUCT ADDITIONS TO
TECHNICAL PERSONNEL RATIO

INDUSTRY CLASS[b]	AGGREGATE ADDITIONS *Frequencies*			ADDITIONS IN NONPRIMARY INDUSTRY GROUP[a] *Frequencies*		
	Actual	Theoretical	Chi-square[c]	Actual	Theoretical	Chi-square[c]
			1929–39			
I	31	142.5		20	80.4	
II	159	190.0		105	107.2	
III	285	142.5		143	80.4	
			234.801			94.161
Total	475			268		
			1939–50			
I	34	133.5		25	85.2	
II	121	178.0		75	113.6	
III	290	133.5		184	85.2	
			275.874			170.223
Total	445			284		
			1950–54			
I	41	120.3		36	79.5	
II	105	160.4		63	106.0	
III	255	120.3		166	79.5	
			86.489			135.361
Total	401			265		

SOURCE: Described in text.

[a] Nonprimary group of company.

[b] Class I comprises deciles 1–3, Class II deciles 4–7, and Class III deciles 8–10 on the basis of the technical personnel ratio. Class III comprises the highest ratios.

[c] All chi-squares are significant at .01 level.

similar patterns to those for all additions, though, on the whole, in a slightly less accentuated form. For all additions and with the three periods combined, the upper 30 per cent of industries in terms of the technical personnel ratio accounted for 830 cases, compared with 491 for the lower 70 per cent of industries. For the aggregate of product additions in the two post-1939 periods, the upper 30 per cent of industries in terms of increase in labor productivity accounted for almost as many cases as the lower 70 per cent (the counts being respectively 402 and 448).

Two aspects are germane to measuring the degree of cyclical stability: first, how frequently does the movement of sales change direction over time; and second, when a change in direction occurs, how sharp is the consequent rise or fall? The frequency of cyclical fluctuations was measured by the number of changes in direction in annual-output indexes for particular commodities. The amplitude of cyclical fluctuations was

TABLE 43
RELATION OF FREQUENCY OF PRODUCT ADDITIONS TO PRODUCTIVITY CHANGE

INDUSTRY CLASS[b]	AGGREGATE ADDITIONS *Frequencies*			ADDITIONS IN NONPRIMARY INDUSTRY GROUP[a] *Frequencies*		
	Actual	Theoretical	Chi-square[c]	Actual	Theoretical	Chi-square[c]
			1929–39			
I	80	141.9		42	80.4	
II	281	189.2		183	107.2	
III	112	141.9		43	80.4	
			77.843			89.335
Total	473			268		
			1939–50			
I	71	135.3		50	86.1	
II	166	180.4		106	114.8	
III	214	135.3		131	86.1	
			77.484			39.226
Total	451			287		
			1950–54			
I	55	119.7		33	79.2	
II	156	159.6		113	105.6	
III	188	119.7		118	79.2	
			74.023			46.477
Total	399			264		

SOURCE: Described in text.

[a] Nonprimary group of company.

[b] Class I comprises deciles 1–3, Class II deciles 4–7, and Class III deciles 8–10 on the basis of productivity change. Class III is the class of highest productivity change.

[c] All chi-squares are significant at .01 level.

measured by averaging trough-to-peak and peak-to-trough changes in the above indexes.

With respect to number of cyclical turning points, the record in all three periods for total product additions shows greater frequencies than expected on the null hypothesis in the lowest class of industries (Table 44).[13] The frequencies in Class III (the class with the highest number of turning points) are consistently less than would be expected in the absence of association between entry and the number of cyclical turning points. This pattern is somewhat more pronounced for the 1929–39 period than for the two later periods. Product additions outside the primary 2-digit industries reveal a similar pattern. However, for these additions, deviations of actual from expected frequencies were significant at the .01 level only for the

[13] As indicated in the table, the data were segregated into three classes with absolute class limits rather than into deciles compressed subsequently into three classes. It was not possible to use deciles for this variable because of the large number of tied ranks on the basis of number of turning points.

TABLE 44
RELATION OF FREQUENCY OF PRODUCT ADDITIONS TO NUMBER OF
TURNING POINTS IN OUTPUT

INDUSTRY CLASS[b]	AGGREGATE ADDITIONS Frequencies			ADDITIONS IN NONPRIMARY INDUSTRY GROUP[a] Frequencies		
	Actual	Theoretical	Chi-square	Actual	Theoretical	Chi-square
	1929–39					
I	189	114.9		63	52.6	
II	189	174.8		110	80.0	
III	13	101.3		6	46.4	
			125.909[c]			48.482[c]
Total	391			179		
	1939–50					
I	181	148.7		98	96.8	
II	180	180.7		135	117.6	
III	83	114.6		56	74.6	
			15.732[c]			7.226[d]
Total	444			289		
	1950–54					
I	169	134.3		102	89.4	
II	142	163.2		100	108.7	
III	90	103.5		65	68.9	
			13.481[c]			2.693[e]
Total	401			267		

SOURCE: Described in text.
[a] Nonprimary industry group of company.
[b] Three classes were selected with absolute class limits. Class III comprises industries with the largest number of turning points.
[c] Significant at the .01 level.
[d] Significant at the .05 level.
[e] Not significant at the .05 level.

first of the three periods, and at the .05 level for the first two but not for the third period. Absence of statistically significant results for the 1950–54 period for product additions in the nonprimary industry categories casts some doubt on the relation between the variables. However, a stronger relation for 1929–39 than for the two later periods has, perhaps, a plausible explanation. Because of the severity of the depression of the early 1930's, greater concern about cyclical stability in selecting industries for diversification would not be surprising in that period. Direct evidence on conscious motives of company managers, however, was not available.

The absence of convincing evidence that industries were systematically selected for diversification with a view to their cyclical stability is most sharply reflected in the analysis of association of additions with amplitude of cyclical fluctuations. Unlike the measure of frequency of turning points, that of cyclical amplitude was at least partially adjusted so as to eliminate the effects of trend. The results show deviations of actual frequencies of product additions from those expected on the null hypothesis that were significant at the .01 level in all three periods, both for all product additions and for those outside primary 2-digit industries (Table 45). The results, however, in all instances reveal a high concentration in the middle four deciles, with substantially smaller frequencies of entry in the deciles at both of the extremes. This would appear to suggest that cyclical stability was not a dominant consideration in the selection of industries for diversification; for if it were, the low-amplitude industries would hardly have been avoided.

The measure of the relative role of large firms in an industry (the "concentration ratio") was based on the ratio of the shipments of the four leading producers in each industry to total industry shipments. The pattern of product additions after 1939 did not deviate with respect

TABLE 45
RELATION OF FREQUENCY OF PRODUCT ADDITIONS TO CYCLICAL AMPLITUDE

INDUSTRY CLASS[b]	AGGREGATE ADDITIONS			ADDITIONS IN NONPRIMARY INDUSTRY GROUP[a]		
	Frequencies			*Frequencies*		
	Actual	Theoretical	Chi-square[c]	Actual	Theoretical	Chi-square[c]
			1929–39			
I	47	116.7		2	49.5	
II	296	155.6		159	66.0	
III	46	116.7		4	49.5	
			211.146			218.449
Total	389			165		
			1939–50			
I	81	132.0		36	84.3	
II	240	176.0		169	112.4	
III	119	132.0		76	84.3	
			44.257			56.992
Total	440			281		
			1950–54			
I	59	117.9		30	79.5	
II	224	157.2		170	106.0	
III	110	117.9		65	79.5	
			49.858			72.107
Total	393			265		

SOURCE: Described in text.

[a] Nonprimary industry group of company.

[b] Class I comprises deciles 1–3, Class II deciles 4–7, and Class III deciles 8–10 on the basis of cyclical amplitude. Class III is the class of highest cyclical amplitudes.

[c] All chi-squares are significant at .01 level.

to this variable from one that could be expected on the null hypothesis (Table 46). In the 1929–39 period, however, frequencies for nonprimary and for all additions deviated significantly from those expected on the null hypothesis. The deviations pointed to lower-than-expected frequencies in the lowest class with respect to the concentration ratio. The most important fact is that in all three periods frequencies of additions were not significantly lower than those expected in the class of industries with high concentration. This appears to show that the forces which produced high concentration were not severe obstacles to entry for our sample of firms. Three factors contribute to explaining these results. First, some of the more concentrated industries are in new and rapidly growing sectors of the economy, and thus offer better than average opportunities for investment. (Older industries tend to have lower concentration ratios.) Second, barriers to entry that stem from large capital requirements may—by

TABLE 46
RELATION OF FREQUENCY OF PRODUCT ADDITIONS TO CONCENTRATION RATIOS

INDUSTRY CLASS[b]	AGGREGATE ADDITIONS Frequencies			ADDITIONS IN NONPRIMARY INDUSTRY GROUP[a] Frequencies		
	Actual	Theoretical	Chi-square[c]	Actual	Theoretical	Chi-square[c]
			1929–39			
I	128	155.7		54	87.7	
II	187	155.7		109	87.7	
III	152	155.7		100	87.7	
			11.308			19.848
Total	467			263		
			1939–50			
I	116	134.7		76	86.1	
II	210	179.6		123	114.8	
III	123	134.7		88	86.1	
			8.758			1.813
Total	449			287		
			1950–54			
I	115	117.0		73	78.0	
II	175	156.0		115	104.0	
III	100	117.0		72	78.0	
			4.818			1.944
Total	390			260		

SOURCE: Described in text.

[a] Nonprimary industry group of company.

[b] For 1929–39, each class comprised a third of all industries. For 1939–50 and 1950–54, Class I comprises deciles 1–3, Class II deciles 4–7, and Class III deciles 8–10 on the basis of concentration ratios. Class III is the class of highest concentration ratios.

[c] Only the chi-squares for the 1929–39 period are significant at .01 level.

reducing entry of smaller firms (and hence competition)—contribute to inducing rather than restricting entry on the part of large firms. Third, a number of product additions were achieved through merger and thus were not subject to the usual barriers to entry.

For the next variable, average plant size,[14] Table 47 indicates a distinct concentration of frequencies in the high, as compared with the low, plant-size industries. The tendency toward more frequent product additions in industries associated with larger plants seemed more accentuated in the 1939–50 and 1950–54 periods than in 1929–39.

The conclusions with respect to firm size were essentially similar. As Table 48 shows, industries in the lower 30 per cent with respect to firm

TABLE 47
RELATION OF FREQUENCY OF PRODUCT ADDITIONS TO PLANT SIZE

INDUSTRY CLASS[b]	AGGREGATE ADDITIONS Frequencies			ADDITIONS IN NONPRIMARY INDUSTRY GROUP[a] Frequencies		
	Actual	Theoretical	Chi-square[c]	Actual	Theoretical	Chi-square[c]
			1929–39			
I	67	120.3		33	65.4	
II	147	160.4		92	87.2	
III	187	120.3		93	65.4	
			61.716			27.963
Total	401			218		
			1939–50			
I	49	95.1		24	61.2	
II	96	126.8		76	81.6	
III	172	95.1		104	61.2	
			92.046			52.928
Total	317			204		
			1950–54			
I	31	80.1		19	51.6	
II	79	106.8		52	68.8	
III	157	80.1		101	51.6	
			111.161			71.992
Total	267			172		

SOURCE: Described in text.

[a] Nonprimary industry group of company.

[b] Class I comprises deciles 1–3, Class II deciles 4–7, and Class III deciles 8–10 on the basis of plant size. Class III is the class of highest plant size.

[c] All chi-squares are significant at .01 level.

[14] It seems likely that in some industries a large number of low-efficiency small plants exist. These plants either serve a local demand where competing firms are not present or survive because of other special circumstances. To improve our measure of differences in optimum plant size, plants with fewer than twenty employees were excluded in computing averages.

TABLE 48

RELATION OF FREQUENCY OF PRODUCT ADDITIONS TO FIRM SIZE

INDUSTRY CLASS[b]	AGGREGATE ADDITIONS Frequencies			ADDITIONS IN NONPRIMARY INDUSTRY GROUP[a] Frequencies		
	Actual	Theoretical	Chi-square[c]	Actual	Theoretical	Chi-square[c]
			1939–50			
I	52	119.7		34	72.9	
II	175	159.6		108	97.2	
III	172	119.7		101	72.9	
			62.627			32.788
Total	399			243		
			1950–54			
I	46	106.8		32	66.9	
II	151	142.4		98	89.2	
III	159	106.8		93	66.9	
			60.645			29.256
Total	356			223		

NOTE: Information on firm size for 1929–39 was not available.
SOURCE: Described in text.
[a] Nonprimary industry group of company.
[b] Class I comprises deciles 1–3, Class II deciles 4–7, and Class III deciles 8–10 on the basis of firm size. Class III is the class of highest firm size.
[c] All chi-squares are significant at .01 level.

size were associated with relatively lower frequencies of product additions in both 1939–50 and 1950–54. Thus, it would seem, high capital requirements did not generate insurmountable barriers to entry for our sample of companies. However, because of the possible effect of other variables which may be correlated with plant and firm size, one cannot say that the latter exerted a positive influence on entry.

The analysis thus far in this chapter has been concerned with the nature of product changes irrespective of the importance of the change to the company in question. It is possible that different considerations apply to decisions to add new products on a large scale relative to total company size from those that are important in minor undertakings. For example, since the risks attached to investments that are large relative to total firm size are considerably greater than those for small undertakings, a more conservative policy may be followed for the former. This conservatism could be reflected in avoidance of very new industries which, though they may currently be growing more rapidly, have a less certain future than the older, more established ones. On the other hand, entry on a fairly large scale may prove difficult in the absence of rapid growth or technological change because of the obstacles to encroaching on the markets of existing producers. In the absence of rapid growth in the entered industry, entry on a large scale may necessitate capturing a significant share of the market of existing producers—a process that is frequently costly.

Information on the relation of growth to the selection of industries for the larger ventures was secured from a special census tabulation. This tabulation brought together all manufacturing plants under common ownership in 1947 and 1954 for our sample of 111 companies. By using 1954 information on plants in conjunction with our record of product additions in the 1939–54 period, it was possible to segregate the larger from the smaller ventures. If the industry appeared in the 1954 Census plant record for a company, and the product record indicated that the industry had been initially entered in the 1939–54 period, the importance of the new activities in 1954 could be measured by taking the ratio of payrolls in the indicated industry to total manufacturing payrolls for the company. In this way the ninety largest product additions (largest as a percentage of manufacturing payrolls for the individual companies) were isolated. Each of the ninety additions accounted in 1954 for at least 2 per cent of manufacturing payrolls of the companies that made the additions.[15]

Table 49 shows the high relative frequencies with which the ninety industries fell in the upper deciles with respect to growth and the technical personnel ratio.[16] The concentration was particularly high in the tenth or highest decile, which accounted for one-half of the industries classified on the basis of the technical personnel ratio and more than one-fourth on the basis of growth. The results for the two variables are substantially similar to the previously reported pattern for all product additions without reference to relative scale of new activities. There seems little doubt that most product additions, irrespective of scale of output, fell into rapidly growing and new industries.

Product Additions and Characteristics of Industries: 2-Digit Industry Data

Table 50 gives the simple correlation coefficients for the relation between frequency of product additions in nineteen industry categories and each

---

[15] The ninety cases represented *all* 1939–54 additions which, on the basis of establishment data, accounted for at least 2 per cent of manufacturing payrolls in 1954.

[16] The classification of the ninety industries according to deciles with respect to each variable was based on their relative position in the ordered list for *all* industries for which information could be secured. Thus, considerably more than one-tenth of the ninety industries could fall in a single decile, while none might fall in other deciles.

TABLE 49

DISTRIBUTION OF 90 INDUSTRIES ENTERED BY 111 COMPANIES, 1939–54,
ACCORDING TO GROWTH AND TECHNICAL PERSONNEL RATIO

Deciles on Basis of 4-Digit Industry Growth, 1939–54	Number of 4-Digit Industries	Deciles on Basis of Technical Personnel Ratio, 1950	Number of 4-Digit Industries
1	1	1	2
2	7	2	10
3	3	3	3
4	1	4	2
5	4	5	4
6	3	6	5
7	12	7	7
8	17	8	4
9	16	9	7
10	26	10	46

NOTE: The plants of each of the industries accounted for at least 2 per cent of manufacturing payrolls in 1954 for the relevant companies. Decile 10 represents highest growth and technical personnel ratio.

SOURCE: U.S. Bureau of the Census, special census tabulation, and product record described in Chapter 2.

of five variables.[17] As may be judged from the table, in each of the three periods studied, the coefficient was highest for the relation between the dependent variable and the technical personnel ratio, being .708, .610, and .664 for the 1929–39, 1939–50, and 1950–54 periods, respectively.[18]

Table 51 shows the multiple correlation coefficients for the relation between frequency of total product additions and various combinations of independent variables. As the table indicates, the highest coefficients were those for equations in which the technical personnel ratio was an independent variable. The addition of a second and third variable to the technical personnel ratio contributed negligibly toward explaining the variance in frequency of product additions, and thus did not improve the predictive power of the hypothesis.

[17] The table also shows the coefficients for the relations between the explanatory variables. Data for cyclical amplitude, frequency of turning points, and the concentration ratio were not developed at the 2-digit level. Data at the 2-digit level were also not available for the 1929–39 period for the plant-size variable. For two of the twenty-one 2-digit industries, measures for some explanatory variables were not available. The analysis was, therefore, restricted to nineteen industries.

[18] The regression equations, with X_1 standing for the number of product additions and X_2 for the technical personnel ratio (in units of number of technical employees per 10,000 of all employees), were as follows:

$$1929–39: \quad X_1 = 11.2996 + .1346\, X_2$$
$$(.0206)$$
$$1939–50: \quad X_1 = 7.2520 + .1101\, X_2$$
$$(.0326)$$
$$1950–54: \quad X_1 = 5.2442 + .0775\, X_2$$
$$(.0041)$$

TABLE 50

SIMPLE CORRELATION COEFFICIENTS FOR FREQUENCY OF PRODUCT
ADDITIONS AND FIVE INDUSTRY VARIABLES

	1950–54[a]		1939–50[a]		1929–39[a]	
Variables	All Products	Nonprimary Products	All Products	Nonprimary Products	All Products	Nonprimary Products
1.2	.608	(.564)	(.583)	(.532)	.303	.103
1.3	.664	(.581)	.610	(.549)	.708	.452
1.4	.450	.420	(.488)	.442	−.104	−.150
1.5	−.138	−.186	−.146	−.169	−.161[b]	−.190[b]
1.6	.179	.086	.047	−.013	c	c
2.3	.698		.711		.409	
2.4	(.569)		d		.672	
2.5	−.157		d		.254[b]	
2.6	.422		d		c	
3.6	.362		.343		c	
3.4	.400		.425		.035	
4.5	−.055		d		.134[b]	

NOTE: The variables are denoted by the numbers 1–6 as follows: frequency of product additions (1), growth (2), technical personnel ratio (3), productivity change (4), firm size (5), plant size (6). Coefficients significant at the .01 level are underlined and those at the .05 level are in parentheses. The coefficients shown for nonprimary products are for data that exclude product additions in the 2-digit industry group of the company from the count of product additions.

[a] The number of observations is 19 in all cases except as indicated in note b.

[b] Results based on seventeen observations.

[c] Data on plant size not available.

[d] Same data used as for 1950–54.

It is possible that, because of technical propinquity, additions that fall in the primary 2-digit industry class of a company are not independent of the latter's primary activity. Entry in these industries may be partly affected by technical propinquity as distinct from the intrinsic attractiveness of the industries as diversification outlets. To free the results from the possible effects of this interdependence, Tables 50 and 51 also show correlation coefficients computed with such additions excluded. Generally, however, the correlations reveal substantially the same pattern whether primary industry product additions are included or excluded. The technical personnel ratio is strongly associated with frequencies of additions on both bases, though the coefficients are somewhat lower with primary industry additions excluded.

A possible bias in the data arises from the fact that the number of 4-digit industries varied among the 2-digit groups. Since additions within 2-digit categories were counted at the 4-digit level of detail, a category with more 4-digit subdivisions would, other things being equal, tend to show a

TABLE 51

MULTIPLE CORRELATION COEFFICIENTS FOR FREQUENCY OF PRODUCT
ADDITIONS AND COMBINATIONS OF INDUSTRY VARIABLES

	1950–54[a]		1939–50[a]		1929–39[a]	
Variables	All Products	Nonprimary Products	All Products	Nonprimary Products	All Products	Nonprimary Products
1.23	.694	(.622)	(.646)	(.585)	.709	.460
1.24	(.621)	(.577)	(.613)	.558	.514	.031
1.25	(.609)	(.569)	(.586)	.539	.452[b]	.396[b]
1.26	(.614)	(.588)	(.623)	(.587)	c	c
1.34	.694	(.616)	(.661)	(.595)	.718	.481
1.36	.667	(.596)	(.634)	(.589)	c	c
1.234	(.705)	(.656)	(.671)	.607	.737	.483
1.245	(.623)	.582	.616	.566	.605[b]	.476[b]
1.236	(.705)	(.654)	(.689)	.589	c	c

NOTE: The variables are denoted by the numbers 1–6 as follows: frequency of product additions (1), growth (2), technical personnel ratio (3), productivity change (4), firm size (5), plant size (6). Coefficients significant at the .01 level are underlined and those at the .05 level are in parentheses. The coefficients shown for nonprimary products are for data that exclude product additions in the 2-digit industry group of the company from the count of product additions.

[a] Based on nineteen observations except as indicated in note b.
[b] Based on seventeen observations.
[c] Data on plant size not available.

larger number of additions. However, the strategic role of the technical personnel ratio is confirmed by the data used in the next section of this chapter. These data are not subject to the indicated bias.

Factors Related to the Magnitude of External Employment

External employment in an industry is that part of total employment contributed by firms external to it. That is, it represents employment in establishments classified in the industry but owned by companies whose primary activities are in other sectors of the economy. A larger external employment usually indicates more diversification *into* the industry. Exceptions, however, arise because companies sometimes shift the locus of their primary operations. Under these circumstances, high external employment will be associated with an industry out of which companies have moved rather than one into which they are moving. High external employment may also result from integration rather than diversification, the most notable examples of this being petroleum refining and crude petroleum extraction. For most industries, however, external employment is likely to measure the attractiveness of the industry as a diversification outlet.

TABLE 52
CLASS FREQUENCIES FOR THE RATIO OF EXTERNAL TO TOTAL EMPLOYMENT,
119 INDUSTRIES, 1954

| Trade and Services | | Manufacturing and Mining | |
External as Percentage of Total Employment	Number of Industries	External as Percentage of Total Employment	Number of Industries
0– 2.5	11	0– 5.0	11
2.6– 5.0	9	5.1–10.0	22
5.1–10.0	9	10.1–15.0	13
Over 10.0	5	15.1–20.0	13
Total	34	20.1–25.0	9
		25.1–30.0	6
		Over 30.0	11
		Total	85

SOURCE: Based on *Company Statistics*, Table 2.

In most industries external employment did not constitute a large percentage of total employment (Table 52).[19] There were, however, substantial differences between industries. In manufacturing and mining, the ratios of external to total employment were substantially higher than in trade and services. In fifty-two of eighty-five manufacturing and mining industries, external employment exceeded 10 per cent of total employment, as compared with only five of thirty-four trade and service industries.

Of the total of 119 industries, 105 showed a higher ratio of external to all activities combined on the basis of data for employment than on the basis of data for number of establishments (without reference to the size of the latter).[20] This clearly shows that in most industries, establishments associated with external employment were larger than average for their industries. Since the size of establishments is positively correlated with company size, the above result suggests that large companies contributed relatively more to external than to total employment.

Table 53, based on data restricted to manufacturing industries, shows the simple correlation coefficients for the ratio of external to total employment and each of five variables. It also shows the multiple correlation

[19] External employment was measured at a modified 3-digit level based on data in *Company Statistics: 1954 Censuses of Business, Manufacturing, Mineral Industries*, U.S. Bureau of the Census, Washington, 1958, Table 2. Since employment that crosses product boundaries within the 3-digit categories is not classified as external, industries that are broader than average in the scope of products they contain will have ratios of external to total employment subject, from this source, to a downward bias. This offsets an upward bias that arises from the fact that the larger the number of markets a 3-digit category contains, the greater is the chance of entry from firms in other sectors.

[20] *Ibid.*

125

coefficients for the ratio and various combinations of the five variables. The only simple correlation coefficient found to be statistically significant was that for the external to total employment ratio and the technical personnel ratio ($r = .608$).[21] All equations in which the latter ratio was one of two or more independent variables generated statistically significant multiple correlation coefficients. However, the contribution of a second, or a second and third, independent variable toward explaining the variance in the ratio of external to total employment proved negligible. In this respect, the results confirmed those based on frequency of product additions.

A limitation of the data for the ratio of external to total employment was that it pertained to a single point in time. External employment may have been generated in a period anteceding that for which the explanatory variables were measured. Since differences between industries in the

TABLE 53
RATIO OF EXTERNAL TO TOTAL EMPLOYMENT
IN RELATION TO FIVE VARIABLES

Simple Correlation Coefficients		Multiple Correlation Coefficients	
1.2	.171[a]	1.23	.619[a]
1.3	.608[b]	1.24	.172[a]
1.4	.051[a]	1.36	.617[b]
1.5	.113[b]	1.35	.610[b]
1.6	.120[b]	1.56	.144[b]
		1.356	.621[b]
		1.234	.623[a]

NOTE: The variables are denoted by the numbers 1–6 as follows: the ratio of external to total employment (1), (2) growth, 1939–53; (3) technical personnel ratio for 1950; (4) productivity change, 1929–53; (5) plant size, 1947; (6) concentration ratio, 1947. Coefficients underlined were significant at the .01 level. The number of observations depended upon the number of industries for which measures of the several explanatory variables were available. These measures were available only for manufacturing industries.

[a] Based on fifty-six observations.
[b] Based on fifty-seven observations.

[21] The equation was $X_1 = 6.0193 + .0494 X_2$, with $X_1 = 100 \left(\dfrac{\text{external}}{\text{total employment}} \right)$ and $(.0081)$

$X_2 = 1950$ technical personnel ratio (in units of number of technical employees per 10,000 of all employees). The widest deviations of observed values from those estimated on the basis of the above equation were for primary metals and petroleum—industries in which external employment was largely a consequence of integration rather than diversification.

technical personnel ratio are likely to be more stable over time than differences in growth, the problem is more serious when the latter is used in the analysis. The relation between the external employment ratio and other variables—for example, change in labor productivity—may also have been obscured. However, it is likely that the volume of external employment undergoes continuous adjustment in response to changes in the relevant variables. This has the effect of reducing the aforementioned limitation of the data.

The Relation of Product Additions to Industry Size

To what extent do differences in the size of industries affect our results? If, for example, industries with a high technical personnel ratio are, in some sense, larger than those with a low one, might not this explain the greater frequency of product additions in the former? An industry that is larger in terms of total output might be entered more frequently for at least two reasons. First, total demand may be growing by larger absolute increments (even when the *rate* of growth is slower); second, the absolute volume of turnover in the population of firms in the industry may be greater. (Assuming only random influences, more firms will be going out of existence in a larger industry, thus creating a larger absolute number of opportunities for new entrants.) There is reason to believe, however, that our results were not materially affected by differences in industry size. Industries characterized by rapid growth and technological change are likely to be newer and, hence, smaller than average. Since these are the industries in which product additions were most frequent, the bias, if any, was in an opposite direction from the observed relations and hence cannot explain the latter. Also, while it is possible that the *absolute* number of additions will be greater in a larger industry, there is no reason to expect that the *relative* magnitude of activities contributed by diversifying firms (as measured, for example, by the ratio of external to total employment) will be larger. It has already been shown that results based on the ratio of external to total employment generally confirm those based on frequency of product additions.

The size of an industry can also be defined in terms of the number of products it contains, with products identified on the basis of a more detailed classification system than that used for industries. In our data, however, the number of recorded product additions is likely to vary with the number of separate markets in which additions could have been made, but not with the number of subclassifications of markets. It is only the former that affects the likelihood an industry will be entered. It will be recalled that several product additions falling within the same 4-digit industry were counted as a single addition precisely to avoid a possible bias arising from differences in the number of 7-digit product classes that 4-digit industries contained. However, even if the extreme assumption were made that the likelihood of entry in an industry is proportional to the number of 7-digit product classes it contains, our results with respect to the two variables, growth and the technical personnel ratio, would not be materially altered. Although industries in the upper deciles with respect to these variables tend to have more 7-digit products, the frequency of additions in industries with high growth and a high technical personnel ratio was, as compared with other industries, far more than proportional to the number of 7-digit products the former contained.

Abandonments of Products

The pattern of product abandonments with respect to the various factors examined was somewhat puzzling in that it tended to be similar to that for product additions. The pattern was, however, considerably less distinct for the former. Similarities between the two have been explained by the fact that an activity cannot be abandoned unless it is first entered into by a company. If, for example, industries associated with a high rate of technological change are entered more frequently, and if, further, some attempts at diversification fail, product abandonments would necessarily fall frequently into industries with rapidly changing technologies. Thus it is to be expected that the pattern of abandonments with respect to industry characteristics will, to a large degree, reproduce that for additions. Appendix Table E–1 indicates by deciles the character of product abandonments with respect to the same variables used to analyze additions.

Diversification and Changes in the Composition of Leading Firms

The discussion thus far has stressed the effect of industry characteristics on the directions of diversification. The effects are, however, to some extent reciprocal. Thus entry into a high-growth industry by large established firms probably increases the total supply of resources in the industry at the prevailing rate of return, and thus accelerates the industry's growth. In the post-1947 period a large number of research laboratories were started by companies in newly entered industries.[22] This probably had the effect of increasing the ratio of technical to all employees in the in-

---

[22] Based on information for company activities derived from public records.

dustries concerned. An effect on competitive relations within industries is likely to result from the frequently large diversification ventures in the more concentrated industries. Indeed, it may well be that in industries with higher than average concentration ratios, threat of entry from potential competitors arises primarily from large established firms in other sectors of the economy. The magnitude of this effect on competitive structures is somewhat difficult to assess. The available information did not permit us to segregate systematically those undertakings which resulted from the construction of new facilities, or the diversion to new uses of existing facilities, from entry achieved exclusively through merger. Mergers and property acquisitions, while they change ownership patterns, need not affect the underlying competitive structure.

In the discussion that follows, two questions are examined. First, in what proportion of the industries entered by the 111 large enterprises did entry lead to a change in the composition of the largest producers? Second, in what types of industries did these changes occur?

There were 218 manufacturing product additions in 1939–54 that were primary to at least one plant in 1954. Of these, fifty-six brought the companies making the additions into the class of leading eight producers in 1954 in the entered industries. Of a list of 158 additions in 1929–39 (once again restricted to those that were primary to at least one plant in 1954), sixty brought the companies into the class of eight leading producers in 1954. These facts point to two important conclusions. First, in a substantial majority of instances, entry on the part of even large firms into industries that are new to them does not result in a leading role in the industry for the entering firm. This apparently was true even after a lapse of roughly two decades following initial entry—a conclusion which is all the more significant since some entries were achieved through merger. Second, comparison of the 1929–39 and 1939–54 records does suggest that the passage of time increases the likelihood that a large company will appear among the leading producers in an industry it has entered. This is further reflected in the fact that, of the sixty additions in 1929–39 which brought companies into the class of largest eight producers, forty also brought the companies into the category of the largest four. On the other hand, of the fifty-six additions in 1939–54 which brought companies into the class of leading eight producers, only 25 also resulted in the companies' appearing among the leading four.

Table 54 shows that a large majority of industries entered in both 1929–39 and 1939–54, in which companies entered the class of leading four or eight producers, fell into the high deciles with respect to the concentration

TABLE 54

CONCENTRATION RATIOS FOR ENTERED INDUSTRIES IN WHICH
ENTRANTS WERE LEADING PRODUCERS IN 1954

Deciles Based on 1947 Concentration Ratios[a]	Industries Entered, 1929–39, in Which Entrants Were Among:		Industries Entered, 1939–54, in Which Entrants Were Among:	
	Four Largest Producers in 1954[b]	Eight Largest Producers in 1954[b]	Four Largest Producers in 1954[b]	Eight Largest Producers in 1954[b]
1	2	1	0	1
2	1	1	2	0
3	1	2	1	1
4	4	3	2	5
5	7	3	1	3
6	2	5	1	5
7	6	9	6	8
8	5	4	5	7
9	8	10	3	9
10	4	22	4	17
Total	40	60	25	56

SOURCE: Special census tabulation and product record described in Chapter 2.

[a] Deciles in ascending order with respect to concentration ratio.

[b] The ranking of industries (and hence the deciles into which industries fall) when concentration ratios are computed for the leading eight firms differs from that when the ratios are computed for the leading four firms. This explains why in some deciles the frequencies shown for the largest four producers are greater than those for the largest eight.

ratio.[23] For example, of the sixty industries entered in 1929–39 in which companies were among the leading eight producers in 1954, thirty-two fell into the two top deciles with respect to the concentration ratio. For industries added in 1939–54, there were twenty-six in the two top deciles out of a total of fifty-six. To an extent, this stems from the greater likelihood that firms will emerge among the leading producers in newly entered industries if the latter are small. Size of industry, on the whole, tends to be inversely related to the concentration ratio. Thus new entrants are more likely to become leading producers in the relatively concentrated industries. Nevertheless, it is significant that diversification frequently alters the relative position of leading firms in the more concentrated industries.

Table 55 indicates that, for the period 1929–54, companies in the electrical machinery, food products, and rubber products industries were

[23] Deciles were determined on the basis of all industries for which data on concentration ratios were available. The frequencies in the various deciles (shown in Table 54) for groupings of industries based on the ratio for the leading four producers are not altogether comparable with the frequencies in the same deciles but with industry groupings based on the ratio for the leading eight. This stems from the fact that a given industry need not appear in the same decile on the basis of the two ratios.

TABLE 55
RELATION BETWEEN INDUSTRY OF COMPANY AND NUMBER OF PRODUCT ADDITIONS THAT
BROUGHT ENTRANTS INTO THE CLASS OF LEADING EIGHT PRODUCERS IN 1954

Primary Industry of Company	Number of Companies	Number of Industries Entered, 1929–54[a]	Number in Which Companies Appeared Among the Leading Eight Producers in 1954
Food products	12	54	22
Tobacco manufactures	5	2	1
Textile mill products	4	11	4
Paper products	8	26	9
Chemicals	14	62	18
Petroleum	10	8	0
Rubber products	5	32	9
Stone, clay, and glass products	7	25	2
Primary metals	10	24	5
Fabricated metal products	5	22	3
Machinery	13	23	9
Electrical machinery	5	41	15
Transportation equipment	13	46	19
Total	111	376	116

SOURCE: Based on record of product changes described in text and on data from special census tabulation.

[a] Product additions which show at least one plant in the industry and for the company in question in the 1954 Census.

responsible for the highest average frequency of additions leading to the emergence of the firms among the largest eight. For the electrical machinery and rubber products companies, however, this reflects primarily the fact that frequencies of total additions per company were high.

We next examine the relation of frequency with which companies were brought into the leading four or eight producers to asset size of company. While these frequencies do not systematically vary with size of firm, they do seem higher in the upper size classes for both the 1929–39 and 1939–54 periods when expressed as a ratio to the total number of industries entered (Tables 56 and 57).[24]

Still another interesting question concerns the rate of growth of newly entered industries in which companies appeared among the leading eight firms in 1954. Generally, one might have expected to find that in older industries—those associated with slower growth—the market structure would be more stable. In the newer industries, on the other hand, the position of the leading firms would seem easier to upset. The more

[24] Counts of the total number of industries entered were restricted to additions that were primary to at least one plant in 1954.

TABLE 56

RELATION OF 1929 ASSET SIZE OF COMPANY TO NUMBER OF ENTERED INDUSTRIES IN WHICH COMPANIES
APPEARED AMONG THE LEADING FOUR AND EIGHT PRODUCERS IN 1954

		Total Number of 4-Digit Industries Added[b]	*Number of Cases in Which Four-Digit Industries Entered, 1929–39, Brought Company into Leading:*			
1929 Asset Size[a] (million dollars)	Number of Companies		Four Companies in 1954	Percentage of All Industries Entered	Eight Companies in 1954	Percentage of All Industries Entered
Under 50	31	41	9	22.0	14	34.1
50 and under 125	27	33	5	15.2	10	30.3
125 and under 250	20	30	9	30.0	12	40.0
250 and under 500	13	25	9	36.0	15	60.0
500 and over	12	15	6	40.0	6	40.0

SOURCE: Based on record of product additions described in text and data from special census tabulation.

[a] Based on total assets as shown in Moody's *Industrials*.

[b] Industries entered in the 1929–39 period which appear in 1954 census establishment data for the relevant companies.

TABLE 57

RELATION OF 1939 ASSET SIZE OF COMPANY TO NUMBER OF ENTERED INDUSTRIES IN WHICH COMPANIES
APPEARED AMONG THE LEADING FOUR AND EIGHT PRODUCERS IN 1954

		Total Number of 4-Digit Industries Added[b]	*Number of Cases in Which Four-Digit Industries Entered, 1939–54, Brought Company into Leading:*			
1939 Asset Size[a] (million dollars)	Number of Companies		Four Companies in 1954	Percentage of All Industries Entered	Eight Companies in 1954	Percentage of All Industries Entered
Under 50	29	89	8	9.0	21	23.6
50 and under 125	32	40	5	12.5	10	25.0
125 and under 250	25	53	6	11.3	12	22.6
250 and under 500	10	10	2	20.0	4	40.0
500 and over	13	24	4	16.7	9	37.5

SOURCE: Based on record of product additions described in text and data from special census tabulation.

[a] Based on total assets as shown in Moody's *Industrials*.

[b] Industries entered in the 1939–54 period which appear in 1954 census establishment data for the relevant companies.

rapidly an industry grows, the easier it is to supplant the position of the leading firm without having to capture an important part of the latter's market. Table 58 shows the industries in which the group of 111 companies entered the class of leading eight producers, distributed according to three classes (lower 30 per cent, middle 40 per cent, and upper 30 per cent of industries) on the basis of growth.[25] It appears that there is a concentration of frequencies in the upper 30 per cent in the 1939–54 period, but not in 1929–39.

An attempt was made to distinguish the characteristics of industries in which entering companies became leading producers from those of newly entered industries generally. Accordingly, to ascertain the special characteristics of industries in which our sample of companies became leading producers, we compared the frequency with which they appear in each growth class with comparable frequencies for *all* the industries entered by the 111 companies. The analysis entailed comparing actual frequencies in each of the three classes for the more restricted group of industries (those in which companies became the leading producers) with null hypothesis frequencies computed on the assumption that the distribution of these industries by growth class was the same as for all those entered.[26]

TABLE 58

ACTUAL AND NULL-HYPOTHESIS FREQUENCIES FOR INDUSTRIES IN WHICH COMPANIES
WERE BROUGHT INTO THE CATEGORY OF LEADING EIGHT PRODUCERS IN 1954

	1929–39		1939–54	
Growth Class[a]	Number of Industries	Number Expected[b]	Number of Industries	Number Expected[b]
I (lower 30 per cent)	15	9.7	12	5.7
II (middle 40 per cent)	24	19.4	15	15.9
III (upper 30 per cent)	21	30.9	29	34.4

SOURCE: Product record described in Chapter 2 and special census tabulation.
[a] Based on a grouping of all industries for which growth information was available.
[b] Chi-squares: 1929–39, 7.159; 1939–54, 7.862.

[25] The classification into lower, middle, and upper growth classes was made on the basis of all industries for which information on growth was available.

[26] The formula was $E_j = T_a \times \dfrac{A_j}{A_t}$, where E_j stands for the null hypothesis frequency in a specified class j, T_a for the actual number of industries in which companies entered the category of leading eight producers, and A_j and A_t respectively, for the actual frequencies in class j and for those in all three classes combined for *all* industries entered by the 111 companies.

The test produced values of chi-square significant at the .05 level in both the 1929–39 and 1939–54 periods. However, the results were opposite to those suggested in the hypothesis. The data show higher-than-expected frequencies in the low-growth industries and lower-than-expected frequencies in high-growth industries. Thus industries in which firms were brought through diversification into the group of leading producers were not among the youngest industries entered by the 111 firms—at least if age is measured by rate of growth.

CHAPTER 8

The Sources of Diversification

THIS chapter studies the nature of the primary industries of diversifying firms. It was shown in Chapter 3 that sharp differences exist in the extent to which firms in various industries (classified by primary activity) tend to diversify. The industry class of a company is associated with a large number of economic variables. Consequently, identification of differences in the extent to which firms in various parts of the economy diversify, while of descriptive interest, represents only a first step in isolating the relevant economic forces.

In the discussion below, attention is first focused on the relation between the degree to which firms with a given primary industry diversify and the economic characteristics of the industry. In this part of the analysis the data consist of industry aggregates showing the volume of employment in nonprimary activities for companies classified by primary industry. Next, for the 111-firm sample, growth rates of primary industries are compared with those of the industries in which the companies added products.

Summary

In the preceding chapter, it was shown that industries which have complex and changing technologies and which require relatively large numbers of technical personnel have proved the most attractive as diversification outlets. It follows, therefore, that firms which have large numbers of technical employees in connection with their primary activities are in a better position to diversify than those that do not. The technical personnel ratio was strongly correlated with the ratio of nonprimary to primary employment in the industry.[1] As a determinant of which firms will diversify, this points to the importance of similarities in requisite skills between primary activities and those attractive as diversification outlets. In a sense, therefore, diversification paradoxically depends upon specialization, except that the relevant form of specialization is in technical skills rather than in the specific goods and services produced. However, even assuming that the advantages of specialization by products rather than by skills were large, one would still expect to find some diversification as a consequence of the effects of random forces in determining which firms discover profitable investment opportunities. These forces render it likely

[1] However, the technical personnel ratio was more strongly associated with the extent to which an industry was an outlet than a source for diversification, the ratio being negatively related to that for nonprimary to external employment. External employment is defined in Chapter 7.

that attractive projects will sometimes be found first by firms with primary activities outside the relevant industries.

To a large degree, firms diversify rather than pursue further growth within their primary industries because of limits to their growth within the latter. These limits are of two types. Type 1 arise from the rate of growth in primary industry demand. Type 2 arise from obstacles to a faster growth in the sales of an individual producer than in market demand.

With respect to Type 1 limits, the net relation (after due account is taken of the role of the technical personnel ratio) between primary industry growth and the ratio of nonprimary to primary employment was negative. Also, for the 111-firm sample, there were roughly twice as many product additions in industries with higher growth than that of primary industries as there were in those with lower growth.

For reasons explained later in the chapter, Type 2 limits are particularly strong in industries in which sellers are large and few in number—a phenomenon roughly measured by the concentration ratio (that is, the proportion of industry sales or shipments contributed by the leading four producers). This ratio was related positively to that of nonprimary to primary employment.

The Magnitude of Nonprimary Activities and Industry Characteristics

In the analysis below, the objective is to establish functional relations between diversification and primary industry characteristics. No attempt is made to identify the conscious motives of managers. Rather the objective is to determine those characteristics of industries that serve as constraints on the alternatives open to firms. For example, managers may wish to enter an industry new to the firm in order to increase earnings—but which of the many industries will they choose? A choice consistent with the purpose of increasing earnings may be affected by a wide array of factors, such as the content of the managers' knowledge and experience, and the ability to use existing machinery, research facilities, or marketing outlets.

Generally, the prospective return on investment in diversification will be higher if the firm undertaking it has, in the new activity, a competitive advantage over most firms in the economy. As shown in Chapter 7, industries that have attracted diversification have been associated with large requirements for technical personnel. Consequently, a firm with a high rate of employment of technical personnel in connection with its primary activity has the advantage of Type 2 technical propinquity (the use of common skills) to the more attractive diversification outlets, and should enter these outlets more frequently than other firms. As a result, a higher technical personnel ratio in the primary activities of firms should produce a lower specialization of output in the primary industry. Further, while most technical employees are not engaged in research and product development, the number so engaged is likely to be positively correlated with the total number employed. Activities in research frequently lead to new or improved products in a variety of industries, thus generating investment opportunities outside the primary one.

Since the managerial resources available to a firm are limited, high rates of growth may entail the dilution of scarce managerial skills over a large number of projects. Capital resources are also limited in the sense that increases in capital requirements will, beyond some level, have to be financed at a rising cost of capital. Thus firms must even choose from among investment opportunities which, if undertaken singly, would yield a rate of return higher than the cost of capital. A high growth rate for the primary industry increases the attractiveness of investment opportunities within the scope of a firm's existing activities and thus tends to reduce diversification.

The opportunity for a faster growth in the sales of an individual firm than in market demand is affected by the concentration ratio for the industry. In a market characterized by high concentration, the outputs of at least the larger producers are interdependent in that a substantial increase in the output of one, not accompanied by a proportionate rise in market demand, must result in a reduction in price or in a significant contraction in output for some or all producers. Thus if the managers of a firm in a concentrated industry seek a faster growth rate than that for primary industry demand, usually they must either diversify or encroach noticeably on the market of a competing producer.[2] Since the latter alternative is frequently expensive and hazardous, a firm in a highly concentrated industry will be more prone to seek investment opportunities outside its primary activity.

The extent of diversification for firms classified in a given industry was measured on the basis of 1954 ratios of employment outside the primary industry to employment in the primary industry (Appendix Table D–6). Analysis was restricted to manufacturing industries for which data on explanatory variables were available. The ratios were taken as of a single point in time, so that nonprimary employment may have been generated in a period which antecedes that to which our measures of explanatory

---

[2] At times the firm can also grow by merger within the primary industry, or through integration. These alternatives are, however, frequently unattractive or not practicable for legal and other reasons.

variables refer. However, inasmuch as nonprimary activities can be contracted as well as expanded, a continuous process of adjustment of nonprimary employment to the relevant variables is at work. This reduces the error of using diversification measures as of a single date. Industry growth was based on data for the period 1939–53, the technical personnel ratio was measured for the year 1950, and concentration ratios were based on 1947 data. An additional variable, average firm size for the industry, was used to test whether the concentration ratio was only a proxy for it in the relation of concentration ratio to diversification. Firm size was measured for the year 1947. The sources of information, methods of measurement used, and units in which these four explanatory variables are expressed are indicated in Appendix D.

Below are the four equations derived from the above-mentioned data. Table 59 shows the relevant multiple and partial correlation coefficients for each of the four equations. In addition, it shows the simple correlations for various pairs of variables.

(1) $$X_1 = 5.8236 + .0004 X_2 + .3605 X_3$$
$$(.0003) \qquad (.1163)$$

(2) $$X_1 = 9.3187 + .0593 X_4 - .0209 X_5$$
$$(.0130) \qquad (.0101)$$

(3) $$X_1 = 9.2734 + .0005 X_2 + .0381 X_4$$
$$(.0002) \qquad (.0085)$$

(4) $$X_1 = -.3923 + .3497 X_3 + .0286 X_4$$
$$(.0998) \qquad (.0090)$$

X_1 is the ratio of nonprimary to primary employment multiplied by 100. X_2 is the firm-size variable, X_3 the concentration ratio, X_4 the technical personnel ratio, and X_5 is industry growth. The standard errors applicable to the regression coefficients are indicated in parentheses.

As may be judged from the table, equation 4, using the concentration ratio and the technical personnel ratio as independent variables, yields the highest correlation coefficient, .614. Both of the partial, as well as the multiple, correlation coefficients for equation 4 were statistically significant at the .01 level.[3] As anticipated, in equation 2 growth exhibited a negative relation to the relative importance of nonprimary operations. The partial correlation coefficient was − .280 and, though small, was significant at the .05 level. Firm size, though correlated with the concentration ratio, contributed less than the latter toward explaining the variance in the

---

[3] The correlation was substantially reduced by one extreme observation, namely, that for the electrical machinery industry. Without the latter, $R_{1\cdot34} = .841$, while $r_{14\cdot3} = .614$ and $r_{13\cdot4} = .743$.

TABLE 59

CORRELATION COEFFICIENTS FOR RATIO OF NONPRIMARY TO PRIMARY
EMPLOYMENT AND INDUSTRY VARIABLES

Equation[a]	Simple Correlation[b]		Multiple Correlation[b]		Partial Correlation[b]	
(1) $N = 54$	r_{12}	(.3071)	$R_{1 \cdot 23}$	.470	$r_{12 \cdot 3}$	.2345
	r_{13}	.4607			$r_{13 \cdot 2}$	(.3731)
	r_{23}	(.3273)				
(2) $N = 55$	r_{14}	.5261	$R_{1 \cdot 45}$	.576	$r_{14 \cdot 5}$	.5419
	r_{15}	.2386			$r_{15 \cdot 4}$	(—.2808)
	r_{45}	.7525				
(3) $N = 62$	r_{12}	(.3160)	$R_{1 \cdot 24}$	.569	$r_{12 \cdot 4}$	(.2882)
	r_{14}	.5325			$r_{14 \cdot 2}$	.4991
	r_{24}	.2254				
(4) $N = 56$	r_{13}	.4942	$R_{1 \cdot 34}$	.614	$r_{13 \cdot 4}$	.4352
	r_{14}	.4811			$r_{14 \cdot 3}$	.4192
	r_{34}	.2617				

[a] The number of observations in each equation was the maximum number of industries for which data were available for all independent variables in the equation. Information was sufficient for only the manufacturing industries. The simple correlation coefficients are based on data for the industries in each equation when two independent variables are used. Thus the simple correlation coefficients for the identical variables show some variation as a result of the fact that they are based on slightly differing groups of industries.

[b] The ratio of nonprimary to primary employment is identified by subscript 1. The independent variables are denoted by subscripts as follows: subscript 2, firm size; subscript 3, concentration ratio; subscript 4, technical personnel ratio; subscript 5, growth. Coefficients significant at the .01 level are underlined. Those significant at the .05 level are in parentheses.

dependent variable (r_{13} was larger than r_{12} and $R_{1 \cdot 34}$ was larger than $R_{1 \cdot 24}$). Thus the concentration ratio cannot be considered a proxy for firm size.

The number of observations for each of the four equations was limited to the maximum number of industries for which information on each set of relevant variables was available; it ranged from fifty-four for equation 1 to sixty-two for equation 3. When all four explanatory variables were used, the number of industries for which data were available was reduced to thirty-six. $R_{1 \cdot 2345}$ was .611 compared with .605 for $R_{1 \cdot 34}$ for the thirty-six observations. Thus it is apparent that the two additional variables— growth and firm size—do not materially contribute toward explaining the variance in the nonprimary to primary employment ratio, once the technical personnel ratio and the concentration ratio are used as independent variables.

The Relation Between Growth of Primary and of Newly Entered Industries
Do companies tend to enter industries that are growing faster than those

in which their largest activities are located? Stated in another way, is diversification associated with the flow of capital funds from slower to faster growing sectors of the economy? In earlier sections of this study it was shown, first, that the rate of growth of the primary industry is inversely related to diversification; and second, that firms when they diversify tend to enter high-growth industries. It follows from these facts that industries into which firms diversify will, on the average, grow faster than the primary industries of diversifying companies. To establish the extent of this, the growth rates of manufacturing industries in which the 111 large companies added products in 1939–50 and 1950–54 were compared with the rates of the primary industries of these companies.[4] This was done by comparing the deciles, on the basis of growth in 1939–54, into which both the primary industries of companies and the industries of product additions were classified.[5]

As may be judged from Table 60, when one compares the number of additions in the growth deciles above and below those of the companies' primary industries, in both periods the former were roughly twice the latter. Thus diversification is strongly associated with the flow of resources from lower- to higher-growth sectors of the economy. Nevertheless, it is interesting that as many as a fourth of all product additions in both 1939–50 and 1950–54 fell into industries growing less rapidly than the companies' primary industries.[6] Clearly, industry growth is not the only factor that affects diversification. Moreover, if the primary industry of a firm is itself associated with a high growth rate, it is difficult for the firm to discover industries for diversification with even faster growth rates.

Companies that diversify into rapidly growing sectors may be expected to increase their growth through diversification more than if they had entered slower growing industries. However, the effect of differences in the growth of newly entered industries was not sufficiently strong to explain the differences in the over-all growth of companies.[7]

---

[4] Primary industry was determined on the basis of 1954 Census data for manufacturing payrolls. Product additions were based on the product record described in Chapter 2.

[5] The loss of detail through the use of deciles was necessitated by restrictions on the use of individual company information. Data on growth rates of individual industries were based on Appendix Table D–3. Deciles were determined on the basis of all the industries in that table.

[6] This proportion was derived after excluding product additions that fell into industries for which no growth measures were available.

[7] Companies were grouped into deciles on the basis of growth in total assets in the period 1939–54. Those in the higher growth deciles, when compared with less rapidly growing firms, did not show a significantly higher ratio of number of entries in high growth to number of entries in all industries.

TABLE 60

COMPARATIVE GROWTH OF PRIMARY INDUSTRIES OF 111 LARGE COMPANIES
AND OF MANUFACTURING INDUSTRIES IN WHICH THE COMPANIES ADDED PRODUCTS

Primary Industry of Company	1950–54 Additions				1939–50 Additions			
	Number in Higher Growth Deciles Than Primary Industry	Number in Lower Growth Deciles Than Primary Industry	Number in Same Growth Decile as Primary Industry	Number of Additions for Which No Growth Measure Was Available	Number in Higher Growth Deciles Than Primary Industry	Number in Lower Growth Deciles Than Primary Industry	Number in Same Growth Decile as Primary Industry	Number of Additions for Which No Growth Measure Was Available
Food products	19	3	1	6	18	3	6	8
Tobacco manufactures	0	0	0	0	1	0	0	0
Textile mill products	3	0	0	0	5	5	2	4
Paper products	15	6	6	10	15	8	8	7
Chemicals	9	32	22	18	11	29	15	18
Petroleum	15	4	2	0	26	4	5	1
Rubber products	29	8	2	15	34	5	0	14
Stone, clay, and glass products	6	3	2	5	12	6	2	5
Primary metals	10	4	3	5	6	0	2	1
Fabricated metal products	9	1	0	4	11	5	1	4
Machinery	14	6	7	6	15	5	5	9
Electrical machinery	8	11	6	16	15	13	10	22
Transportation equipment	38	10	10	21	31	9	11	13
Total	175	88	61	106	200	92	67	106

NOTE: Growth measured for 1939–54. The 4-digit level of industry detail was used.

SOURCE: Product record described in Chapter 2 and 1954 census data. The latter were used to determine primary 4-digit industries on the basis of information for payrolls. Growth deciles were based on information described in Appendix B.

The Technical Personnel Ratio and the Flow of Resources

It will be recalled that the technical personnel ratio was found to be positively correlated with both the nonprimary employment ratio and the ratio of external to total employment.[8] The non-primary employment ratio purports to measure the extent to which companies with specified primary industries diversify, and the latter measures the attractiveness of industries as outlets for diversification. The question that is now examined is whether a high technical personnel ratio for a given industry is associated more strongly with a flow of resources into that industry (from firms outside it) than with the flow of resources into other sectors from firms in the industry.

For fifty-six industries,[9] the simple correlation between the technical personnel ratio and the ratio of nonprimary to external employment[10] was only $-.214$, and hence not acceptable at the .05 level of significance. However, the relation was obscured by the influence of another variable. It will be recalled that concentration ratios were positively related to nonprimary employment. When the ratio of nonprimary to external employment was taken as the dependent variable, and both the 1950 technical personnel ratio and 1947 concentration ratio as independent variables, the following equation was derived for the fifty-six industries:

$$X_1 = 34.1224 + 7.1780 \ X_2 - .4652 \ X_3,$$
$$(2.0937) \quad (.1879)$$

where X_1 stands for the ratio of nonprimary to external employment multiplied by 100, X_2 the concentration ratio, and X_3 the technical personnel ratio.[11] The standard errors for the regression coefficients are indicated in parentheses. The coefficient of multiple correlation was .469 and the two partial correlation coefficients were as follows: $r_{12 \cdot 3} = .428$ and $r_{13 \cdot 2} = -.337$.[12] All three coefficients were significant at the .01 level. Thus the technical personnel ratio is related inversely to the ratio of nonprimary to external employment. That is, the higher the technical personnel ratio, the greater will be employment (and presumably other resources) within the industry emanating from firms outside it, relative to employment outside the industry emanating from firms within it.

[8] As expected data for eighty-five manufacturing and mining industries also produced a positive coefficient of rank correlation (.461) for the nonprimary and external employment ratios.

[9] Manufacturing industries for which data on explanatory variables were available.

[10] The ratio of nonprimary to external employment for all manufacturing and mining industries is shown in Appendix Table D–8.

[11] Expressed in units of number of technical employees per 10,000 of all employees.

[12] The correlation coefficients were materially reduced by the single observation for the meat-packing industry. Excluding meat packing, $R = .679$, $r_{12 \cdot 3} = .663$, $r_{13 \cdot 2} = -.451$.

As a last comment, the positive association between the technical personnel ratio and the extent to which an industry was both a source and an outlet for diversification is, at first view, somewhat puzzling since better than average investment opportunities within the industry entail a larger demand therein for limited capital resources. This should exert a negative influence on the amount of diversification undertaken by firms classified in the industry. Apparently, however, the positive effect of technical propinquity to diversification outlets more than offset the negative effect of a higher demand for scarce resources within the primary industry.

APPENDIX A

Composition of Sample 111 Large Enterprises

TABLE A–1
TOTAL ASSETS AND RATES OF RETURN FOR 111 LARGE CORPORATIONS

	Total Assets			Net Income[a]
	1929 ($000)	1939 ($000)	1954 ($000)	Net Worth 1947–54 (%)
Food products				
Armour & Co. (Ill.)	452,313	302,506	469,915	5.45
Swift & Co.	351,252	312,453	495,264	7.36
Coca-Cola Co.	55,062	93,414	236,726	19.03
National Biscuit Co.	133,225	125,471	218,051	16.45
Borden Co.	174,046	125,714	301,066	12.35
National Dairy Products Corp.	224,533	193,666	446,465	14.26
Corn Products Refining Co.	126,726	115,935	181,781	11.93
General Foods Corp.	70,504	90,915	357,696	13.95
Campbell Soup Co.	n.a.	n.a.	233,106	n.a.
National Distillers Products Corp.	28,347	74,398	387,820	9.61
Distillers Corp.-Seagrams, Ltd.	21,456	77,447	478,269	16.49
Hiram Walker-Gooderham & Worts, Ltd.	39,803	58,753	198,240	15.90
Tobacco manufactures				
P. Lorillard Co.	106,780	57,504	184,210	10.79
Liggett & Myers Tobacco Co.	160,123	181,453	491,309	11.66
R. J. Reynolds Tobacco Co.	163,187	176,710	617,636	15.93
American Tobacco Co.	265,406	291,230	775,364	12.95
Philip Morris & Co., Ltd., Inc.	6,378	37,143	255,131	11.22
Textile mill products				
Armstrong Cork Co.	58,248	55,290	142,188	9.76
United Merchants & Manufacturers, Inc.	n.a.	27,118	189,530	16.36
Cannon Mills Co.	37,718	46,656	132,675	12.33
Pacific Mills	54,556	30,608	79,134	7.13
Paper products				
International Paper Co.	333,348	219,169	549,403	15.11
Marathon Corp.	11,708	14,307	122,221	11.19
Container Corp. of America	23,354	26,110	98,332	15.52
West Virginia Pulp & Paper Co.	56,666	61,553	176,487	11.73
Kimberly-Clark Corp.	48,686	50,858	152,080	9.55
St. Regis Paper Co.	86,448	59,123	216,565	12.51
Crown Zellerbach Corp.	117,710	102,171	315,776	13.63
Minnesota Mining & Manufacturing Co.	5,452	15,140	185,502	18.25
Chemicals				
Allied Chemical & Dye Corp.	277,147	236,698	688,832	14.41
Koppers Co.	n.a.	109,943	158,183	10.41
Monsanto Chemical Co.	24,333	54,752	376,516	12.97
Merck & Co., Inc.	8,293	12,230	148,513	12.47
American Cyanamid Co.	46,167	77,346	499,938	11.83
Colgate-Palmolive Co.	63,984	70,898	174,516	13.43

(continued)

TABLE A-1 (continued)

	Total Assets			Net Income[a]
				Net Worth 1947–54 (%)
	1929 ($000)	1939 ($000)	1954 ($000)	
Chemicals (cont.)				
E. I. du Pont de Nemours & Co.	541,986	857,618	1,946,073	17.36
Union Carbide & Carbon Corp.	306,618	336,845	1,251,636	18.06
Olin Mathieson Chemical Corp.	21,534	24,857	474,225	12.52
Celanese Corp. of America	40,159	66,297	320,412	12.02
Sherwin-Williams Co.	51,259	56,759	137,239	10.22
Procter & Gamble Co.	133,238	150,821	476,930	15.71
Dow Chemical Co.	21,549	40,664	704,804	12.51
Food Machinery & Chemical Corp.	6,521	11,978	224,697	9.25
Petroleum				
Standard Oil Co. (New Jersey)	1,767,378	2,034,989	6,614,743	5.80
Standard Oil Co. (Indiana)	697,034	723,080	2,187,358	9.88
Socony-Vacuum Oil Co.	708,406	930,067	2,256,691	11.14
Texas Co.	609,853	661,067	1,945,509	14.15
Gulf Oil Corp.	430,845	523,293	1,969,052	14.31
Standard Oil of California	604,724	628,618	1,677,849	15.81
Cities Service Co.	989,881	1,068,579	1,053,527	14.07
Sinclair Oil Corp.	400,647	357,849	1,186,771	13.47
Phillips Petroleum Co.	145,385	223,280	1,092,745	12.46
Atlantic Refining Co.	167,249	203,400	611,682	10.88
Rubber products				
Goodyear Tire & Rubber Co.	243,282	191,554	668,664	15.72
Firestone Tire & Rubber Co.	161,647	174,753	576,717	15.54
United States Rubber Co.	304,557	182,295	497,040	19.72
B. F. Goodrich Co.	181,204	133,164	464,136	16.48
General Tire & Rubber Co.	15,537	16,600	150,812	10.52
Stone, clay, and glass products				
National Gypsum Co.	7,352	18,876	118,827	13.84
Libbey-Owens-Ford Glass Co.	30,737	46,948	132,498	22.69
Corning Glass Works	n.a.	n.a.	122,407	19.12
Johns-Manville Corp.	43,938	53,750	198,251	14.22
United States Gypsum Co.	64,384	64,857	228,510	14.97
Owens-Illinois Glass	48,413	87,337	258,198	12.19
Pittsburgh Plate Glass Co.	101,681	124,151	443,099	14.10
Primary metals				
Aluminum Co. of America	234,729	251,421	1,002,210	12.80
Anaconda Copper Mining Co.	680,548	587,933	870,324	6.64
Kennecott Copper Corp.	337,808	361,182	730,867	15.12
United States Steel Corp.	2,286,184	1,768,524	3,348,696	8.59
Bethlehem Steel Corp.	801,631	732,932	1,613,444	12.47
Republic Steel Corp.	331,758	365,050	747,971	12.17
Jones & Laughlin Steel Corp.	222,026	230,865	576,868	8.81
National Steel Corp.	120,829	218,028	547,925	13.50
Armco Steel Corp.	104,250	144,317	490,197	13.83

(continued)

TABLE A–1 (concluded)

	Total Assets			Net Income[a] Net Worth 1947–54 (%)
	1929 ($000)	1939 ($000)	1954 ($000)	
Primary metals (cont.)				
Youngstown Sheet & Tube Co.	235,741	247,655	500,543	10.98
Fabricated metal products				
American Can Co.	191,336	190,903	456,858	10.73
Continental Can Co. Inc.	83,170	126,145	358,072	7.92
American Radiator & Standard Sanitary Corp.	199,307	146,183	218,358	13.32
A. O. Smith Corp.	34,349	17,400	121,019	10.82
Babcock & Wilcox Co.	35,409	26,561	161,459	14.26
Machinery				
Crane Co.	115,919	109,410	214,170	8.70
Allis-Chalmers Manufacturing Co.	73,023	108,060	410,575	10.37
Fairbanks, Morse & Co.	40,780	31,822	89,141	9.91
Ingersoll-Rand Co.	52,920	43,144	159,947	23.64
International Business Machines Corp.	40,404	79,028	565,475	18.81
Deere & Co.	107,238	105,849	430,379	13.41
Caterpillar Tractor Co.	53,125	49,898	263,803	15.43
International Harvester Co.	384,078	402,434	940,053	9.12
Burroughs Corp.	40,913	36,673	138,418	15.44
National Cash Register Co.	55,474	56,935	183,424	19.83
Baldwin-Lima-Hamilton Corp.	98,856	61,071	131,345	5.00
Singer Manufacturing Co.	182,894	158,116	412,558	6.60
Remington Rand, Inc.	72,211	43,240	207,712	18.16
Electrical machinery				
General Electric Co.	515,776	392,223	1,803,661	20.08
Radio Corp. of America	158,680	93,740	548,325	18.11
Westinghouse Electric Corp.	253,928	217,158	1,329,120	12.91
Electric Auto-Lite Co.	30,861	36,480	157,209	12.00
Sylvania Electric Products, Inc.	3,480	7,597	191,380	9.52
Transportation equipment				
Borg-Warner Corp.	39,068	49,497	269,430	16.69
General Motors Corp.	1,324,890	1,706,940	5,130,094	24.11
American Motors Corp.	64,087	48,519	266,711	12.60
Chrysler Corp.	209,741	222,495	1,034,592	17.20
Boeing Airplane Co.	n.a.	9,254	252,643	20.78
Bendix Aviation Corp.	70,986	34,909	285,431	13.34
Lockheed Aircraft Corp.	n.a.	15,547	280,822	13.47
American Locomotive Co.	106,242	56,131	99,254	9.49
Douglas Aircraft Co., Inc.	3,283	24,584	258,496	10.68
United Aircraft Corp.	41,335	67,047	261,938	10.98
Pullman, Inc.	315,555	221,885	210,586	6.91
Ford Motor Co.	761,078	691,912	2,585,337	13.25
ACF Industries, Inc.	119,519	89,989	153,109	5.14

SOURCE: Moody's *Industrials*.
[a] After taxes.

TABLE A–2
COMPANIES GROUPED BY INDUSTRY AND DISTRIBUTED BY DECILES
ACCORDING TO GROWTH IN TOTAL ASSETS, 1929–39

| Industry | Number of Companies in each Decile[a] on Basis of 1929–39 Growth | | | | | | | | | | |
	I	II	III	IV	V	VI	VII	VIII	IX	X	Total[b]
Food products		1	2	2				2	1	2	10
Tobacco manufactures	1					2	1			1	5
Textile mill products	1			1				1			3
Paper products	2		1		1	1	2			1	8
Chemicals			1			3	2	1	4	2	13
Petroleum			1		2	2	3	1	1		10
Rubber	1	2			1	1					5
Stone, clay, and glass products				1			2		2	1	6
Primary metals		1	1	1	3	2		1	1		10
Fabricated metal products	1	2		1				1			5
Machinery	2	1	3	3	2			1		1	13
Electrical machinery	1	1	1				1			1	5
Transportation equipment	2	3		1	1			2	1	1	11
Total[b]	11	11	10	10	10	11	11	10	10	10	104

SOURCE: Moody's *Industrials*.
[a] Deciles in ascending order with respect to growth.
[b] Information for some companies in the sample of 111 was not available.

TABLE A–3
COMPANIES GROUPED BY INDUSTRY AND DISTRIBUTED BY DECILES
ACCORDING TO GROWTH IN TOTAL ASSETS, 1939–54

| Industry | Number of Companies in each Decile[a] on Basis of 1939–54 Growth | | | | | | | | | | |
	I	II	III	IV	V	VI	VII	VIII	IX	X	Total[b]
Food products	3	2	2			1	1	1		1	11
Tobacco manufactures			2	1		1			1		5
Textile mill products			2	1					1		4
Paper products			1	1	2	1	1			2	8
Chemicals	1	1	2	1	1		1	1	2	4	14
Petroleum	1		1	1	4	1	1	1			10
Rubber			1		3					1	5
Stone, clay, and glass products				1	1	3			1		6
Primary metals	1	5	2			1	1				10
Fabricated metal products	1		1	1					2		5
Machinery		3		2	1		4	2	1		13
Electrical machinery								3	1	1	5
Transportation equipment	3				1		2	3	1	3	13
Total-	10	11	11	11	11	11	11	11	11	11	109

SOURCE: Moody's *Industrials*.
[a] Deciles in ascending order with respect to growth.
[b] Information for some companies in the sample of 111 was not available.

TABLE A–4

COMPANIES GROUPED BY INDUSTRY AND DISTRIBUTED ACCORDING TO FIVE
CLASSES ON THE BASIS OF 1954 TOTAL ASSETS

Industry	Under $150 Million	$150 Million and Under $250 Million	$250 Million and Under $500 Million	$500 Million and Under $1 Billion	$1 Billion and over	Total
Food products		5	7			12
Tobacco manufactures		1	2	2		5
Textile mill products	3	1				4
Paper products	2	4	1	1		8
Chemicals	2	3	5	2	2	14
Petroleum				1	9	10
Rubber		1	2	2		5
Stone, clay, and glass products	3	2	2			7
Primary metals			1	6	3	10
Fabricated metal products	1	2	2			5
Machinery	3	4	4	2		13
Electrical machinery		2		1	2	5
Transportation equipment	1	2	7		3	13
Total	15	27	33	17	19	111

SOURCE: Moody's *Industrials*.

151

APPENDIX B

Product Record for 111
Large Enterprises

TABLE B–1
1954 PRODUCT STRUCTURES OF 111 LARGE COMPANIES

	Total Number of Products in 1954	Number of Products in Manufacturing Industries	Number of Products in Primary 2-digit Industry
Food products	203	156	85
Swift & Co.	30	26	12
National Distillers Products Corp.	13	9	3
Armour & Co.	36	27	8
General Foods Corp.	30	24	15
Campbell Soup Co.	6	4	3
Coca-Cola Co.	2	2	1
National Dairy Products Corp.	22	20	16
National Biscuit Co.	17	12	8
Distillers Corp.-Seagrams	3	1	1
Borden Co.	21	18	11
Hiram Walker-Gooderham & Worts, Ltd.	7	4	3
Corn Products Refining Co.	16	9	4
Tobacco manufactures	35	26	18
American Tobacco Co.	12	9	4
R. J. Reynolds Tobacco Co.	8	5	3
Liggett and Myers Tobacco Co.	5	4	4
Philip Morris & Co., Ltd., Inc.	4	3	3
P. Lorillard Co.	6	5	4
Textile mill products	54	39	16
United Merchants & Manufacturers, Inc.	18	12	6
Cannon Mills Co.	5	4	3
Armstrong Cork Co.	24	17	3
Pacific Mills	7	6	4
Paper products	153	117	39
International Paper Co.	20	14	8
Crown Zellerbach Corp.	17	10	5
St. Regis Paper Co.	19	12	6
Kimberly-Clark Corp.	15	13	6
West Virginia Pulp & Paper Co.	8	6	3
Container Corp. of America	13	10	4
Marathon Corp.	24	19	5
Minnesota Mining & Manufacturing Co.	37	33	2
Chemicals	371	280	161
Celanese Corp. of America	12	10	5
E. I. du Pont de Nemours & Co.	29	26	12
Allied Chemical & Dye Corp.	26	19	14
Union Carbide & Carbon Corp.	37	25	8
Dow Chemical Co.	31	18	13

(continued)

TABLE B–1 (continued)

	Total Number of Products in 1954	Number of Products in Manufacturing Industries	Number of Products in Primary 2-digit Industry
Chemicals (cont.)			
Procter & Gamble Co.	16	10	7
American Cyanamid Co.	24	20	15
Olin Mathieson Chemical Corp.	56	40	16
Monsanto Chemical Co.	24	21	19
Colgate-Palmolive Co.	5	4	4
Koppers Co.	40	28	9
Merck & Co., Inc.	28	28	27
Sherwin-Williams Co.	14	11	6
Food Machinery & Chemical Corp.	29	20	6
Petroleum	211	84	17
Standard Oil Co. (New Jersey)	19	9	1
Standard Oil Co. of Indiana	25	12	1
Socony-Vacuum Oil Co.	19	6	1
Texas Co.	23	11	3
Gulf Oil Corp.	24	6	1
Standard Oil Co. of California	21	9	2
Cities Service Co.	18	7	3
Sinclair Oil Corp.	20	7	1
Phillips Petroleum Co.	23	9	1
Atlantic Refining Co.	19	8	3
Rubber products	173	153	17
Goodyear Tire & Rubber Co.	25	22	3
United States Rubber Co.	57	56	4
Firestone Tire & Rubber Co.	32	22	3
B. F. Goodrich Co.	22	20	4
General Tire & Rubber Co.	37	33	3
Stone, clay, and glass products	135	92	35
Pittsburgh Plate Glass Co.	34	24	6
Owens-Illinois Glass Co.	20	15	5
United States Gypsum Co.	21	13	5
Johns-Manville Corp.	21	15	9
Libbey-Owens-Ford Glass Co.	16	10	4
National Gypsum Co.	15	9	5
Corning Glass Works	8	6	1
Primary metals	288	153	49
United States Steel Corp.	56	32	7
Bethlehem Steel Corp.	37	26	7
Anaconda Copper Mining Co.	45	26	9
Kennecott Copper Corp.	24	13	4
Aluminum Co. of America	39	16	4
Republic Steel Corp.	21	12	4
Jones & Laughlin Steel Corp.	18	8	3

(continued)

TABLE B-1 (concluded)

	Total Number of Products in 1954	Number of Products in Manufacturing Industries	Number of Products in Primary 2-digit Industry
Primary metals (cont.)			
National Steel Corp.	16	8	6
Armco Steel Corp.	15	7	3
Youngstown Sheet & Tube Co.	17	5	2
Fabricated metal products	98	87	20
American Can Co.	11	10	5
Continental Can Co., Inc.	22	18	3
American Radiator & Standard Sanitary Corp.	24	22	6
Babcock & Wilcox Co.	20	17	2
A. O. Smith Corp.	21	20	4
Machinery	209	159	74
Fairbanks, Morse & Co.	19	16	7
International Harvester Co.	26	15	6
International Business Machines Corp.	12	9	3
Allis-Chalmers Manufacturing Co.	32	27	18
Deere & Co.	13	10	5
Singer Manufacturing Co.	12	8	2
Caterpillar Tractor Co.	7	5	4
Remington Rand, Inc.	15	11	3
National Cash Register Co.	6	4	2
Ingersoll-Rand Co.	12	8	6
Burroughs Corp.	13	12	3
Baldwin-Lima-Hamilton Corp.	23	20	13
Crane Co.	19	14	2
Electrical machinery	205	179	53
General Electric Co.	79	74	17
Westinghouse Electric Corp.	61	54	14
Radio Corp. of America	23	10	6
Electric Auto-Lite Co.	16	15	6
Sylvania Electric Products, Inc.	26	26	10
Transportation equipment	250	204	44
Ford Motor Co.	21	15	3
General Motors Corp.	52	41	9
Chrysler Corp.	22	17	2
Bendix Aviation Corp.	25	25	5
Boeing Airplane Co.	4	4	2
Lockheed Aircraft Corp.	5	2	2
Borg-Warner Corp.	31	28	4
American Motors Corp.	15	11	3
United Aircraft Corp.	9	5	4
Douglas Aircraft Co., Inc.	3	1	1
American Locomotive Co.	17	16	3
Pullman, Inc.	19	16	3
A.C.F. Industries, Inc.	27	23	3

SOURCE: The sources of information are described in Chapter 2.

Industry Group of Company	No. of Co's in Group	Ord-nance & Access.	Food Prod.	To-bac-co Mfs.	Tex-tile Mill Prod.	Appar-el	Lum-ber & Wood Prod.	Furni-ture & Fix-tures	Pa-per Prod.	Print. & Publ.
Food products	12		12		1		2		3	2
Tobacco manufactures	5			5	1	1	1		1	1
Textile mill products	4				4	3			1	
Paper products	8				1		7	1	8	2
Chemicals	14	5	3		3		3	1	2	2
Petroleum	10									
Rubber products	5	3			5	2	1	3	1	
Stone, clay, and glass products	7	1			2		2	2	5	
Primary metals	10	1					1	1		1
Fabricated metal products	5	1					1		2	2
Machinery	13	3	1		1		2	4	2	4
Electrical machinery	5	1			2		1	2	2	2
Transportation equipment	13	5					1	1	1	1
Total no. of companies		20	16	5	20	6	22	15	28	17
Total less primary group companies		20	4	0	16	6	22	15	20	17

E B–2

of Products

Chemicals[a]	Petr. & Coal Prod.	Rubber Prod.	Leather Prod.	Stone, Clay, & Glass Prod.	Primary Metals	Fabr. Metal Prod.	Mach.[b]	Elec. Mach.	Trans. Equip.	Instrument	Misc. Mfg.
7			2	1		3	4		1		1
1						2					
2		1		1		1	1				1
6	1	1		2		1	6	1		1	3
14	3	1		4	6	3	7	2	1	2	3
10	10				1	3	1		1	1	3
4	1	5	2	4	1	4	5	3	5	3	5
4	2	1		7	1	4		1		2	4
5	7			3	10	10	37	5	2		3
		1		2	3	5	5	3	3	3	2
	1			1	8	4	13	7	5	7	3
3				3	4	5	4	5	3	4	4
5	1	2		5	8	8	10	7	13	4	1
61	26	12	4	33	42	53	66	34	34	27	33
47	16	7	4	26	32	48	53	29	21	27	33

SOURCE: Product record described in Chapter 2.
[a] And allied products.
[b] Except electrical machinery.

TAB|
Number of 4-digit Products and Services in
Large Enterprises Gro|

| | | | | | *Industries of* |
Industry Group of Product Additions	Food Products (12)	Tobacco (5)	Textile Mill Products (4)	Paper Products (8)	Chemicals (14)
Farms	2	1	1		
Forestry	1			9	2
Fisheries	1				
Metal mining	1				7
Coal mining					
Crude petroleum and natural gas extraction	1				6
Mining and quarrying of nonmetallic minerals	3		1	3	15
Building construction	1				
Construction other than building			1		5
Railroads	4			2	5
Water transportation	2			1	5
Transportation by air					
Pipeline transportation					3
Services incidental to transportation				1	1
Telecommunications					
Utilities and sanitary services	2	1		7	4
Merchant wholesalers	6	1	3	3	1
Retail trade	3		2		2
Banking	1				1
Credit agencies other than banks			1		1
Insurance	2				1
Real estate	1	1		2	9
Holding and other investment companies			1		1
Misc. business services	2	1	2	2	5
Automobile repair services and garages					
Misc. repair services	1				
Radio and television broadcasting					1
Motion pictures					1
Amusement and recreation services	1				
Medical and other health services					
Educational services				2	
Automotive dealers and gasoline service stations					
Average per company	2.92	1.0	3.0	4.0	5.42

E B-3
PECIFIED NONMANUFACTURING INDUSTRIES FOR 111
PED BY INDUSTRY, 1954

Companies[a]

Petroleum (10)	Rubber Products (5)	Stone, Clay, and glass Products (7)	Primary Metals (10)	Fabricated Metal Products (5)	Machinery (13)	Electrical Machinery (5)	Trans. Equip. (13)	Total (111)
	1							5
		2	2		1			17
								1
		1	21		2			32
		1	7		1			9
24		4	1					36
3		11	17	1	2			56
			5					6
		1	4		2		1	14
7		1	15		2	2	1	39
15		2	8		1		2	36
1								1
15		2	1					21
1			2				3	8
3						3	1	7
4	1	1	16		2	1	2	41
								14
	4	2	6		2			21
					1			3
	1		1	1	3	2	5	15
4	1		2				2	12
12	2	3	7	1	7	2	4	51
2		1	3		1	1	2	12
		1			6		6	25
	1						1	2
				2	1	1	4	9
	2					4		7
								1
						1	1	3
						1		1
						1	2	5
16	6							22
10.70	3.80	4.71	11.80	1.0	2.62	3.80	2.85	4.79

SOURCE: Product record for 111 large enterprises described in Chapter 2.
[a] Numbers in parentheses refer to number of companies in the specified industry.

TABLE B–4
ADDITIONS AND ABANDONMENTS OF PRODUCTS BY 111 LARGE COMPANIES, 1929–1939

	Total Number of Products Added 1929–39	Number of Products Added in Manufacturing Industries	Number of Products Added in Primary 2-digit Industry	Total Number of Products Deleted
Food products	73	52	38	5
Swift & Co.	20	14	8	1
National Distillers Products Corp.	3	2	2	0
Armour & Co.	9	5	3	3
General Foods Corp.	12	8	7	0
Campbell Soup Co.	1	1	1	0
Coca-Cola Co.	0	0	0	0
National Dairy Products Corp.	9	9	8	0
National Biscuit Co.	6	5	5	0
Distillers Corp.-Seagrams	2	1	1	0
Borden Co.	4	4	2	1
Hiram Walker-Gooderham & Worts, Ltd.	2	1	1	0
Corn Products Refining Co.	5	2	0	0
Tobacco manufactures	3	2	1	1
American Tobacco Co.	0	0	0	1
R. J. Reynolds Tobacco Co.	2	1	0	0
Liggett and Myers Tobacco Co.	0	0	0	0
Philip Morris and Co., Ltd., Inc.	1	1	1	0
P. Lorillard Co.	0	0	0	0
Textile mill products	21	18	2	1
United Merchants & Manufacturers, Inc.	6	5	1	1
Cannon Mills Co.	0	0	0	0
Armstrong Cork Co.	13	11	0	0
Pacific Mills	2	2	1	0
Paper products	36	31	22	2
International Paper Co.	10	8	7	1
Crown Zellerbach Corp.	3	3	3	0
St. Regis Paper Co.	3	3	3	1
Kimberly-Clark Corp.	1	1	1	0
West Virginia Pulp & Paper Co.	4	3	2	0
Container Corp. of America	6	4	4	0
Marathon Corp.	3	3	2	0
Minnesota Mining & Manufacturing Co.	6	6	0	0
Chemicals	89	71	53	11
Celanese Corp. of America	0	0	0	0
E. I. du Pont de Nemours & Co.	23	21	13	3

(continued)

TABLE B–4 (continued)

	Total Number of Products Added 1929–39	Number of Products Added in Manufacturing Industries	Number of Products Added in Primary 2-digit Industry	Total Number of Products Deleted
Chemicals (cont.)				
Allied Chemical & Dye Corp.	4	3	3	0
Union Carbide & Carbon Corp.	12	10	7	2
Dow Chemical Co.	13	9	9	1
Procter & Gamble Co.	3	3	3	1
American Cyanamid Co.	8	7	5	0
Olin Mathieson Chemical Corp.	8	4	3	2
Monsanto Chemical Co.	7	6	6	1
Colgate-Palmolive Co.	1	1	1	1
Koppers Co.	3	3	0	0
Merck & Co., Inc.	0	0	0	0
Sherwin-Williams Co.	2	1	1	0
Food Machinery & Chemical Corp.	5	3	2	0
Petroleum	41	24	10	8
Standard Oil Co. (New Jersey)	4	4	1	0
Standard Oil Co. of Indiana	5	2	0	1
Socony-Vacuum Oil Co.	7	5	1	0
Texas Co.	3	2	2	2
Gulf Oil Corp.	7	3	1	2
Standard Oil Co. of California	1	1	1	1
Cities Service Co.	2	2	2	0
Sinclair Oil Corp.	5	3	1	1
Phillips Petroleum Co.	5	2	1	0
Atlantic Refining Co.	2	0	0	1
Rubber products	42	39	5	10
Goodyear Tire & Rubber Co.	12	11	1	2
United States Rubber Co.	11	11	1	4
Firestone Tire & Rubber Co.	8	7	1	4
B. F. Goodrich Co.	6	6	1	0
General Tire & Rubber Co.	5	4	1	0
Stone, clay, and glass products	49	37	13	4
Pittsburgh Plate Glass Co.	13	10	3	0
Owens-Illinois Glass Co.	6	6	2	2
United States Gypsum Co.	10	7	1	0
Johns-Manville Corp.	3	2	1	1
Libbey-Owens-Ford Glass Co.	4	4	2	1
National Gypsum Co.	9	6	3	0
Corning Glass Works	4	2	1	0
Primary metals	59	41	12	14
United States Steel Corp.	8	7	0	2
Bethlehem Steel Corp.	1	0	0	1

(continued)

TABLE B–4 (continued)

	Total Number of Products Added 1929–39	Number of Products Added in Manufacturing Industries	Number of Products Added in Primary 2-digit Industry	Total Number of Products Deleted
Primary metals (cont.)				
Anaconda Copper Mining Co.	2	2	1	0
Kennecott Copper Corp.	4	3	1	3
Aluminum Co. of America	3	2	1	0
Republic Steel Corp.	15	11	3	2
Jones & Laughlin Steel Corp.	4	3	1	3
National Steel Corp.	7	4	1	0
Armco Steel Corp.	9	7	3	0
Youngstown Sheet & Tube Co.	6	2	1	3
Fabricated metal products	14	10	1	2
American Can Co.	0	0	0	0
Continental Can Co., Inc.	5	3	1	0
American Radiator & Standard Sanitary Corp.	1	1	0	2
Babcock & Wilcox Co.	4	4	0	0
A. O. Smith Corp.	4	2	0	0
Machinery	43	35	20	5
Fairbanks, Morse & Co.	4	3	3	2
International Harvester Co.	1	1	1	1
International Business Machines Corp.	9	7	2	0
Allis-Chalmers Manufacturing Co.	7	6	5	0
Deere & Co.	1	1	1	0
Singer Manufacturing Co.	3	2	0	0
Caterpillar Tractor Co.	1	1	1	1
Remington Rand, Inc.	4	3	0	0
National Cash Register Co.	0	0	0	0
Ingersoll-Rand Co.	2	0	0	1
Burroughs Corp.	4	4	2	0
Baldwin-Lima-Hamilton Corp.	6	6	5	0
Crane Co.	1	1	0	0
Electrical machinery	76	61	20	4
General Electric Co.	25	23	7	0
Westinghouse Electric Corp.	16	13	3	3
Radio Corp. of America	16	6	5	0
Electric Auto-Lite Co.	16	16	4	1
Sylvania Electric Products, Inc.	3	3	1	0
Transportation equipment	73	63	10	24
Ford Motor Co.	0	0	0	12
General Motors Corp.	12	9	2	5
Chrysler Corp.	7	6	0	2

(continued)

PRODUCT RECORD

TABLE B–4 (concluded)

	Total Number of Products Added 1929–39	Number of Products Added in Manufacturing Industries	Number of Products Added in Primary 2-digit Industry	Total Number of Products Deleted
Transportation equipment (cont.)				
Bendix Aviation Corp.	16	15	3	0
Boeing Airplane Co.	0	0	0	0
Lockheed Aircraft Corp.	0	0	0	0
Borg-Warner Corp.	20	19	2	1
American Motors Corp.	5	4	0	2
United Aircraft Corp.	2	1	1	2
Douglas Aircraft Co., Inc.	1	0	0	0
American Locomotive Co.	4	4	1	0
Pullman, Inc.	1	0	0	0
A.C.F. Industries, Inc.	5	5	1	0

SOURCE: The sources are described in Chapter 2.

TABLE B–5

ADDITIONS AND ABANDONMENT OF PRODUCTS BY 111 LARGE COMPANIES 1939–50

	Total Number of Products Added 1939–50	Number of Products Added in Manufacturing Industries	Number of Products Added in Primary 2-digit Industry	Total Number of Products Deleted
Food products	50	36	21	27
Swift & Co.	2	1	0	12
National Distillers Products Corp.	7	4	1	1
Armour & Co.	3	3	0	3
General Foods Corp.	10	8	7	2
Campbell Soup Co.	2	2	1	0
Coca-Cola Co.	1	1	0	2
National Dairy Products Corp.	2	1	1	3
National Biscuit Co.	1	1	1	1
Distillers Corp.-Seagrams	0	0	0	0
Borden Co.	11	10	7	1
Hiram Walker-Gooderham & Worts, Ltd.	5	3	2	0
Corn Products Refining Co.	6	2	1	2
Tobacco manufactures	2	1	0	3
American Tobacco Co.	0	0	0	3
R. J. Reynolds Tobacco Co.	2	1	0	0
Liggett & Myers Tobacco Co.	0	0	0	0
Philip Morris & Co., Ltd., Inc.	0	0	0	0
P. Lorillard Co.	0	0	0	0
Textile mill products	22	17	7	4
United Merchants & Manufacturers, Inc.	10	6	4	0
Cannon Mills Co.	0	0	0	2
Armstrong Cork Co.	8	7	0	1
Pacific Mills	4	4	3	1
Paper products	50	38	12	15
International Paper Co.	7	5	3	5
Crown Zellerbach Corp.	5	4	2	0
St. Regis Paper Co.	4	1	1	2
Kimberly-Clark Corp.	3	3	2	1
West Virginia Pulp & Paper Co.	2	2	2	4
Container Corp. of America	2	2	1	1
Marathon Corp.	4	1	1	2
Minnesota Mining & Manufacturing Co.	23	20	0	0
Chemicals	98	76	48	30
Celanese Corp. of America	4	4	1	1
E. I. du Pont de Nemours & Co.	8	8	5	6
Allied Chemical & Dye Corp.	3	2	2	0

(continued)

TABLE B–5 (continued)

	Total Number of Products Added 1939–50	Number of Products Added in Manufacturing Industries	Number of Products Added in Primary 2-digit Industry	Total Number of Products Deleted
Chemicals (cont.)				
Union Carbide & Carbon Corp.	16	11	6	5
Dow Chemical Co.	12	8	6	5
Procter & Gamble Co.	5	4	2	2
American Cyanamid Co.	7	6	6	2
Olin Mathieson Chemical Corp.	7	5	5	3
Monsanto Chemical Co.	3	3	3	1
Colgate-Palmolive Co.	0	0	0	2
Koppers Co.	14	10	5	3
Merck & Co., Inc.	2	2	2	0
Sherwin-Williams Co.	0	0	0	0
Food Machinery & Chemical Corp.	17	13	5	0
Petroleum	57	37	4	16
Standard Oil Co. (New Jersey)	3	3	1	3
Standard Oil Co. of Indiana	11	8	1	3
Socony-Vacuum Oil Co.	3	1	0	3
Texas Co.	8	8	0	1
Gulf Oil Corp.	8	2	1	0
Standard Oil Co. of California	4	2	0	2
Cities Service Co.	8	5	1	1
Sinclair Oil Corp.	2	1	0	1
Phillips Petroleum Co.	7	4	0	1
Atlantic Refining Co.	3	3	0	1
Rubber products	60	53	5	9
Goodyear Tire & Rubber Co.	8	7	1	3
United States Rubber Co.	10	9	1	0
Firestone Tire & Rubber Co.	14	12	1	5
B. F. Goodrich Co.	11	11	1	1
General Tire & Rubber Co.	17	14	1	0
Stone, clay, and glass products	29	25	10	12
Pittsburgh Plate Glass Co.	5	4	1	5
Owens-Illinois Glass Co.	9	6	2	2
United States Gypsum Co.	2	2	1	1
Johns-Manville Corp.	2	2	1	0
Libbey-Owens-Ford Glass Co.	6	6	3	1
National Gypsum Co.	2	2	1	3
Corning Glass Works	3	3	1	0
Primary metals	24	9	5	34
United States Steel Corp.	1	0	0	6
Bethlehem Steel Corp.	1	0	0	2
Anaconda Copper Mining Co.	2	2	2	4

(continued)

TABLE B–5 (continued)

	Total Number of Products Added 1939–50	Number of Products Added in Manufacturing Industries	Number of Products Added in Primary 2-digit Industry	Total Number of Products Deleted
Primary metals (cont.)				
Kennecott Copper Corp.	3	1	1	5
Aluminum Co. of America	12	3	1	1
Republic Steel Corp.	0	0	0	3
Jones & Laughlin Steel Corp.	1	0	0	1
National Steel Corp.	1	1	0	1
Armco Steel Corp.	3	2	1	5
Youngstown Sheet & Tube Co.	0	0	0	6
Fabricated metal products	22	21	3	14
American Can Co.	0	0	0	0
Continental Can Co., Inc.	7	7	0	6
American Radiator & Standard Sanitary Corp.	3	3	0	6
Babcock & Wilcox Co.	0	0	0	0
A. O. Smith Corp.	12	11	3	2
Machinery	42	36	14	15
Fairbanks, Morse & Co.	6	5	1	0
International Harvester Co.	7	3	0	3
International Business Machines Corp.	2	2	2	0
Allis-Chalmers Manufacturing Co.	2	2	0	4
Deere & Co.	2	2	2	2
Singer Manufacturing Co.	4	4	1	4
Caterpillar Tractor Co.	2	2	2	0
Remington Rand, Inc.	2	2	1	1
National Cash Register Co.	0	0	0	0
Ingersoll-Rand Co.	3	2	0	0
Burroughs Corp.	5	5	1	0
Baldwin-Lima-Hamilton Corp.	7	7	4	1
Crane Co.	0	0	0	0
Electrical machinery	63	62	21	12
General Electric Co.	23	23	4	2
Westinghouse Electric Corp.	18	18	6	3
Radio Corp. of America	4	4	3	2
Electric Auto-Lite Co.	2	1	0	5
Sylvania Electric Products, Inc.	16	16	8	0
Transportation equipment	73	63	16	29
Ford Motor Co.	2	1	0	1
General Motors Corp.	17	17	5	6
Chrysler Corp.	9	9	1	1
Bendix Aviation Corp.	9	9	3	6

(continued)

PRODUCT RECORD

TABLE B–5 (concluded)

	Total Number of Products Added 1939–50	Number of Products Added in Manufacturing Industries	Number of Products Added in Primary 2-digit Industry	Total Number of Products Deleted
Transportation equipment (cont.)				
Boeing Airplane Co.	1	1	1	0
Lockheed Aircraft Corp.	4	1	0	0
Borg-Warner Corp.	7	7	2	5
American Motors Corp.	3	1	0	1
United Aircraft Corp.	2	2	2	0
Douglas Aircraft Co., Inc.	2	1	1	1
American Locomotive Co.	3	3	0	0
Pullman, Inc.	11	9	0	3
A.C.F. Industries, Inc.	3	2	1	5

SOURCE: The sources are described in Chapter 2.

TABLE B–6

ADDITIONS AND ABANDONMENTS OF PRODUCTS BY 111 LARGE COMPANIES, 1950–54

	Total Number of Products Added 1950–54	Number of Products Added in Manufacturing Industries	Number of Products Added in Primary 2-digit Industry	Total Number of Products Deleted
Food products	34	29	11	22
Swift & Co.	3	3	0	1
National Distillers Products Corp.	8	7	0	6
Armour & Co.	5	3	0	2
General Foods Corp.	4	4	3	7
Campbell Soup Co.	3	2	2	0
Coca-Cola Co.	0	0	0	0
National Dairy Products Corp.	2	2	1	0
National Biscuit Co.	3	3	3	1
Distillers Corp.-Seagrams	1	0	0	0
Borden Co.	3	3	0	2
Hiram Walker-Gooderham & Worts, Ltd.	1	1	1	0
Corn Products Refining Co.	1	1	1	3
Tobacco manufactures	2	0	0	0
American Tobacco Co.	0	0	0	0
R. J. Reynolds Tobacco Co.	0	0	0	0
Liggett & Myers Tobacco Co.	0	0	0	0
Philip Morris & Co., Ltd., Inc.	2	0	0	0
P. Lorillard Co.	0	0	0	0
Textile mill products	6	3	1	4
United Merchants & Manufacturers, Inc.	1	1	0	0
Cannon Mills Co.	0	0	0	0
Armstrong Cork Co.	5	2	1	2
Pacific Mills	0	0	0	2
Paper products	41	38	11	2
International Paper Co.	3	2	2	0
Crown Zellerbach Corp.	5	4	2	0
St. Regis Paper Co.	4	4	3	0
Kimberly-Clark Corp.	2	2	2	0
West Virginia Pulp & Paper Co.	1	1	1	0
Container Corp. of America	5	5	1	0
Marathon Corp.	6	6	0	0
Minnesota Mining & Manufacturing Co.	15	14	0	2
Chemicals	98	83	40	17
Celanese Corp. of America	7	5	4	1
E. I. du Pont de Nemours & Co.	5	5	2	0
Allied Chemical & Dye Corp.	6	6	6	0

(continued)

TABLE B–6 (continued)

	Total Number of Products Added 1950–54	Number of Products Added in Manufacturing Industries	Number of Products Added in Primary 2-digit Industry	Total Number of Products Deleted
Chemicals (cont.)				
Union Carbide & Carbon Corp.	5	4	2	5
Dow Chemical Co.	3	2	2	2
Procter & Gamble Co.	0	0	0	0
American Cyanamid Co.	2	2	1	0
Olin Mathieson Chemical Corp.	42	34	10	0
Monsanto Chemical Co.	9	8	7	1
Colgate-Palmolive Co.	2	2	2	0
Koppers Co.	4	4	0	5
Merck & Co., Inc.	3	3	2	2
Sherwin-Williams Co.	1	1	0	1
Food Machinery & Chemical Corp.	9	7	2	0
Petroleum	23	21	4	9
Standard Oil Co. (New Jersey)	1	1	0	2
Standard Oil Co. of Indiana	1	1	0	0
Socony-Vacuum Oil Co.	0	0	0	1
Texas Co.	0	0	0	2
Gulf Oil Corp.	3	3	1	0
Standard Oil Co. of California	3	3	0	1
Cities Service Co.	0	0	0	2
Sinclair Oil Corp.	6	5	0	0
Phillips Petroleum Co.	4	4	0	0
Atlantic Refining Co.	5	4	3	1
Rubber products	57	54	6	8
Goodyear Tire & Rubber Co.	8	8	2	3
United States Rubber Co.	18	18	1	1
Firestone Tire & Rubber Co.	9	7	0	2
B. F. Goodrich Co.	7	6	2	2
General Tire & Rubber Co.	15	15	1	0
Stone, clay, and glass products	19	16	5	7
Pittsburgh Plate Glass Co.	5	3	1	0
Owens-Illinois Glass Co.	1	1	1	2
United States Gypsum Co.	1	0	0	0
Johns-Manville Corp.	1	1	0	1
Libbey-Owens-Ford Glass Co.	6	6	1	4
National Gypsum Co.	3	3	1	0
Corning Glass Works	2	2	1	0
Primary metals	32	22	5	11
United States Steel Corp.	11	11	1	0
Bethlehem Steel Corp.	2	2	0	0
Anaconda Copper Mining Co.	4	2	1	0

(continued)

TABLE B–6 (continued)

	Total Number of Products Added 1950–54	Number of Products Added in Manufacturing Industries	Number of Products Added in Primary 2-digit Industry	Total Number of Products Deleted
Primary metals (cont.)				
Kennecott Copper Corp.	2	2	1	2
Aluminum Co. of America	3	1	0	6
Republic Steel Corp.	5	3	1	1
Jones & Laughlin Steel Corp.	0	0	0	2
National Steel Corp.	1	0	0	0
Armco Steel Corp.	4	1	1	0
Youngstown Sheet & Tube Co.	0	0	0	0
Fabricated metal products	16	14	2	5
American Can Co.	0	0	0	0
Continental Can Co., Inc.	7	5	0	2
American Radiator & Standard Sanitary Corp.	3	3	1	2
Babcock & Wilcox Co.	2	2	0	0
A. O. Smith Corp.	4	4	1	1
Machinery	42	33	18	4
Fairbanks, Morse & Co.	5	5	3	2
International Harvester Co.	4	3	3	0
International Business Machines Corp.	2	1	1	1
Allis-Chalmers Manufacturing Co.	4	3	2	0
Deere & Co.	2	2	1	0
Singer Manufacturing Co.	0	0	0	0
Caterpillar Tractor Co.	2	1	1	0
Remington Rand, Inc.	1	1	0	1
National Cash Register Co.	1	1	1	0
Ingersoll-Rand Co.	0	0	0	0
Burroughs Corp.	5	5	2	0
Baldwin-Lima-Hamilton Corp.	8	6	4	0
Crane Co.	8	5	0	0
Electrical machinery	42	38	12	1
General Electric Co.	12	10	3	0
Westinghouse Electric Corp.	14	12	3	0
Radio Corp. of America	4	4	2	1
Electric Auto-Lite Co.	0	0	0	0
Sylvania Electric Products, Inc.	12	12	4	0
Transportation equipment	85	80	22	13
Ford Motor Co.	2	2	2	3
General Motors Corp.	21	20	4	1
Chrysler Corp.	4	3	2	3
Bendix Aviation Corp.	3	3	0	0

(continued)

TABLE B–6 (concluded)

	Total Number of Products Added 1950–54	Number of Products Added in Manufacturing Industries	Number of Products Added in Primary 2-digit Industry	Total Number of Products Deleted
Transportation equipment (cont.)				
Boeing Airplane Co.	2	2	0	0
Lockheed Aircraft Corp.	1	1	1	1
Borg-Warner Corp.	17	16	4	1
American Motors Corp.	8	8	2	0
United Aircraft Corp.	3	3	2	0
Douglas Aircraft Co., Inc.	1	0	0	1
American Locomotive Co.	9	9	2	0
Pullman, Inc.	3	3	2	1
A.C.F. Industries, Inc.	11	10	1	2

SOURCE: The sources are described in Chapter 2.

TABL
Number of Companies that Added Products in
Enterpri

		Industries of								
Industry Group of Company	No. of Co's in Group	Ord-nance & Access.	Food Prod.	To-bac-co Mfs.	Tex-tile Mill Prod.	Appar-el	Lum-ber & Wood Prod.	Furni-ture & Fix-tures	Pa-per Prod.	Print. & Publ.
Food products	12		10				1		1	
Tobacco manufactures	5			1						
Textile mill products	4				2	2			1	
Paper products	8								8	
Chemicals	14	1			1					
Petroleum	10									
Rubber products	5				4		1	1	1	
Stone, clay, and glass products	7								3	1
Primary metals	10						1	1		
Fabricated metal products	5							1	1	1
Machinery	13							2		
Electrical machinery	5	1			1			2	1	1
Transportation equipment	13	1								
Total no. of co's. adding products		3	10	1	8	2	3	7	16	3
Total less co's. whose primary activities are in the industry		3	0	0	6	2	3	7	8	3

B–7
SPECIFIED MANUFACTURING INDUSTRIES, 111 LARGE
s, 1929–39

Product Additions

Chemicals[a]	Petr. & Coal Prod.	Rubber Prod.	Leather Prod.	Stone, Clay, & Glass Prod.	Primary Metals	Fabr. Metal Prod.	Mach.[b]	Elec. Mach.	Trans. Equip.	Instrument	Misc. Mfg.
5							1				
						1					
2		1		1		1	1				1
3		1		1						1	
10		1		4	2	1	2		1	1	1
4	8					1	2			1	1
4		5		3		1	1	3	3	2	2
3	1			7		4	2				1
				1	8	6	2	1			
				1	1	1	2			1	
						1	8	4		2	2
			1	1	2	4	2	5	1	3	3
2		1		1	3	5	6	4	6	2	
33	9	9	1	20	16	26	29	17	11	13	11
23	1	4	1	13	8	25	21	12	5	13	11

SOURCE: Product record described in Chapter 2.
[a] And allied products.
[b] Except electrical machinery.

TA
NUMBER OF COMPANIES THAT ADDED PRODUCTS
ENTERPR

									Industries of	
Industry Group of Company	No. of Co's in Group	Ord- nance & Access.	Food Prod.	To- bac- co Mfs.	Tex- tile Mill Prod.	Appar- el	Lum- ber & Wood Prod.	Furni- ture & Fix- tures	Pa- per Prod.	Print. & Publ.
Food products	12		8				2			1
Tobacco manufactures	5									
Textile mill products	4				2	2			1	
Paper products	8								8	1
Chemicals	14	2	1		2				1	
Petroleum	10									
Rubber products	5	3			3			1		
Stone, clay, and glass products	7						1	2	3	
Primary metals	10									
Fabricated metal products	5	1							1	
Machinery	13	3					1			1
Electrical machinery	5	2						2		1
Transportation equipment	13	2								
Total no. of co's. adding products		13	9	0	7	2	4	5	14	4
Total less co's. whose primary activities are in the industry		13	1	0	5	2	4	5	6	4

, B–8
SPECIFIED MANUFACTURING INDUSTRIES, 111 LARGE
s, 1939–50

Product Additions

Chemicals[a]	Petr. & Coal Prod.	Rubber Prod.	Leather Prod.	Stone, Clay, & Glass Prod.	Primary Metals	Fabr. Metal Prod.	Mach.[b]	Elec. Mach.	Trans. Equip.	Instrument	Misc. Mfg.
4						1			1		
1											
2				1			1				
1	1	1		2			3	1		1	2
12	1			1	1	1	4	1	1	1	1
10	4				1	1					
5		5	1	2	1	3	1	1	5	1	3
3	1	1		7						1	
1					4	3					
1						1	2	1			2
					2	2	9	4	1	3	
1				2	2	3	2	4	3	2	2
1	1	1		2	3	5	6	3	8	2	
42	8	8	1	17	14	20	28	15	19	11	10
30	4	3	1	10	10	19	19	11	11	11	10

SOURCE: Product record described in Chapter 2.
[a] And allied products.
[b] Except electrical machinery.

TAB▮
NUMBER OF COMPANIES THAT ADDED PRODUCTS I▮
ENTERPR▮

		Industries of								
Industry Group of Company	No. of Co's in Group	Ord- nance & Access.	Food Prod.	To- bac- co Mfs.	Tex- tile Mill Prod.	Appar- el	Lum- ber & Wood Prod.	Furni- ture & Fix- tures	Pa- per Prod.	Print. & Publ.
Food products	12		6						1	
Tobacco manufactures	5									
Textile mill products	4				1					
Paper products	8				1		2	1	7	1
Chemicals	14	2	2		3		1	1	1	1
Petroleum	10									
Rubber products	5	1			4	2	1	1		
Stone, clay, and glass products	7	1			2				1	
Primary metals	10	1								
Fabricated metal products	5								1	1
Machinery	13							1		
Electrical machinery	5						1			
Transportation equipment	13	4						1		
Total no. of co's. adding products		9	8	0	11	2	5	5	11	3
Total less co's. whose primary activities are in the industry		9	2	0	10	2	5	5	4	3

B–9
Specified Manufacturing Industries, 111 Large
s, 1950–54

Product Additions

Chemicals[a]	Petr. & Coal Prod.	Rubber Prod.	Leather Prod.	Stone, Clay, & Glass Prod.	Primary Metals	Fabr. Metal Prod.	Mach.[b]	Elec. Mach.	Trans. Equip.	Instrument	Misc. Mfg.
5											
1											1
3		1		1			2				1
10	2			1	1	1	4	1	2	1	2
6	2								1	1	
2	1	4	1			1	2	1	5	2	3
2				5				1		1	1
		1		2	5	2	1	2	1		2
		1			1	2	1	1	3		1
1					1		9	2	2	2	2
2				1	2	2	4	4	1	1	1
2					3	3	7	4	10	2	1
34	5	7	1	10	13	11	30	16	25	10	15
24	3	3	1	5	8	9	21	12	15	10	15

Source: Product record described in Chapter 2.
[a] And allied products.
[b] Except electrical machinery.

TA▮

NUMBER OF COMPANIES THAT ABANDONED PRODUCTS
ENTERPI▮

Industry Group of Company	No. of Co's in Group	Industries of								
		Ord- nance & Access.	Food Prod.	To- bac- co Mfs.	Tex- tile Mill Prod.	Appar- el	Lum- ber & Wood Prod.	Furni- ture & Fix- tures	Pa- per Prod.	Print. & Publ.
Food products	12	2								
Tobacco manufactures	5									
Textile mill products	4				1					
Paper products	8								2	
Chemicals	14								1	1
Petroleum	10									
Rubber products	5				2					
Stone, clay, and glass products	7									
Primary metals	10									
Fabricated metal products	5									
Machinery	13									
Electrical machinery	5									
Transportation equipment	13						1			
Total no. of co's. deleting products		0	2	0	3	0	1	0	3	1
Total less co's. whose primary activities are in the industry		0	0	0	2	0	1	0	1	1

E B–10
SPECIFIED MANUFACTURING INDUSTRIES, 111 LARGE
ES, 1929–39

Product Abandonments

Chemicals[a]	Petr. & Coal Prod.	Rubber Prod.	Leather Prod.	Stone, Clay, & Glass Prod.	Primary Metals	Fabr. Metal Prod.	Mach.[b]	Elec. Mach.	Trans. Equip.	Instrument	Misc. Mfg.
						1					
4				1		1					
1	3					4					
1		1	1								1
1				1							
1					2				1		
							1		1		
							2		1		
				1		1	1	1			
1	1			1		1		1	3	1	
9	4	1	1	4	2	8	4	2	6	1	1
5	1	0	1	3	0	8	2	1	3	1	1

SOURCE: Product record described in Chapter 2.
[a] And allied products.
[b] Except electrical machinery.

Industry Group of Company	No. of Co's in Group	Industries of								
		Ord-nance & Access.	Food Prod.	To-bac-co Mfs.	Tex-tile Mill Prod.	Appar-el	Lum-ber & Wood Prod.	Furni-ture & Fix-tures	Pa-per Prod.	Print. & Publ.
Food products	12		6				1		1	
Tobacco manufactures	5				1				1	
Textile mill products	4				3					
Paper products	8						1		4	
Chemicals	14									
Petroleum	10						1			
Rubber products	5									
Stone, clay, and glass products	7									
Primary metals	10							1		
Fabricated metal products	5						2		1	
Machinery	13									
Electrical machinery	5									
Transportation equipment	13						1			
Total no. of co's. deleting products		0	6	0	4	0	6	1	7	0
Total less co's. whose primary activities are in the industry		0	0	0	1	0	6	1	3	0

E B–11
IN SPECIFIED MANUFACTURING INDUSTRIES, 111 LARGE
1939–50

Product Abandonments

Chemicals[a]	Petr. & Coal Prod.	Rubber Prod.	Leather Prod.	Stone, Clay, & Glass Prod.	Primary Metals	Fabr. Metal Prod.	Mach.[b]	Elec. Mach.	Trans. Equip.	Instrument	Misc. Mfg.
1							1				
2										1	
5				2	3	1			1		
4	1					2	1			1	1
								1	1	2	1
2				1		2	1				
1	1			1	2	2	2		2		
	1				2	1					
							6	1	1		
			1					1	1		1
2					1	1	4	2	1	1	
17	3	0	1	4	8	9	15	5	7	5	3
12	2	0	1	3	6	8	9	4	6	5	3

SOURCE: Product record described in Chapter 2.
[a] And allied products.
[b] Except electrical machinery.

TABL
NUMBER OF COMPANIES THAT ABANDONED PROD
111 LARGE ENTER

										Industries of
Industry Group of Company	No. of Co's in Group	Ord- nance & Access.	Food Prod.	To- bac- co Mfs.	Tex- tile Mill Prod.	Appar- el	Lum- ber & Wood Prod.	Furni- ture & Fix- tures	Pa- per Prod.	Print. & Publ.
Food products	12		5			1				
Tobacco manufactures	5									
Textile mill products	4				1					
Paper products	8									
Chemicals	14				1					1
Petroleum	10									
Rubber products	5				1					
Stone, clay, and glass products	7									1
Primary metals	10									
Fabricated metal products	5									
Machinery	13									
Electrical machinery	5									
Transportation equipment	13						1			
Total no. of co's. deleting products		0	5	0	3	1	1	0	0	2
Total less co's. whose primary activities are in the industry		0	0	0	2	1	1	0	0	2

E B–12
UCTS IN SPECIFIED MANUFACTURING INDUSTRIES,
PRISES, 1950–54

Product Abandonments

Chemicals[a]	Petr. & Coal Prod.	Rubber Prod.	Leather Prod.	Stone, Clay, & Glass Prod.	Primary Metals	Fabr. Metal Prod.	Mach.[b]	Elec. Mach.	Trans. Equip.	Instrument	Misc. Mfg.
3			1								
1				1							
		1		1							
4	1				1	1	1				2
1						1					
		1						1	1		
1				2							1
											1
1					1	1					1
							1	1			
								1			
		1		1		1	4		2	1	
11	1	3	1	5	2	4	7	2	3	1	5
7	1	2	1	3	2	3	6	1	1	1	5

SOURCE: Product record described in Chapter 2.
[a] And allied products.
[b] Except electrical machinery.

APPENDIX C

Census Data for Multiestablishment Companies
with 2,500 and over Employees

TABLE C-1

AVERAGE COMPANY EMPLOYMENT FOR 711 MULTIESTABLISHMENT COMPANIES
SEGREGATED BY INDUSTRY AND EMPLOYMENT SIZE CLASS, 1954[a]

Industry	Average Employment									
	4 cos.	4 cos.	12 cos.	10 cos.	10 cos.	10 cos.	10 cos.	10 cos.	10 cos.	10 cos.
Food and kindred products	52,667	21,589	10,602	8,143	6,857	5,219	3,919	3,061	2,708(8)	
Textile mill products	27,961	13,320	8,372	5,166	3,939	3,308	2,869	2,626(6)		
Paper and allied products	15,985	10,093	6,058	3,608	2,900(9)					
Chemicals and allied products	60,560	21,244	11,056	6,425	4,820	3,479	2,756			
Products of petroleum and coal	44,149	28,989	11,890	3,754(7)						
Rubber products	50,427	7,158	2,985(4)							
Stone, clay, and glass products	19,655	11,331	5,317							
Primary metal industries	124,521	33,444	17,459	6,566	3,967	3,128				
Fabricated metal products	24,921	8,817	4,439	2,828(7)						
Machinery (except electrical)	41,078	23,154	11,502	7,054	5,402	4,612	3,786	3,398	2,930	2,615(8)
Electrical machinery	127,056	18,726	7,732	4,937	3,612	2,793				
Transportation equipment	206,366	54,129	25,164	11,847	6,959	4,099	2,912(4)			
Instruments	23,743	7,845	3,862(10)							
Mining	12,212	5,481	3,535(10)							
Retail grocers	56,883	13,389	4,427							
Other retail	84,246	26,638	10,464	5,217	3,957	2,852				
Drug and variety stores	44,498	16,265	5,783(8)							
Restaurants and bars	6,527	3,467	2,745(6)							
Merchant wholesalers	8,555									

SOURCE: Special census tabulation.

[a] All multiestablishment companies in the specified industries with 2,500 and over employees are included (except ten companies for which information could not be shown because of disclosure of individual company information). Numbers in parentheses indicate exceptions to number of companies as given in column head. The first class consists of the largest four, the second of the next four, etc.

TABLE C-2

AVERAGE COMPANY EMPLOYMENT IN MANUFACTURING FOR 589 MULTIESTABLISHMENT MANUFACTURING COMPANIES, SEGREGATED BY INDUSTRY AND EMPLOYMENT SIZE CLASS, 1954[a]

Industry	Average Employment									
	4 cos.	4 cos.	12 cos.	10 cos.	10 cos.	10 cos.	10 cos.	10 cos.	10 cos.	10 cos.
Food and kindred products	39,783	16,164	8,719	6,361	5,131	4,059	3,089	2,502	1,923(8)	
Textile mill products	26,764	11,003	7,786	4,881	3,766	3,168	2,730	2,440(6)		
Paper and allied products	14,597	8,923	5,577	3,416	2,726(9)					
Chemicals and allied products	50,012	17,603	9,103	4,955	3,613	2,668	1,678			
Products of petroleum and coal	16,426	9,137	3,721	999(7)						
Rubber products	41,285	6,312	2,685(4)							
Stone, clay, and glass products	15,252	10,124	4,748							
Primary metal industries	96,437	27,924	14,652	5,662	3,504	2,564				
Fabricated metal products	22,058	7,901	4,161	2,390(7)						
Machinery (except electrical)	30,644	15,143	9,335	5,866	4,625	3,957	3,366	2,936	2,595	1,665(8)
Electrical machinery	99,681	16,989	7,046	4,779	3,472	2,519				
Transportation equipment	184,235	53,789	23,937	11,042	6,217	3,658	2,726(4)			
Instruments	20,673	6,521	3,622(10)							

SOURCE: Special census tabulation.

[a] All multiestablishment companies in the specified industries with *total* employment of 2,500 and over are included (except six companies for which information could not be shown because of disclosure of individual company information). Numbers in parentheses indicate exceptions to number of companies as given in column head. The first class consists of the largest four, the second of the next four, etc.

TABLE C-3

AVERAGE NONPRIMARY EMPLOYMENT FOR 711 MULTIESTABLISHMENT COMPANIES
GROUPED BY INDUSTRY AND EMPLOYMENT SIZE, 1954[a]

Industry	Average Employment									
	4 cos.	4 cos.	12 cos.	10 cos.	10 cos.	10 cos.	10 cos.	10 cos.	10 cos.	10 cos.
Food and kindred products	10,691	6,196	1,463	643	1,015	1,482	705	288	918(8)	
Textile mill products	8,472	5,768	2,570	1,023	693	906	580	412(6)		
Paper and allied products	5,882	4,148	2,532	855	989(9)					
Chemicals and allied products	37,426	10,027	4,555	1,632	1,518	1,486	1,022			
Products of petroleum and coal	33,730	21,452	8,192	1,768(7)						
Rubber products	30,357	3,679	701(4)							
Stone, clay, and glass products	6,388	2,867	1,473							
Primary metal industries	53,420	17,324	6,285	2,784	770	710				
Fabricated metal products	9,694	3,439	1,980	478(7)						
Machinery (except electrical)	19,471	4,399	3,600	2,546	897	1,250	1,041	635	460	706(8)
Electrical machinery	63,274	6,067	1,229	642	585	528				
Transportation equipment	48,083	11,529	7,121	4,443	1,106	889	874(4)			
Instruments	11,990	2,612	911(10)							
Mining	4,714	981	544(10)							
Retail grocers	6,143	1,004	212							
Other retail	16,091	1,465	900	323	135	180				
Drug and variety stores	311	98	237(8)							
Restaurants and bars	849	49	228(6)							
Merchant wholesalers	4,466									

SOURCE: Special census tabulation.

[a] All multiestablishment companies in the specified industries with 2,500 and over employees are included (except ten companies for which information could not be shown because of disclosure of individual company information). Numbers in parentheses indicate exceptions to number of companies as given in column head. The first class consists of the largest four, the second of the next four, etc.

TABLE C-4
AVERAGE CENTRAL OFFICE EMPLOYMENT FOR 711 MULTIESTABLISHMENT COMPANIES GROUPED BY INDUSTRY AND EMPLOYMENT SIZE, 1954[a]

Industry	Average Employment									
	4 cos.	4 cos.	12 cos.	10 cos.	10 cos.	10 cos.	10 cos.	10 cos.	10 cos.	10 cos.
Food and kindred products	4,213	1,339	816	513	782	412	114	150	357(8)	
Textile mill products	615	506	193	98	91	79	86	76(6)		
Paper and allied products	160	464	333	112	84(9)					
Chemicals and allied products	6,783	1,615	475	700	275	268	174			
Products of petroleum and coal	12,538	7,856	2,925	450(7)						
Rubber products	2,521	236	137(4)							
Stone, clay, and glass products	1,474	499	213	263	274	84				
Primary metal industries	5,479	2,174	681	141(7)						
Fabricated metal products	1,520	705	115	127						
Machinery (except electrical)	2,506	1,320	506	127	297	106	87	251	94	42(8)
Electrical machinery	8,767	974	294	30	54	176				
Transportation equipment	13,207	325	478	509	104	111	131(4)			
Instruments	427	173	8(10)							
Mining	806	312	265(10)							
Retail grocers	10,978	1,888	673							
Other retail	4,212	320	471	235	91	14				
Drug and variety stores	1,468	1,041	601(8)							
Restaurants and bars	281	218								
Merchant wholesalers	205		107(6)							

SOURCE: Special census tabulation.

[a] All multiestablishment companies in the specified industries with 2,500 and over employees are included (except ten companies for which information could not be shown because of disclosure of individual company information). Numbers in parentheses indicate exceptions to number of companies as given in column head. The first class consists of the largest four, the second of the next four, etc.

APPENDIX D

Industry Data

THIS appendix describes the sources and methods used to develop information on an industry basis for a number of variables which contribute in differing degree toward explaining patterns of diversification and integration. The tables are generally limited to variables whose sources are diverse or methods of computation relatively complex, or for which basic information is unpublished and hence not readily available. Data developed in other National Bureau studies are, of course, not reproduced here. Measures for "explanatory variables" were developed only for manufacturing industries.

In addition to those concerned with "explanatory variables," three tables derived from U.S. Bureau of the Census, *Company Statistics: 1954 Censuses of Business, Manufacturing, Mineral Industries,* Washington 1958, are presented.

In some instances, particularly for data used in conjunction with diversification measures derived from *Company Statistics,* information for explanatory variables was on an industry basis somewhat different in scope from that used for measures of diversification. The comparability, however, was deemed to be close enough to render the errors not crucial to the findings.

Growth

For the periods 1929-39 and 1939-54, measures of growth were obtained for totals of 223 and 271 industries, respectively. The levels of detail in classification of these industries are given below:

	1929–39	*1939–54*
4-digit industries	150	232
3-digit industries	22	22
Combinations of two or more 4-digit industries	34	11
Combinations of two or more 3-digit industries	17	6

Measures of growth were also obtained for eighteen major manufacturing groups and one combination of two such groups[1] for the periods 1929–39, 1939–54, 1929–37, and 1937–53.

Three measures of growth were used: (1) changes in output indexes, (2) changes in deflated value of product, and (3) changes in number of

---

[1] "Professional, scientific, and controlling instruments" was combined with "miscellaneous manufacturing industries." A measure for "ordnance and accessories" was not available.

production workers. These were expressed as a percentage of initial-year values.

The measures based on changes in output were obtained from output indexes developed by Kendrick.[2] The terminal year of these indexes is 1953. To obtain measures of growth for the period 1939–54, changes in output for 1939–53 were projected to 1954 on the basis of the ratio of value added in 1954 to that in 1953 (adjusted for price changes) for the relevant 2-digit groups in which the individual 3- or 4-digit industries fell.

In all cases for which 1937, 1939, 1952, and 1953 index numbers were given, the higher for each set of adjacent years was used to approximate more closely cyclical peaks in output. This was designed to eliminate the effect of excess capacity on measures of growth.[3] The breakdown of industries for which growth during the two periods was measured on the basis of relative changes in output follows:

	1929–39	*1939–54*
4-digit industries	103	25
3-digit industries	21	20
Combinations of two or more 4-digit industries	31	9
Combinations of two or more 3-digit industries	17	6

In addition, the growth of the major (2-digit) groups was measured on this basis for the periods 1929–39 and 1939–53.

The number of industries for which growth could be measured according to available output indexes was insufficient for our purposes, since it provided no measure of growth for broad sectors of the industrial spectrum. Accordingly, other measures of growth were used.

Value-of-product data were obtained from the 1929, 1939, and 1954 Censuses of Manufactures for industries which remained comparable throughout each of the two periods 1929–39 and 1939–54. The data were adjusted for price changes on the basis of those BLS wholesale price indexes which most closely approximated, in terms of commodities to which the indexes referred, the composition of census industries. Measures

---

[2] John W. Kendrick, *Productivity Trends in the United States*, Princeton University Press for National Bureau of Economic Research, 1961. The data were obtained from worksheets developed for this study and may show minor differences from data eventually published.

[3] The 1939 index number was not available for SIC industries 3331, 3332, and 3333, thus necessitating the use of 1937 index numbers.

of growth for the two periods were obtained on this basis for the following
industry classifications:

	1929–39	1939–54
4-digit industries	47	142
3-digit industries	1	2
Combinations of two or more 4-digit industries	3	0

The reclassification of census industries and the formation of new industries
for the 1947 Census of Manufactures still left serious gaps in the measures
of growth, particularly for chemicals, electrical machinery, and primary
metals. However, the 1947 Census of Manufactures shows 1939 census data
for number of establishments and number of production workers according
to the 1947 Census classification. Thus a third measure of growth, namely,
the percentage change in number of production workers, was used for some
industries for the period 1939–54. The data were adjusted for changes in
productivity on the basis of productivity indexes (output/employment)
developed by Kendrick.[4] The value of the index number for 1953 (the
terminal year of Kendrick's study) was used for 1954. A breakdown by
major industry groups of the 4-digit industries for which growth was
measured on this basis is shown below:

	Industries
Chemicals	11
Stone, clay, and glass products	4
Primary metals	8
Machinery	20
Electrical machinery	11
Transportation equipment	5
Instruments	6

	Combination Industries
Transportation equipment	2
Instruments	2
Total	69

For twelve of the sixty-five industries, data on production workers were
not available in the Preliminary Report of the 1954 Census of Manufactures.[5] The number of production workers in 1954 was estimated for
these industries on the basis of either 1952 or 1953 (obtained from the

[4] *Productivity Trends.*
[5] These measures were developed prior to the publication of the 1954 Census.

Annual Surveys of Manufactures). To bring the 1952 or 1953 statistic to a 1954 basis, an adjustment was made according to the change from 1952, or 1953, to 1954 (at the relevant 3-digit level) in price-deflated value added.

Growth measured by percentage change in value of product was compared with change in the number of production workers for a sample of thirty-five industries. The coefficient of rank correlation was .78, indicating at least a tolerable degree of similarity in results.

Productivity

Changes in labor productivity in 171 industries during 1929–37 and forty-six during 1937–53 were computed from productivity indexes (output/man-hours) developed by Kendrick.[6] These changes were expressed as a percentage of initial-year values. A breakdown follows:

	1929–37	1937–53
4-digit industries	93	15
3-digit industries	26	18
Combinations of two or more 4-digit industries	39	4
Combinations of two or more 3-digit industries	13	9

Percentage change in labor productivity as well as in total factor productivity (capital and labor) was computed also from the same source for eighteen major manufacturing groups and one combination of two such groups.[7] Because indexes for 1939 included only 65 of the 171 industries, 1937 was used. For the 1937–53 period, the 1953 productivity nipex number was estimated for 21 of the 46 industries. Indexes for these 21 industries were available only to 1950, 1951, or 1952. The extrapolation was made on the basis of the change in productivity at the relevant 2-digit level from 1950, 1951, or 1952 (the last year for which the index was available at a 4- or 3-digit level) to 1953.

Average Size of Plant

Measures of average plant size in 1947 were obtained for 444 4-digit manufacturing industries and twenty major manufacturing groups. Measures for 1935 were obtained for two major groups and a total of 233 individual industries at the following levels of detail:

    202 4-digit industries

---

[6] *Productivity Trends.*
[7] See note 1.

16 3-digit industries

13 Combinations of two or more 4-digit industries

2 Combinations of two or more 3-digit industries

For each industry, average size of plant was computed by dividing the number of employees in establishments with twenty or more employees by the total number of such establishments. The data were obtained from the Census of Manufactures for 1947, and the "Supplement on Wage Earners in Establishments Classified According to Number of Wage Earners, by Industry," Census of Manufactures, 1935. Data on establishments with twenty or fewer employees were omitted to obtain a better indication of differences among industries in the most efficient plant size. The most efficient size of plant is probably more closely related to average plant size if the large numbers of very small, low-efficiency establishments, likely to exist in some industries, are excluded. The Spearman coefficients of rank correlation for average plant size, using all establishments, and average plant size derived from data excluding establishments with twenty or fewer employees, were .95 for the fifty industries with highest average plant size and .74 for the twenty-five with lowest size.

Measures of average size of plant in 1947 were also computed for manufacturing industry groupings used in *Company Statistics*. The two bodies of data (information on plant size and data from *Company Statistics*) were made comparable by combining 1947 census industries into *Company Statistics* industries. Data for all establishments, including those with fewer than twenty employees, were used.

Average Size of Firm

Measures of average firm size in 1947 were obtained for 101 *Statistics of Income* "minor industries,"[8] a level of classification roughly comparable to that of the 3-digit SIC code. For each industry, average size of firm was computed by dividing total corporate assets by number of corporate returns. In addition, based on published data from *Statistics of Income*, average firm size in 1948 was computed for eighteen major manufacturing groups and one combination of two such groups.[9] Corporations with total assets of $50,000 and under were omitted from the 1948 computations. This was done with the objective of eliminating the effect of low-efficiency small firms which may be present in some industries, but the adjustment was not made for other years. Average firm size (total assets/number of

---

[8] Internal Revenue Service, *Source Book for Statistics of Income.*

[9] See note 1.

firms) for 1938 was also computed for sixteen major manufacturing groups and one combination of two groups.

Technical Personnel Ratio

Measures of the number of technical personnel (engineers, surveyors, and chemists) per 10,000 of all personnel were developed by Nestor Terleckyj at the 3- and 4-digit levels for 68 industries in 1930, 54 in 1940, and 53 in 1950, as well as for 19 major manufacturing groups for 1930, 1940, and 1950.[10] The individual ratios for three major groups[11] in 1930 were estimated on the assumption that they were the same relative to their 1940 values as for the three groups combined. The data were drawn from the Census of Population for 1930, 1940, and 1950.

Concentration Ratios

Concentration ratios for 1947, based on the ratio of value of product contributed by the four leading producers in an industry to value of product for the industry, were obtained for 350 4-digit manufacturing industries from U.S. Federal Trade Commission, *Changes in Concentration in Manufacturing, 1935–1947 and 1950, 1954*, Table 1. This source also indicates 1935 concentration ratios for some industries. When these data were used in connection with information on product additions for 1929–39, 1935 concentration ratios were substituted for 1947 values for a few industries in which a sizable change in concentration occurred between 1935 and 1947.

Concentration indexes developed by Stigler[12] were available at the *Statistics of Income* "minor industry" level (roughly comparable to the SIC 3-digit level). For each 3-digit industry, the concentration index is a weighted average, using value added as weights, of the component 4-digit-industry concentration ratios.

Cyclical Variability[13]

Measures of cyclical variability were developed for those production series which are included in the Federal Reserve System's Index of Industrial Production.[14] Measures for two periods were developed. The first period was from 1923 through 1941, and the second from 1947 through

---

[10] Nestor Terleckyj, unpublished study of factors affecting changes in productivity.

[11] "Fabricated metal products," "machinery," and "electrical machinery."

[12] George J. Stigler "The Mobility of Capital in Manufacturing Industries," MS., NBER.

[13] These measures were prepared by the author jointly with Nestor Terleckyj and Jerome Strong.

[14] The data were obtained from the *Federal Reserve Bulletin* for August 1940, October 1943, December 1953, January 1956, and July 1957.

1955. For some series only one period could be covered; for others, both. When series were combined to conform with SIC industries, weights used in the Index of Industrial Production were used.

Measures of Cyclical Amplitude

All turning points in the relevant period were marked off and identified as troughs and peaks. The first and last years of the periods were treated as peaks or troughs even though they may not have constituted turning points. A turning point was defined as a change in direction in annual data.

The periods were then divided into trough-to-trough cycles and measures of amplitude computed in the following way:

1. The changes from trough to peak were divided by number of years in the relevant expansion phase of the cycle. Similarly, peak-to-trough changes were divided by the number of years in the relevant cyclical contraction.

2. The average annual changes of the two phases were added and then divided by the value of the index at the peak. Thus average annual changes were expressed as a percentage of the peak value, rendering measures for different cycles comparable. The use of the number of years in each phase of the specific cycle as a denominator eliminates much of the effect of differences in trends in particular industries.

3. If at the beginning or at the end of the series only one phase was left over, the average annual change of this phase was divided by the adjacent peak value and multiplied by two to make it comparable with measures for full cycles.

4. All amplitude measures for individual cycles were added and divided by the number of cycles times two. The resulting average was thus interpreted as representing an annual cyclical percentage change (relative to peak) found in the cycles of the relevant period.

Measure of Cyclical Frequency

To measure the frequency of cyclical fluctuations, the turning points within the period were counted and their number divided by the number of years in the period covered by data for particular indexes.

The Level-of-Industry Detail

The level-of-industry detail for each explanatory variable used in Chapter 7 to analyze product additions is shown in Table D-1 for 1929–39, 1939–50, and 1950–54.

TABLE D–1
THE CLASSIFICATION OF PRODUCT CHANGES
ACCORDING TO EIGHT VARIABLES

Variable	Period	No. of Product Additions Classified at: 3- and 4-digit Levels	2-digit Levels	Total No. of Product Additions Classified	Unclassified	Total No. of Product Additions
Concentration	1929–1939	467	0	467	17	484
ratio	1939–1950	449	0	449	25	474
	1950–1954	390	0	390	41	431
Amplitude of	1929–1939	111	278	389	95	484
cyclical	1939–1950	324	116	440	34	474
fluctuations	1950–1954	256	137	393	38	431
Frequency of	1929–1939	84	307	391	93	484
cyclical	1939–1950	330	114	444	30	474
fluctuations	1950–1954	264	137	401	30	431
Technical	1929–1939	185	290	475	9	484
personnel	1939–1950	162	283	445	29	474
ratio	1950–1954	178	223	401	31	431
Average size	1929–1939	395	6	401	83	484
of plant	1939–1950	317	0	317	157	474
	1950–1954	267	0	267	164	431
Productivity	1929–1939	233	240	473	11	484
change	1939–1950	118	333	451	23	474
	1950–1954	106	293	399	32	431
Growth	1929–1939	319	28	347	137	484
	1939–1950	365	0	365	109	474
	1950–1954	323	0	323	108	431
Average size	1939–1950	399	0	399	75	474
of firm	1950–1954	356	0	356	75	431

SOURCES: Described in text of Appendix D.

TABLE D–2

THE GROWTH OF 3- AND 4-DIGIT INDUSTRIES, 1929–39

SIC. Industry Number	Industry	Percentage Growth 1929–39	Measure Used[a]
3741	Locomotives and parts	−7.06	2
3492	Safes and vaults	−6.91	1
3294	Graphite, ground and refined	−6.32	1
374	Locomotives and parts and railroad and street cars	−6.18	2
3985	Fireworks	−5.38	1
3742	Railroad and street cars	−5.28	2
3493	Steel springs	−5.12	1
2445	Cooperage	−4.91	2
3799	Carriage, wagons, sleighs, etc.	−4.63	2
3192	Saddlery, harnesses and whips	−4.62	2
3393	Welded and heavy-riveted pipe	−4.56	2
2863	Gum naval stores	−4.52	1
3576	Scales and balances	−4.44	1
3522	Agricultural equip. (except tractors)	−4.44	2
2491	Wood preserving	−4.40	1
3441	Structural and ornamental products	−4.32	2
3332	Primary lead	−4.17[b]	2
3161	Luggage	−3.98	1
3442	Metal doors, sash, frames and trim	−3.89	1
325+ 3297	Clay products, n.e.c.	−3.60	2
2444	Wooden boxes (except cigar boxes)	−3.49	1
3931	Pianos	−3.48	2
2991	Fuel briquets and packaged fuel	−3.43	2
3391	Iron and steel forgings	−3.35	1
3444	Sheet metal work	−3.32	2
2863	Gum naval stores	−3.29	2
3296	Sand-lime products	−3.28	2
371	Motor vehicles and equipment	−3.22	2
2425	Excelsior mills	−3.19	2
2383	Suspenders and garters	−3.09	2
2091	Baking powder, leavening compounds	−3.09	2
2493	Mirror frames and picture frames	−3.07	1
333	Primary nonferrous metals	−2.83	2
c	Lumber mill products	−2.81	2
242+ 243	Lumber and timber mill products, n.e.c. planing mill products, excelsior	−2.81	2
3241	Hydraulic Cement	−2.77	2
3421+ 3422	Cutlery and edge tools	−2.75	2
2882	Linseed oil mills	−2.69	2
3293	Gaskets and asbestos insulation	−2.65	2
Part of 3321	Cast-iron pipe	−2.64	2
2296	Linen goods	−2.51	2
2097	Manufactured ice	−2.49	2
3583	Sewing machines	−2.48	1
3121	Industrial leather belting	−2.45	2
2131	Chewing and smoking tobacco	−2.44	2

(continued)

TABLE D-2 (continued)

SIC. Industry Number	Industry	Percentage Growth 1929–39	Measure Used[a]
3311 + 3313	Blast furnaces and electrometallurgical products	−2.40	2
Part of 3341	Secondary nonferrous metals, nonprecious	−2.43[b]	2
2043	Cereal preparations	−2.38	2
3424 + 3425 + 3423	Hand tools, n.e.c., files, hand saws and saw blades	−2.37	2
3424	Files	−2.27	1
3495	Screw machine products and wood screws	−2.25	1
2121	Cigars	−2.21	2
2443	Cigar boxes	−2.11	2
3494 + 3495	Bolts, nuts, washers and screw machine products	−2.09	2
326	Pottery	−2.09	2
c	Primary nonferrous metals	−2.08	2
3466	Galvanizing and other hot dip coating	−2.08	1
2441 + 2442	Basket and rattan and willowware, not including furniture	−2.01	1
2325	Men's and boys' cloth hats and caps	−1.98	2
3331	Primary copper	−1.96[b]	2
3425	Saws	−1.95	1
283	Drugs and medicine (not including drug grinding)	−1.94	1
3021	Rubber footwear	−1.92	2
3494	Bolts, nuts and rivets	−1.92	1
c	Brooms	−1.79	2
2062	Cane sugar refining	−1.73	2
3572 + 3571	Computing and related machines and typewriters	−1.69	2
3011	Tires and inner tubes	−1.65	2
c	Primary iron and steel	−1.63	2
2881	Cottonseed oil mills	−1.59	2
3953	Hand stamps, stencils, and brands	−1.53	1
3982	Cork products	−1.52	1
3872	Watchcases	−1.48	1
3471	Lighting fixtures	−1.48	1
2651	Envelopes	−1.47	1
3333	Primary zinc	−1.39[b]	2
3423	Hand tools (except edge tools, machine tools, files and saws)	−1.38	1
3543	Machine-tool accessories and machinists' precision tools	−1.38	1
293	Coke oven products (beehive and coke-oven)	−1.31	2
2492	Lasts and related products	−1.30	1
2693	Wallpaper	−1.30	1
c	Fabricated iron and steel	−1.16	2
3943	Children's vehicles	−1.13	2
3552	Textile machinery	−1.05	1
2388	Handkerchiefs	−0.99	2

(continued)

TABLE D–2 (continued)

SIC. Industry Number	Industry	Percentage Growth 1929–39	Measure Used[a]
315	Leather gloves and mittens	−0.95	2
3392	Wire drawing	−0.92	2
3432 + 3439	Oil burners and heating and cooking apparatus	−0.91	2
2271	Wool carpets, rugs, and carpet yarn	−0.87	2
c	Fabricated nonferrous	−0.86	2
2041 + 2045	Flour and meal and blended and prepared flour	−0.78	2
2298	Cordage and twine	−0.72	2
3265	China decorating for the trade	−0.63	1
227	Carpets, rugs and other floor coverings	−0.51	2
2381 + 2382	Fabric and combination dress and work gloves	−0.53	2
2898	Salt	−0.39	2
2094	Corn products	−0.25	2
2826	Explosives	−0.22	2
2051	Baked goods and other bakery products	−0.09	2
324 + 327	Cement, lime and concrete, wall plaster and board	−0.04	2
2562	Window shades	0.05	2
2073	Chewing gum	0.08	1
205	Bakery products	0.15	2
Part of 3497	Tin and other foils	0.15	2
3481	Nails and spikes	0.23	2
c	Foundry and machine shop products	0.23[b]	2
2897	Insecticides and fungicides and foundry supplies	0.34	1
204	Grainmill products	0.42	2
3995	Umbrellas, parasols and canes	0.45[b]	2
205 + 207	Bakery products and confectionery and related products	0.46	2
2851 + 2852	Paints, varnishes, lacquers and color pigments	0.46	1
3988	Morticians' goods	0.48	2
3489	Wirework, n.e.c.	0.57	2
2223 + 2224 + 2233	Cotton goods	0.58	2
c	Allied chemical substances	0.58	2
287	Fertilizers	0.59[b]	2
2274	Hardsurface floor coverings	0.63	2
2515	Mattresses and bed springs	0.67	2
1951	Small arms	0.71[b]	2
2281	Fur felt hats and hat bodies	0.83	2
285	Paints and allied products	0.90[b]	2
231 + 232	Men's and boys' outerwear	0.92	2
2861 + 2862	Hardwood and softwood distillation	0.93	2

(continued)

TABLE D–2 (continued)

SIC. Industry Number	Industry	Percentage Growth 1929–39	Measure Used[a]
2254	Knit underwear mills	0.93	2
2992	Lubricating oils and greases not made in petroleum refineries	0.95	1
3981	Brooms and brushes	0.96	1
373	Ships and boats	1.02	2
2327+ 2328+ 2311+ 2329+ 2312+ 2386	Men's and boys' suits and coats, separate trousers and work shirts, boys' work clothes, leather and sheep-lined clothing	1.16	2
2321	Men's dress shirts and nightwear	1.19	2
206	Sugar	1.19	2
3111	Leather tanning and finishing	1.21[b]	2
2052	Biscuits, crackers, and pretzels	1.27	2
2031+ 2032	Canned seafood and cured fish	1.28	2
2071	Confectionery products	1.31	2
2021	Creamery butter	1.52	2
2096	Vinegar and cider	1.52	2
2295	Coated fabrics except rubberized	1.56	2
314	Footwear (except rubber)	1.57	2
2024	Ice cream and ices	1.58	2
221	Woolen and worsted manufactures	1.61	2
2095	Flavoring extracts	1.68	1
3468	Electroplating	1.77	1
3274	Lime	1.82	2
3491	Steel barrels, kegs and drums	1.93	1
Part of 3341	Secondary nonferrous metals, precious	1.94	2
302+ 303+ 309	Rubber footwear, reclaimed rubber, rubber, n.e.c.	2.06	2
2044	Rice cleaning and polishing	2.09	2
202	Dairy products	2.11	2
2253+ 2255	Knit outerwear mills and knit glove mills	2.20	2
2612	Paper and board mills	2.35	2
2865+ 2843	Natural tanning and dyeing materials, sulfonated oils and assistants	2.36	2
3949	Sporting and athletic goods	2.38	2
3496	Collapsible tubes	2.55	2
2841	Soap and glycerine	2.57	2
3292	Asbestos products	2.60[b]	2
2093	Oleomargarine	2.61[b]	2
2952	Roofing felts and coatings	2.70	2
2911	Petroleum refining	2.75	2
3963	Buttons	2.76	2
261	Paper and pulp mills	2.77	2
2098	Macaroni and spaghetti	2.79	2

(continued)

TABLE D-2 (continued)

SIC. Industry Number	Industry	Percentage Growth 1929–39	Measure Used[a]
2111 + 2121	Cigarettes and cigars	2.80	2
3231	Products of purchased glass	2.92[b]	2
3952	Lead pencils and crayon	2.96[b]	2
2042	Prepared animal feeds	2.99	2
3431	Metal plumbing fixtures	2.99	2
3842	Surgical and orthopedic appliances and related products	3.03	1
225	Knitting mills	3.26	2
3461 + 3462 + 3463 + 3465	Stamped and pressed metal products; enameling, japanning and lacquering	3.46	1
2891	Printing ink	3.48	1
3581	Domestic laundry equipment	3.51	1
303 + 309	Reclaimed rubber and rubber products, n.e.c.	3.56	2
3871	Watches and clocks	3.92[b]	2
2251 + 2252	Full-fashioned and seamless hosiery mills	3.73	2
2896	Compressed and liquified gases	3.85	2
2661	Paper bags	3.85	1
2894	Glue and gelatin	3.87	2
2886	Grease and tallow	3.88	2
2895	Carbon black	3.99	2
c	Wall plaster and board	4.00	2
2893	Perfumes, cosmetics, and other toilet preparations	4.02	1
3955	Carbon paper and inked ribbons	4.10	1
Part of 2297	Jute goods	4.34[b]	2
2111	Cigarettes	4.40	2
2023	Concentrated milk	4.44	2
233 + 236 + 234	Women's clothing	4.46	2
2072	Chocolate and cocoa products	4.54	2
2842	Cleaning and polishing preparations and blackings, stains and dressings	4.56	1
2611	Pulp mills	4.68	2
264–9	Converted paper products	4.71	2
2022	Natural cheese	4.73	2
2092	Shortenings and cooking oils	4.78[b]	2
3861	Photographic equipment	4.84	2
2063	Beet sugar	4.90	2
Part of 3999	Fire extinguishers	5.00	2
3271	Concrete products	5.25	2
2292	Lace goods	5.35[b]	2
203	Canning, preserving and freezing	5.43	2
2899	Chemicals, n.e.c.	5.47	2

(continued)

TABLE D-2 (concluded)

SIC. Industry Number	Industry	Percentage Growth 1929–39	Measure Used[a]
2283	Straw hats	5.84[b]	2
2256+ 2259	Knit fabric mills and knitting mills, n.e.c.	5.86	2
2034+ 2033+ 2035+ 2037	Canned fruits and vegetables, dried and dehydrated fruits and vegetables, pickled fruits and vegetables, frozen foods	5.89	2
c	Aluminum manufactures	6.06	2
3211+ 3221+ 3229	Glass	6.26[b]	2
3411	Tin cans and other tinwear	6.52	2
2222+ 2225+ 2234	Silk and rayon goods	7.52	2
281+ 282	Industrial chemicals	7.61	2
2081	Bottled soft drinks	8.14	2
2011–13	Meat packing, wholesale and prepared meats	8.70	2
c	Chemicals, n.e.c.; rayons and gases	8.77	2
3951	Pens and mechanical pencils	12.52	2
3964	Needles, pins, hooks, and eyes	13.50	1
2061	Raw cane sugar	14.45	2
2083	Malt	14.50[b]	2
3295	Minerals and earths	15.75	1
2892	Essential oils	16.87	1
2951	Paving mixtures and blocks	17.33	1
372	Aircraft	18.59	2
2282	Wool felt hats and hat bodies	20.80	2
2825	Synthetic fibers	24.58	2
208	Beverages	63.78	2
2084	Wines and brandy	193.8	2
2085	Distilled liquors, except brandy	1,059.6[b]	2

NOTE: For fuller explanation of sources and methods, see text of Appendix D.

[a] Measure 1 equals relative change in value of product (deflated for price changes). Source: 1929 and 1939 Censuses of Manufactures. Measure 2 equals relative change in output. Source: Kendrick's output indexes (preliminary worksheets).

[b] Growth for period 1929–37.

[c] Composition differs somewhat from industry classes in the SIC Code so that no three- or four-digit industries, alone or in combination, contain precisely the activities covered by the indicated categories in the table.

TABLE D-3
THE GROWTH OF 3- AND 4-DIGIT INDUSTRIES, 1939–54

SIC. Industry Number	Industry	Percentage Growth 1939–54	1939–53	Measure Used[a]
2383	Suspenders and garters	−69.6		1
2443	Cigar boxes	−64.9		1
2216	Finishing wool textiles	−60.7		1
2331	Blouses	−59.5		1
2284	Hatter's furs	−58.6		1
2328	Work shirts	−57.2		1
2445	Cooperage	−56.9		1
2492	Lasts and related products	−54.9		1
2097	Manufactured ice	−49.7		1
2131	Tobacco (chewing and smoking) and snuff	−40.6		1
2371	Fur goods	−38.6		1
2693	Wallpaper	−31.3		1
2442	Rattan and willow ware	−27.1		1
3568	Mechanical stokers	−25.7[b]		3
3461	Vitreous-enameled products	−25.6		1
2061	Cane sugar (except refining)	−21.4		1
3296	Sand-lime products	−20.4	−20.5	2
2021	Creamery butter	−19.8	−17.7	2
2931	Beehive coke ovens	−18.0		1
2085	Distilled liquor (except brandy)	−17.8[c]	−15.9[d]	2
2251	Full-fashioned hosiery mills	−14.6		1
2032	Cured fish	−11.5		1
3982	Cork products	−9.2		1
2326	Hat and cap materials	−9.0		1
315	Leather gloves and mittens	−4.6		1
2493	Mirror and picture frames	−2.4		1
2041 + 2045	Flour and meal and blended and prepared flour	1.5	1.3	2
3111	Leather tanning and finishing	1.7[c]	1.7[d]	2
221	Woolen and worsted manufactures	1.8	2.1	2
c	Other leather products	4.2	4.2	2
2425	Excelsior mills	5.2		1
2323	Men's and boys' neckwear	5.7		1
2562	Window shades	5.9		1
2063	Beet sugar	6.8	6.0	2
3131	Footwear cut stock	6.8		1
2051	Bread and other bakery products	9.1		1
314	Footwear (except rubber)	11.4[e]	11.4[e]	2
3843	Dental equipment and supplies	12.1		1
2251 + 2252	Full-fashioned and seamless hosiery mills	12.4[e]	14.0[e]	2
2388	Handkerchiefs	13.4		1
2292	Lace goods	13.6		1
2821	Cyclic (coal-tar) crudes	14.3		3
2121	Cigars	15.1	15.7	2
2043	Cereal preparations	18.0		1
2091	Baking powder, yeast, and other leavening compounds	18.3		1

(continued)

TABLE D-3 (continued)

SIC. Industry Number	Industry	Percentage Growth 1939–54	1939–53	Measure Used[a]
3424	Files	18.7		1
2041	Flour and other grain mill products	19.1		1
231+ 232	Men's and boys' outerwear	22.2	23.7	2
2223+ 2224+ 2233	Cotton goods	22.6	25.6	2
206	Sugar	24.0	21.4	2
2033	Canning and preserving, except fish	27.7		1
314	Footwear (except rubber)	28.1		1
3586	Measuring and dispensing pumps	30.0		1
295	Paving and roofing materials	30.7		1
2861	Hardwood distillation	36.4[b]		3
2071	Candy and other confectionery products	37.0		1
2081	Bottled soft drinks	38.4		1
3263	Earthenware food utensils	39.5		1
2252	Seamless hosiery mills	40.2		1
2062	Cane-sugar refining	41.5	37.1	2
3262	Vitreous china food utensils	−42.5		1
205	Bakery products	43.0	38.4[e]	2
3981	Brooms and brushes	43.8		1
205+ 207	Bakery products and confectionery and related products	43.9[e]	39.2[e]	2
3631	Insulated wire and cable	44.7		1
3121	Industrial leather belting	44.7		1
242+ 243	Sawmills, veneer, and cooperage stock mills, planing mills, plywood mills, excelsior mills	46.7	50.5	2
2271	Wool carpets, rugs, and carpet yarn	50.2	56.9	2
3351	Copper rolling and drawing	51.3		3
2031	Canned seafood	51.6		1
2222+ 2225+ 2234	Silk and rayon goods	51.7	58.6	2
2841	Soap and glycerine	52.0	53.6	2
3572	Typewriters	52.3		3
233+ 234+ 236	Women's clothing	53.2[e]	56.8[e]	2
225	Knitting mills	53.3	60.4	2
3192	Saddlery, harnesses, and whips	53.6		1
3255	Clay refractories	54.0		1
2098	Macaroni, spaghetti, vermicelli, etc.	54.0		1
2011–3	Meat packing, wholesale and prepared meats	54.3	48.5	2
2851	Paints, varnishes and lacquers	55.1		3
3251	Brick and hollow tile	55.2		1
3297+ 325	Clay products, n.e.c.	57.2[e]	57.6[e]	2

(continued)

TABLE D–3 (continued)

SIC. Industry Number	Industry	Percentage Growth 1939–54	Percentage Growth 1939–53	Measure Used[a]
3871	Watches and clocks	57.2		3
2082	Malt liquors	57.3		1
2083	Malt	58.1		1
3872	Watchcases	58.5		1
3851	Ophthalmic goods	59.5		1
2094	Corn products	60.3		1
2052	Biscuits, crackers, and pretzels	60.9		1
3955	Carbon paper and inked ribbons	64.4		1
293	Coke oven products (beehive and by-product)	65.4	70.0	2
3312	Steel works and rolling mills	65.6		3
2831	Biological products	66.7[b]		3
2334	Dresses, dozen price	68.9		1
2023	Concentrated milk	71.2	63.6	2
202	Dairy products	71.7	64.1	2
2111 + 2121	Cigarettes and cigars	73.7	76.7	2
2261	Finishing textiles, except wool	75.0		1
2951	Paving mixtures and blocks	76.3		1
3254	Sewer pipe	76.8		1
3552	Textile machinery	77.2		1
204	Grain mill products	79.2	70.7	2
3717 + 3713	Motor vehicles and parts	79.4		3
2072	Chocolate and cocoa products	79.9		1
2952	Roofing felts and coating	82.9[e]	88.7[e]	2
227	Carpets, rugs and other floor coverings	84.3	95.6	2
2035	Pickles and sauces	84.4		1
301	Tires and inner tubes	84.9	91.5	2
2651	Envelopes	85.3		1
2881	Cottonseed oil mills	86.4		1
3211	Flat glass	87.6		1
3171	Handbags and purses	88.9		1
2022	Natural cheese	89.6	80.1	2
2322	Men's and boys' underwear	90.0		1
264–269	Converted paper products	90.9	89.5	2
2612	Paper and board mills	91.4	90.0	2
3741	Locomotives and parts	91.9		3
3211 + 3221 + 3229	Glass	92.8[c]	93.5[d]	2
3953	Handstamps and stencils	93.6		1
3323	Steel foundries	93.6		1
2893	Toilet preparations	94.1		1
3842	Surgical appliances and supplies	94.3		1
3274	Lime	96.7[f]	97.5[f]	2
373	Ships and boats	96.8[e]	102.7[e]	2
2896	Compressed and liquified gases	97.4		1
285	Paints and allied products	98.2[c]	101.2[d]	2

(continued)

TABLE D-3 (continued)

SIC. Industry Number	Industry	Percentage Growth 1939–54	1939–53	Measure Used[a]
3322	Malleable iron foundries	100.4		1
3496	Collapsible tubes	100.7		1
208	Beverages	101.3	90.5	2
2342	Corsets and allied garments	103.3		1
2852	Inorganic color pigments	104.9		1
261	Paper and pulp mills	105.2	103.5	2
2911	Petroleum refining	105.8	113.1	2
3949	Sporting and athletic goods	106.9		1
2321	Men's dress shirts and nightwear	108.2		1
2111	Cigarettes	109.0[e]	113.4[e]	2
333	Primary nonferrous metals	109.6	129.4	2
2843	Sulfonated oils and assistants	110.0		3
3411	Tin cans and other tinwear	110.4	116.8	2
3467	Engraving on metal	111.5		1
3583	Sewing machines	111.5		1
2674	Fibre cane, tubes, drums, etc.	111.9		1
3253	Floor and wall tile	113.8[b]		3
3264	Porcelain electrical supplies	113.8[b]		3
203	Canning, preserving and freezing	113.8	101.7	2
3651	Electric lamps	114.2		1
3241	Hydraulic cement	114.8	115.8	2
2325	Men's and boys' cloth hats	115.4		1
3491	Metal barrels, drums, and pails	116.5		1
3691	Storage batteries	117.6		1
2515	Mattresses and bedsprings	118.0		1
3984	Candles	119.2		1
371	Motor vehicles and equipment	120.1	127.5	2
3751	Autos, motorcycles, and bicycles	120.3	127.7	2
3293	Gaskets and asbestos insulation	120.9		1
3555	Printing-trades machinery	120.9		1
3341	Secondary nonferrous metals	121.2		3
2561	Window and door screens	121.4		1
3576	Scales and balances	123.2		1
3221	Glass containers	123.8		1
2886	Grease and tallow	123.9		1
2274	Hard surface floor coverings	125.2	142.0	2
2293	Padding and upholstery filling	125.5		1
3425	Hand saws and saw blades	125.7		1
3021	Rubber footwear	125.9		1
3172	Small leather goods	127.6		1
3272	Gypsum products	127.8[b]		3
2093	Oleomargarine	128.6		1
2024	Ice cream and ices	128.7	115.0	2
3489	Wirework, n.e.c.	129.8		1
3742	Railroad and street cars	130.1	138.1	2
3532	Oil field machinery and tools	133.3[g]		3
3521	Tractors	135.5		3
3311	Blast furnaces	136.5		3
2611	Pulp mills	142.4	140.1	2

(continued)

TABLE D–3 (continued)

SIC. Industry Number	Industry	Percentage Growth 1939–54	1939–53	Measure Used[a]
2894	Glue and gelatin	143.7		1
3229	Pressed and blown glass, n.e.c.	144.7		1
3985	Fireworks and pyrotechnics	145.0		1
287	Fertilizers	145.2[c]	149.7[c]	2
3551	Food products machinery	145.5		3
3493	Steel springs	145.8		1
2812	Alkalies and chlorine	145.9		3
3471	Lighting fixtures	153.5		1
2387	Belts	153.6		1
3161	Luggage	155.7		1
3582	Laundry and dry-cleaning machinery	161.5		3
2361	Children's dresses	161.8		1
3541	Machine tools	162.3		1
2671	Paperboard boxes	165.6		1
3444	Sheet-metal work	165.7		1
3522	Farm machinery	168.4		3
2044	Rice cleaning and polishing	170.0		1
3231	Products of purchased glass	179.7[g]		3
2363	Children's coats	185.9		1
374	Locomotive and parts, railroads and street cars	187.7[e]	199.2[e]	2
3562	Elevators and escalators	187.9		3
2534	Public-building furniture	191.6		1
2042	Prepared animal feeds	192.2		1
3261	Vitreous plumbing fixtures	195.0		1
3561	Pumps and compressors	196.3		3
3554	Paper industries machinery	198.0		1
2691	Die-cut paper and board	202.7		1
3566	Power-transmission equipment	204.1		3
3441	Structural and ornamental work	209.4		1
3614	Motors and generators	216.5		3
2826	Explosives	217.7		1
3321	Gray-iron foundries	225.3		1
2842	Cleaning and polishing products	232.2		1
3861	Photographic equipment and supplies	240.1		3
3723 + 3729	Aircraft propellers and equipment	241.1		3
3612	Carbon and graphite products	242.4		1
2895	Carbon black	242.5		1
3392	Wire drawing	243.1		1
3391	Iron and steel forgings	244.2		3
2661	Paper bags	244.4		1
2641	Paper coating and glazing	248.2		1
3841	Surgical and medical instruments	256.5		3
3492	Safes and vaults	258.3		1
3542	Metalworking machinery	261.9		3
3466	Galvanizing	266.7		1
3553	Woodworking machinery	269.7		3
3031	Reclaimed rubber	279.0		1

(continued)

TABLE D–3 (concluded)

SIC. Industry Number	Industry	Percentage Growth 1939–54	1939–53	Measure Used[a]
3641	Engine electrical equipment	280.2		3
3585	Refrigeration machinery	280.6		3
2887	Fatty acids	283.3[b]		3
3361	Nonferrous foundries	289.5		3
3271	Concrete products	293.0	295.3	2
3571	Computing and related machines	297.4		3
3715	Truck trailers	303.2		3
281 + 282	Industrial chemicals	309.2	318.8	2
3611	Wiring devices and supplies	313.9		3
3519	Internal combustion engines	324.4		1
3099	Rubber industries, n.e.c.	330.3		1
3465	Enameling and lacquering	332.1		1
3821	Mechanical measuring instruments	333.1		3
3565	Industrial trucks and tractors	338.2		3
2825	Synthetic fibers	345.2	355.9	2
2694	Pulp goods, pressed and molded	354.5		1
3352	Aluminum rolling and drawing	355.0		3
3621	Electrical appliances	361.0		3
3531	Construction and mining machinery	361.6[g]		3
2853	Whiting and fillers	366.7		3
3613	Electrical measuring instruments	372.8		1
3313	Electrometallurgical products	373.9		3
3581	Domestic laundry equipment	376.3		1
3443	Boiler shop products	378.1		1
3564	Blowers and fans	397.4		3
3664	Telephone and telegraph equipment	404.3		3
3468	Plating and polishing	427.7		1
3615	Transformers	434.3		3
3563	Conveyors	460.4		3
3831	Optical instruments and lenses	465.4		3
3567	Industrial furnaces and ovens	466.7		3
3617	Electrical welding apparatus	489.5		3
3616	Electrical distribution and control apparatus	519.3		3
2823	Plastic materials	522.0		3
3811	Scientific instruments	528.2		3
3663	Phonograph records	650.0		3
3971	Plastic products, n.e.c.	656.4		1
3661	Radios and related products	680.2		3
3511	Steam engines and turbines	681.6		3
2834	Pharmaceutical preparations	682.3[g]		3
2273	Carpets and rugs, except wool	693.5		1
2045	Flour mixes	741.9		1
3662	Electron tubes	753.5		3
3716	Automobile trailers	783.3		3
2883	Soybean oil mills	1,028.0		1
3721	Aircraft	1,314.3		3
372	Aircraft	1,543.1	1,638.1	2
3722	Aircraft engines	1,879.6		3
2833	Medicinal chemicals	2,259.1[g]		3

Notes to Table D-3

For fuller explanation of sources and methods, see text of this appendix.

ᵃ Measure 1 equals relative change in value of product (deflated for price changes). Source: 1939 and 1954 censuses of manufactures. Measure 2 equals relative change in output. Source: Kendrick's output indexes (preliminary worksheets). Measure 3 equals relative change in number of production workers (deflated for productivity changes). Source: 1939 and 1954 Censuses of Manufactures.

ᵇ 1954 number of production workers estimated from 1952 number of production workers.

ᶜ 1937–54.

ᵈ 1937–53.

ᵉ 1952 output index number used.

ᶠ 1953 output index number estimated.

ᵍ 1954 number of production workers estimated from 1953 number of production workers.

TABLE D–4
AVERAGE ASSET SIZE OF FIRMS IN 101 MANUFACTURING INDUSTRIES, 1947

Industry	Average Size of Firm (assets in thousands of dollars)
Bakery products	469.90
Confectionery	838.31
Canning	789.61
Meat products	1,387.23
Grain mill products	857.59
Cereal preparations	3,147.77
Dairy products	636.77
Sugar	6,887.92
Miscellaneous foods	640.82
Breweries	2,386.59
Distilled and rectified liquor	4,715.02
Wines	482.85
Nonalcoholic beverage	199.25
Tobacco	8,783.94
Cotton manufactures	2,291.70
Woolen and worsted	1,352.91
Rayon and silk	1,516.57
Knit goods	423.20
Hats, excluding cloth and millinery	412.43
Carpets	2,142.33
Dyeing and finishing	521.93
Miscellaneous textile	814.08
Men's clothing	353.68
Women's clothing	138.95
Furs	75.61
Millinery	50.65
Miscellaneous apparel	175.05
Tanning, currying and finishing	885.81
Footwear, excluding rubber	505.59
Miscellaneous leather	130.49
Logging camps and miscellaneous	631.94
Planing mills	380.05
Wooden containers	295.04
Furniture	297.20
Partitions and fixtures	141.66
Miscellaneous furniture	268.15
Pulp, paper and paperboard	5,137.76
Miscellaneous paper	572.55
Newspapers	553.63
Periodicals	427.24
Books	363.88
Commercial printing and lithographing	192.92
Miscellaneous printing	143.24
Paints and varnishes	779.54
Industrial chemicals	5,160.56
Soap and glycerin	1,951.42
Drugs and toilet preparations	492.63
Oils	2,151.55
Rayon	32,601.56

(continued)

TABLE D-4 (continued)

Industry	Average Size of Firm (assets in thousands of dollars)
Plastic materials	509.12
Fertilizers	976.82
Miscellaneous chemicals	586.31
Petroleum refining	38,153.14
Miscellaneous petroleum and coal	2,433.89
Tires and tubes	27,325.60
Miscellaneous rubber	624.96
Pottery and porcelain	519.66
Concrete	314.45
Cut stone	139.04
Structural clay	447.85
Glass	1,041.38
Cement	4,250.23
Miscellaneous stone, clay, and glass	1,133.64
Blast furnaces and rolling mills	37,672.22
Structural steel	426.64
Tin cans	5,698.83
Hand tools, cutlery, etc.	665.20
Heating apparatus	885.22
Miscellaneous iron and steel	608.48
Nonferrous metals, basic	5,421.96
Miscellaneous nonferrous	415.51
Electrical equipment for public utilities, etc.	1,896.65
Automotive electrical equipment	1,369.00
Communications equipment	2,012.03
Electrical appliances	696.58
Miscellaneous electrical equipment	1,374.43
Engines and turbines	2,814.56
Agricultural machinery	2,902.87
Special industry machinery	850.54
General industry machinery	647.02
Metalworking machinery	529.27
Construction and mining machinery	1,821.55
Office and store machinery	2,617.85
Household and service industry machinery	1,544.67
Miscellaneous machinery	1,201.34
Motor vehicles, including truck bodies and industrial trailers	10,356.90
Motor vehicle parts and accessories	1,627.20
Railroad and railway equipment	8,309.94
Aircraft and parts	5,019.51
Ship and boat building	878.35
Motorcycles and bicycles	904.21
Miscellaneous transport equipment	159.22
Firearms	1,442.33
Ammunition	13,426.80
Tanks	90.33
Sighting and fire control equipment	1,930.13
Ordnance n.e.c.	661.14
Clocks and watches	1,355.38

(continued)

TABLE D–4 (concluded)

Industry	Average Size of Firm (assets in thousands of dollars)
Jewelry, excluding costume	258.50
Matches	3,959.90
Miscellaneous manufacturing	275.69

Source: Internal Revenue Service, *Source Book for Statistics of Income*, 1947.

TABLE D–5
AMPLITUDE OF CYCLICAL FLUCTUATIONS; 1923–41 AND 1947–55

	1923–41	1947–55
All Manufacturing	14.97	7.06
Food products	3.85	1.70
Meat products[a]	8.09	5.19
Dairy products	4.91	3.35
Butter	3.03	8.26
Cheese	6.57	4.97
Concentrated milk	3.82	2.99
Ice cream	6.72	4.13
Canned and frozen foods	—	4.86
Grain mill products	—	1.94
Wheat flour	2.32	4.07
Cereals and feeds	—	2.90
Sugar	—	8.66
Cane sugar (meltings)	5.35	7.08
Beet sugar	—	12.98
Confectionery	—	2.36
Miscellaneous foods[a]	6.29	1.53
Beverages	—	2.67
Soft drinks	—	5.81
Alcoholic beverages[b]	8.49	3.27
Malt liquors[b]	7.50	2.10
Liquor distilling	—	20.38
Whiskey[b]	21.19	—
Other distilled spirits	14.86	—
Rectified spirits	10.44	—
Liquor bottling	—	7.11
Tobacco manufactures	3.57	2.16
Cigarettes	5.74	3.11
Cigars	3.44	2.47
Tobacco and snuff	1.45	—
Textile mill products	12.56	8.15
Textile fabrics	12.44	—
Cotton fabrics (consumption)	12.82	7.52
Rayon and silk (deliveries)	9.88	—
Silk (and nylon after 1940)	6.76	—
Rayon	15.08	—
Woolen textiles	16.64	12.18
Apparel wool[a]	19.03	9.60
Woolen yarn	12.62	—
Worsted yarn	21.61	—
Wool fabrics	17.11	12.09
Knit goods	—	5.06
Hosiery	—	3.16
Full fashioned	—	3.36
Seamless	—	4.90
Knit garments	—	8.44
Floor coverings	—	11.81
Carpets[a]	22.10	15.86
Cotton and synthetic fabrics	—	8.02
Synthetic fabrics	—	12.71
Fabric finishing	—	5.71

(continued)

TABLE D–5 (continued)

	1923–41	1947–55
Apparel and fabricated textiles	—	4.51
Men's outerwear	—	6.17
Suits and coats	—	11.14
Suits	—	11.38
Outercoats	—	12.91
Shirts and work clothing	—	6.42
Women's outerwear	—	4.26
Suits and coats	—	7.51
Miscellaneous apparel and allied products	—	5.04
Lumber and products	—	7.87
Lumber	9.05	7.09
Millwork and plywood	—	9.89
Millwork	—	10.47
Softwood plywood	—	8.61
Wooden containers	—	5.22
Furniture and fixtures	12.47	8.55
Household furniture	—	9.92
Fixtures and office furniture	—	6.13
Paper and products	9.30	5.93
Pulp and paper	9.10	6.78
Wood pulp	8.77	6.32
Paper and board	9.16	6.61
Printing paper	7.90	5.34
Fine paper	11.13	7.13
Tissue (sanitary)	7.54	6.16
Paperboard	10.09	8.16
Wrapping	7.40	—
Newsprint production	4.61	—
Coarse paper	—	7.26
Building paper and board	—	9.91
Miscellaneous paper products	—	6.66
Paperboard containers	10.79	7.15
Printing and publishing	8.16	3.91
Newsprint consumption	6.11	3.32
Job printing and periodicals	—	4.34
Chemicals	8.89	5.23
Industrial chemicals	—	9.53
Basic inorganic chemicals	—	11.67
Industrial organic chemicals	—	10.79
Plastic materials	—	7.39
Synthetic rubber	—	19.62
Synthetic fibers	—	11.40
Miscellaneous organic chemicals	—	9.37
Vegetable and animal oils	—	6.77
Vegetable oils	—	2.77
Grease and tallow	—	8.41
Soap and allied products	—	4.53
Paints	—	7.19
Fertilizers	—	2.47

(continued)

TABLE D–5 (continued)

	1923–41	1947–55
Petroleum and coal products	8.01	6.02
Petroleum refining	6.43	5.33
Gasoline	5.25	5.63
Automotive	—	5.64
Aviation	—	6.05
Fuel oil	6.33	7.43
Distilled	—	10.42
Residual	—	3.87
Lubricating oil	7.54	6.59
Kerosene	5.29	10.02
Coke	16.58	14.39
By-product	13.92	—
Beehive	32.77	—
Asphalt roofing and siding	—	9.41
Rubber products	10.60	11.98
Rubber consumption	10.70	—
Tires and tubes	10.91	12.31
Auto tires	—	13.81
Truck and bus tires	—	14.65
Miscellaneous rubber products	—	11.83
Leather and products	9.08	6.41
Leather (tanning, etc.)	12.48	6.76
Shoes (footwear)	8.65	5.90
Stone, clay, and glass products	12.77	7.94
Cement	10.94	9.32
Structural clay[a]	12.79	7.30
Glass products[a],[c]	11.36	7.48
Flat glass[a]	20.55	11.18
Glass containers	11.07	7.11
Home glassware and pottery	—	6.02
Concrete and plaster products	—	8.45
Miscellaneous stone and earth mfs.	—	10.96
Primary metals	—	14.73
Ferrous metals	—	15.78
Pig iron and steel	18.67	15.72
Pig iron	20.18	16.18
Steel	18.69	17.40
Carbon steel	—	15.48
Alloy steel	—	21.51
Ferrous castings and forgings	—	13.66
Iron and steel castings	—	14.99
Steel forgings	—	17.99
Nonferrous metals[a]	15.98	12.18
Primary nonferrous metals	13.35	4.09
Copper smelting	13.63	9.38
Copper refining	—	10.10
Lead[c]	19.16	6.35
Zinc	12.59	7.79
Tin (consumption)	24.98	—
Copper deliveries	19.59	—
Aluminum	—	4.80

(continued)

TABLE D–5 (concluded)

	1923–41	1947–55
Secondary nonferrous metals	—	13.43
Nonferrous shapes and castings	—	14.29
Copper mill shapes	—	12.59
Aluminum mill shapes	—	18.99
Nonferrous castings	—	16.04
Fabricated metal products	—	7.66
Structural metal	—	7.42
Furnaces, ranges, etc.	—	15.41
Tin cans	—	4.50
Stampings and miscellaneous	—	9.46
Machinery, All	11.89	16.67
Machinery, non-electrical	—	8.93
Farm and industrial machinery	—	8.31
Farm machinery	—	10.83
Industrial and commercial machinery	—	8.64
Machine tools and presses	—	10.39
Appliances (laundry and refrig.)	—	19.13
Electrical machinery	—	6.94
Electrical apparatus and parts	—	8.35
Radio and TV sets	—	13.29
Transportation equipment	20.05	10.80
Motor vehicles and parts	19.62	18.45
Autos	—	22.48
Trucks	—	15.81
Light	—	12.58
Medium	—	17.16
Heavy	—	23.18
Truck trailers	—	26.98
Vehicle parts		
Aircraft[a],[d]	27.70	20.42
Ships and boats	16.44	9.49
Railroad equipment	24.63	13.58
Locomotives	32.11	—
Railroad cars	24.10	20.02
Instruments and miscellaneous mfg.	—	7.34
Instruments	—	7.62
Miscellaneous manufacturing	—	7.15

SOURCE: The sources are indicated in the text of this appendix.
[a] Not identical composition in the two periods.
[b] 1934–41 instead of 1923–41.
[c] 1926–41 instead of 1923–41.
[d] 1931–41 instead of 1923–41.

TABLE D–6
NONPRIMARY EMPLOYMENT AS A PERCENTAGE OF PRIMARY EMPLOYMENT
FOR 86 MANUFACTURING AND MINING INDUSTRIES, 1954[a]

Industry	Nonprimary Employment Primary Employment (per cent)	Industry	Nonprimary Employment Primary Employment (per cent)
Metal mining	15.60	Periodicals	12.79
Anthracite mining	02.36	Books, misc. publishing and	
Bituminous coal and lignite		greeting cards	07.30
mining	07.48	Commercial printing and	
Crude petroleum and natural		lithographing	03.42
gas extraction	03.87	Bookbinding and printing	
Nonmetallic minerals, except		trade services	01.37
fuels, mining	07.24	Inorganic and organic	
Meat-packing plants	22.34	chemicals	41.21
Dairy products	08.94	Drugs and medicines	23.17
Canned and frozen foods	04.75	Soap and related products	26.60
Grainmill products	20.29	Paints and allied products,	
Bakery products	06.09	gum and wood chemicals	50.79
Candy and related products	07.64	Fertilizers	55.98
Bottled soft drinks	00.95	Vegetable and animal oils	24.58
Beverages, except bottled		Chemical products, n.e.c.	22.00
soft drinks	08.10	Petroleum refining	24.08
Tobacco manufactures	03.58	Integrated petroleum extrac-	
Woolen and worsted		tion and refining	54.41
manufactures	02.84	Other petroleum and coal	
Yarn and thread mills, broad-		products	29.50
woven fabrics, and		Rubber products	35.29
finishing textiles	12.81	Footwear (except rubber)	09.89
Knitting mills	93.34	Leather and leather products	
Carpets and rugs	75.31	except footwear	03.74
Other textile mill products	08.71	Glass products	15.28
Men's and boys' clothing	03.17	Cement, hydraulic	02.28
Women's and children's		Structural clay products	05.08
clothing (except millinery		Concrete and plaster products	18.92
and fur goods)	01.55	Other metallic mineral	
Millinery, fur goods, and		products	13.77
misc. apparel	02.56	Blast furnaces and steel mills	48.47
Fabricated textiles, n.e.c.	02.98	Iron and steel foundries	13.43
Logging and lumber and		Nonferrous smelting, refining,	
basic products	06.17	rolling and nonferrous	
Millwork and related products	09.40	foundries	53.57
Other wood products	05.13	Primary metal industries,	
Household furniture	03.73	n.e.c.	15.20
Furniture and fixtures, except		Tin cans and other tinware	42.75
household furniture	05.39	Cutlery, hand tools and	
Pulp, paper and board	40.97	hardware	13.60
Paperboard containers	18.30	Heating and plumbing	
Other pulp, paper and		equipment	25.79
products	17.38	Structural metal products	09.37
Newspapers	03.43	Metal stamping and coating	07.14

(continued)

223

TABLE D–6 (concluded)

Industry	Nonprimary Employment Primary Employment (per cent)	Industry	Nonprimary Employment Primary Employment (per cent)
Other fabricated metal products	10.08	Other electrical machinery, equipment and supplies	25.22
Engines and turbines	27.16	Motor vehicles and equipment	49.96
Tractors and farm machinery	43.71	Aircraft	04.49
Construction and mining machinery	25.21	Aircraft parts	37.01
Metalworking machinery	09.52	Ships and boats	12.22
Special-industry machinery, n.e.c.	11.20	Other transportation equipment	68.39
General industrial machinery	17.63	Scientific and mechanical measuring instruments	25.27
Office and store machines	16.00	Optical, medical, and ophthalmic goods	14.19
Service and household machines	22.89	Photographic equipment	42.83
Misc. machinery parts	12.58	Watches and clocks	23.12
Electrical industrial apparatus	80.61	Misc. manufactures (incl. ordnance and accessories)	09.78
Communication equipment	21.88		

Source: Data derived from *Company Statistics*, Table 2.

[a] For definitions of primary and nonprimary employment, see Chapter 2.

TABLE D–7
NONPRIMARY EMPLOYMENT AS A PERCENTAGE OF PRIMARY EMPLOYMENT
FOR 34 NONMANUFACTURING INDUSTRIES, 1954[a]

Industry	Nonprimary Employment / Primary Employment (per cent)
Public warehouses	01.25
Wholesale trade	
Food products wholesalers	04.01
Drugs, chemicals, allied prod. wholesalers	07.19
Automotive wholesalers	01.68
Electrical, electronics appliance distributors	02.00
Hardware, plumbing, heating goods wholesalers	03.23
Lumber, construction materials distributors	03.66
Machinery, equipment supplies distributors	03.10
Miscellaneous merchant wholesalers	04.75
Petroleum bulk, plant, terminals, and LP gas facilities	07.54
Merchandise agents, brokers	01.81
Assemblers of farm products	03.06
Retail trade	
Grocery stores	04.92
Food stores except grocery stores	01.66
Eating, drinking places	01.03
General merchandise group, except variety stores	01.13
Variety stores	00.60
Shoe stores	07.17
Apparel, accessories except shoe stores	01.74
Furniture, home furnishings, appliance dealers	01.60
Automotive group and gasoline service stations	00.71
Lumber, building material, hardware, farm equipment dealers	02.20
Drug stores, proprietary stores	00.95
Other retail stores	02.13
Nonstore retailers	12.44
Service trades	
Personal services	00.30
Advertising	01.10
Business services, except accounting, auditing, bookkeeping and advertising	01.20
Automobile repair shops, garages	00.62
Miscellaneous repair services	01.74
Motion picture theaters	03.78
Motion picture production and distribution	01.72
Amusement, recreation except motion pictures	00.78
Hotels, motels, tourist courts, camps	00.79

SOURCE: Data derived from *Company Statistics*, Table 2.

[a] For definitions of primary and nonprimary employment, see Chapter 2.

TABLE D-8

NONPRIMARY EMPLOYMENT AS A PERCENTAGE OF EXTERNAL EMPLOYMENT
FOR 86 MANUFACTURING AND MINING INDUSTRIES, 1954[a]

Industry	Nonprimary Employment External Employment (per cent)	Industry	Nonprimary Employment External Employment (per cent)
Metal mining	14.6	Newspapers	361.9
Anthracite mining	38.8	Periodicals	169.0
Bituminous coal and lignite mining	27.3	Books, miscellaneous publishing and greeting cards	105.3
Crude petroleum and natural gas extraction	8.6	Commercial printing and lithographing	56.8
Nonmetallic minerals (except fuels) mining	30.4	Bookbinding and printing trade services	22.7
Meat-packing plants	1961.1	Inorganic and organic chemicals	164.3
Dairy products	177.9	Drugs and medicines	124.2
Canned and frozen foods	53.2	Soap and related products	257.0
Grainmill products	176.5	Paints and allied products; gum and wood chemicals	129.2
Bakery products	76.9	Fertilizers	109.3
Candy and related products	63.7	Vegetable and animal oils	61.4
Bottled soft drinks	12.6	Chemical products, n.e.c.	71.4
Beverages, except bottled soft drinks	338.2	Petroleum refining	2.2
Tobacco manufactures	750.1	Integrated petroleum extraction and refining	—
Woolen and worsted manufactures	12.9	Other petroleum and coal products	14.6
Yarn and thread mills, broad-woven fabrics, and finishing textiles (except wool)	182.5	Rubber products	390.0
		Footwear (except rubber)	527.1
Knitting mills	79.8	Leather and leather products except footwear	28.4
Carpets and rugs	244.5	Glass products	254.2
Other textile mill products	67.0	Cement, hydraulic	14.7
Men's and boys' clothing	72.2	Structural clay products	42.5
Women's and children's clothing (except millinery and fur goods)	71.3	Concrete and plaster products	120.4
		Other nonmetallic mineral products	55.5
Millinery, fur goods, and miscellaneous apparel	55.9	Blast furnaces and steel mills	559.1
Fabricated textiles, n.e.c.	15.8	Iron and steel foundries	40.6
Logging and lumber and basic products	111.5	Nonferrous smelting, refining, rolling and nonferrous foundries	284.1
Millwork and related products	97.7		
Other wood products	32.7	Primary metal industries, n.e.c.	19.7
Household furniture	43.4	Tin cans and other tinware	258.1
Furniture and fixtures, except household furniture	66.6	Cutlery, hand tools, and hardware	31.9
Pulp, paper, and board	152.9	Heating and plumbing equipment	119.2
Paperboard containers	66.3		
Other pulp, paper and products	41.6	Structural metal products	43.1

(continued)

TABLE D–8 (concluded)

Industry	Nonprimary Employment External Employment (per cent)	Industry	Nonprimary Employment External Employment (per cent)
Metal stamping and coating	31.9	Other electrical machinery, equipment and supplies	31.0
Other fabricated metal products	44.2	Motor vehicles and equipment	617.3
Engines and turbines	20.5	Aircraft	88.8
Tractors and farm machinery	377.5	Aircraft parts	57.9
Construction and mining machinery	69.2	Ships and boats	46.1
Metalworking machinery	75.1	Other transportation equipment	75.3
Special-industry machinery, n.e.c.	79.8	Scientific and mechanical measuring instruments	70.1
General industrial machinery	69.3	Optical, medical, and ophthalmic goods	94.7
Office and store machines	567.7	Photographic equipment	587.9
Service and household machines	33.8	Watches and clocks	238.9
Miscellaneous machinery parts	66.1	Miscellaneous manufactures (including ordnance and accessories)	35.8
Electrical industrial apparatus	408.0		
Communication equipment	102.0		

SOURCE: Data derived from *Company Statistics*, Table 2.

a For definition of nonprimary employment, see Chapter 2. For definition of external employment, see Chapter 7.

APPENDIX E

		1929–1939			
		Product Additions		*Product Abandonments*	
VARIABLE	Decile	All	Those Falling Out of Primary 2-Digit Group of Company	All	Those Falling Out of Primary 2-Digit Group of Company
Concentration ratio	1				
	2				
	3				
	4				
	5				
	6				
	7				
	8				
	9				
	10				
	Total				
Average size of plant	1	20	4	3	2
	2	20	8	0	0
	3	27	21	3	2
	4	26	15	3	3
	5	31	18	4	0
	6	48	33	4	3
	7	42	26	5	5
	8	47	24	6	2
	9	81	37	16	7
	10	59	32	8	4
	Total	401	218	52	28
Technical personnel ratio	1	0	0	1	1
	2	13	7	2	1
	3	18	13	1	1
	4	13	8	4	2
	5	25	6	3	1
	6	66	61	14	10
	7	32	30	5	2
	8	104	67	8	3
	9	71	29	5	3
	10	110	47	15	9
	Total	475	268	58	33

E E–1
ons and Abandonments to Industry Characteristics,
fied into Deciles on the Basis of Six Variables,
–54

	1939–1950				1950–1954			
	Product Additions		*Product Abandonments*		*Product Additions*		*Product Abandonments*	
All	Those Falling Out of Primary 2-Digit Group of Company	All	Those Falling Out of Primary 2-Digit Group of Company	All	Those Falling Out of Primary 2-Digit Group of Company	All	Those Falling Out of Primary 2-Digit Group of Company
26	15	15	6	27	20	4	3
49	38	9	5	45	29	5	2
41	23	13	10	43	24	6	3
48	29	10	9	37	19	7	5
60	36	23	17	56	37	12	9
57	32	7	1	50	36	7	5
45	26	16	9	32	23	6	3
40	35	10	8	36	27	7	6
39	23	19	10	31	16	5	3
44	30	12	8	33	29	8	4
449	287	134	83	390	260	67	43
10	5	5	0	5	4	2	1
18	6	4	2	6	3	3	2
21	13	9	7	20	12	3	3
15	12	7	5	14	8	4	2
25	20	10	7	23	17	7	4
38	31	17	13	25	18	1	1
18	13	5	3	17	9	6	5
48	27	13	6	41	27	8	4
70	47	11	8	47	31	11	8
54	30	20	14	69	43	8	4
317	204	101	65	267	172	53	34
4	3	2	2	11	11	4	4
16	14	6	5	10	10	1	1
14	18	5	2	20	15	6	1
17	11	9	2	12	2	3	0
12	2	3	2	27	21	4	4
31	14	15	8	29	16	7	3
61	48	24	15	37	24	8	8
33	15	13	7	31	19	5	4
113	77	28	22	97	71	10	7
144	92	29	18	127	76	17	11
445	284	134	83	401	265	65	43

(continued)

VARIABLE	Decile	Product Additions		Product Abandonmen	
		All	Those Falling Out of Primary 2-Digit Group of Company	All	Those Falling Out of Primary 2-Digit Group of Company
Productivity change	1	24	13	2	0
	2	39	18	6	1
	3	17	11	8	4
	4	53	46	5	5
	5	18	5	2	0
	6	113	82	8	6
	7	97	50	12	7
	8	7	5	0	0
	9	81	33	10	6
	10	24	5	5	2
	Total	473	268	58	31
Growth	1	21	16	9	5
	2	20	13	1	0
	3	15	7	3	0
	4	39	32	7	5
	5	29	19	2	2
	6	20	10	4	2
	7	24	11	6	4
	8	55	27	5	2
	9	46	17	3	2
	10	78	31	9	4
	Total	347	183	49	26
Average size of firm	1				
	2				
	3				
	4				
	5				
	6				
	7				
	8				
	9				
	10				
	Total				

The header "1929–1939" spans the Product Additions and Product Abandonmen columns.

(concluded)

	1939–1950				1950–1954			
	Product Additions		*Product Abandonments*		*Product Additions*		*Product Abandonments*	
All	Those Falling Out of Primary 2-Digit Group of Company	All	Those Falling Out of Primary 2-Digit Group of Company	All	Those Falling Out of Primary 2-Digit Group of Company	All	Those Falling Out of Primary 2-Digit Group of Company
---	---	---	---	---	---	---	---
11	6	5	3	17	9	5	3
48	37	16	10	27	19	5	4
12	7	0	0	11	5	5	4
11	4	6	4	7	3	3	1
25	8	15	5	20	7	5	0
76	52	25	13	69	47	9	6
54	41	16	13	60	56	16	11
26	17	14	9	28	19	2	2
67	37	13	12	68	40	3	2
121	77	24	12	92	59	14	10
451	287	134	81	399	264	67	43
6	6	4	3	3	1	2	1
16	7	6	1	11	10	5	1
19	12	12	6	14	12	6	1
17	10	6	4	18	8	4	2
29	14	17	7	25	15	3	2
21	10	13	10	30	17	5	3
33	17	15	12	23	11	6	3
52	36	10	9	35	22	1	1
97	62	26	14	96	62	11	8
75	51	9	6	68	43	9	8
365	225	118	72	323	201	52	30
6	4	2	1	3	3	5	4
23	19	6	6	19	16	4	4
23	11	8	8	24	13	2	0
55	33	16	7	50	31	8	6
47	32	13	4	37	24	8	4
38	22	8	5	31	18	8	3
35	21	12	8	33	25	4	1
54	35	12	8	45	31	6	4
45	20	15	5	57	31	2	2
73	46	19	10	57	31	9	6
399	243	111	62	356	223	56	34

Source: Product record described in Chapter 2. For explanation of methods of classifying products according to variables, see Chapter 7.

INDEX

Capital requirements, as factor in choice of diversification outlets, 4, 103, 107, 137

Central office activity, relation of, to size of firm, 7, 14, 87-91

Central office employment, relation of, to integration, 7, 13, 79, 80

Chemicals industries:
as industry of nonprimary products, 40
choice of, as diversification outlet, 50
number of products per company as measure of diversification in, 40

Company, *see* Firm

Concentration ratio:
as factor in choice of diversification outlet, 107, 108, 112, 117, 118, 130
definition of, 107, 108, 117
primary industry of firm and, 137
ratio of external to total employment and, 126
ratio of nonprimary to primary employment and, 136
sources of data on, 200

Crowder, Walter F., 6, 6n

Cyclical stability:
as factor in choice of diversification outlet, 4, 106, 107, 114-117
sources of data on, 200, 201, 219-223

Diversification:
consequences of, for individual firm, 3, 4
definition of, 3, 8, 9
effects of, on economy, 3
as countercyclical device, 4, 104
as source of competition, 4, 104, 129

Diversification measures, relations among, 23-26

Diversification outlets, 110, 111, 202
See also Capital requirements; Concentration ratio; Cyclical stability; Employment, external; Growth; Labor productivity; Size of plant or firm; Technical personnel ratio

Electrical machinery industry:
as industry of nonprimary products, 40
number and diversification of firms in, 35-37
number of products per firm as measure of diversification in, 40

Employment:
ratio of nonprimary to external, 226, 227
ratio of nonprimary to primary, 31, 32, 223-225
ratio of nonprimary to total, 31, 62, 66-73
share of multi-industry firms in total of, 30

Employment, auxiliary:
and integration, 55, 80-84

Employment, external:
as factor in choice of diversification outlets, 124, 125
as percentage of total employment, 125, 126
definition of, 124
ratio of nonprimary employment to, 226, 227

Enterprise, *see* Firm

Establishments, *see* Plants

Extractive industries, choice of, as diversification outlet, 96, 97, 102

Fabricated metal products industries:
as industry of nonprimary products, 40
number of products per firm as measure of diversification in, 40

Finance, importance of, for diversification or integration, 102

Food industry:
characteristics of nonprimary products in, 40, 41
characteristics of product additions in, 50
number of activities of firms in, 60
relative homogeneity of plants in, 40

Firm, definition of, 17

Firms, sample of, 111:
asset size of, 19, 216-218
basis of selection for, 18, 19
composition of, 147-151
effect of, on entered industries, 130-134
effect of diversification on composition of, 129-131
number of products and services of, 34-37, 60-63
product structure of, 155-185
representativeness of, 19

Growth of firm:
relation of, to diversification, 65, 74-76
relation of, to frequency of product additions, 76